Private Screenings

A camera obscura *Book*

Private Screenings

Television and the Female Consumer

Lynn Spigel and Denise Mann, editors

University of Minnesota Press
Minneapolis

Mary Beth Haralovich, "Sit-coms and Suburbs: Positioning the 1950s
Homemaker," reprinted from *Quarterly Review of Film and Video,* 11
(1989), pp. 61–83, copyright Harwood Academic Publishers GmbH;
George Lipsitz, "The Meaning of Memory: Family, Class, and Ethnicity
in Early Network Television Programs," first appeared in *Cultural
Anthropology,* 1 (November 1986), pp. 355–387, copyright American
Anthropological Association.

Photographs:
Cover photo courtesy of Keith de Lellis Gallery, © Keith de Lellis.
© Emerson Radio Corp., 1953. Reprinted with the permission of
Emerson Radio Corporation.
© Sparton Corp., 1953.
© Kimberly-Clark Corp., 1949. Kotex® is a registered trademark of
Kimberly-Clark Corporation. Used with permission.
© Allied-Signal Inc., 1948. Reprinted with the permission of Allied-Signal
Incorporated.

Published by the University of Minnesota Press
2037 University Avenue Southeast, Minneapolis, MN 55414
Printed in the United States of America on acid-free paper

Library of Congress Cataloging-in-Publication Data

Private screenings : television and the female consumer / Lynn Spigel and
Denise Mann, editors.
     p.   cm. — (A Camera obscura book)
   An expanded version of issue no. 16, winter 1988, of Camera obscura.
   Includes bibliographical references and index.
   ISBN 0-8166-2052-0 (hc : acid-free paper).
   ISBN 0-8166-2053-9 (pb : acid-free paper)
   1. Television and women — United States.   2. Television viewers —
United States.   3. Women in television — United States.
4. Television programs for women — United States.   I. Spigel, Lynn.
II. Mann, Denise.   III. Series.
HQ1233.P755   1992
302.23'45'082 — dc20   91-40919
                                                                      CIP

The University of Minnesota is an
equal-opportunity educator and employer.

Contents

Introduction
Lynn Spigel and Denise Mann

Television has always had its eye on women. Since its arrival in the late 1940s, it has particularly tried to attract female viewers, who, the industry assumes, are the primary consumers for their households. In this regard, television has much in common with other mass media (film, radio, magazines, romance fiction), which have also historically targeted women as their key source of revenue. But television's pervasiveness as a domestic medium, a medium that is literally a piece of furniture in our homes, makes it a particularly important site for feminist analysis.

Private Screenings brings together essays that focus on the relationship among women, television, and consumer culture. Chief concerns are the way television tries to appeal to women consumers and the way it inserts itself into their everyday lives, both at home and in the marketplace. Consumption, a central theme in this book, is conceptualized in two ways. First, we are interested in its literal sense — television's display of commodities and consumer lifestyles. Our second concern is with the consumption of television itself — how audiences understand television programs and, in particular, how the medium defines femininity and female desire.

Insofar as television attempts to attract women shoppers with buying power, its definition of femininity works to exclude many women in the population. Historically, women of color and lesbians have not fit the mold of television's ideal feminine type, and thus have been omitted from or marginalized in its representational system. And even when, in the late 1960s, television discovered that it needed to revamp its model of femininity from its zany housewives and loving mothers to new, more independent working women, the mold it cast for femininity and the appeals it made to female desire still worked to limit the

---

The special issue of *Camera Obscura* (no. 16, Winter 1988) on which this book is based was edited by Lynn Spigel and Denise Mann.

range of female identities. This book, then, illuminates the ways television has historically addressed (and not addressed) its female audiences and how it has worked within the wider logic of postwar consumer culture.

Private Screenings is an expanded version of a special issue of *Camera Obscura* that was published in 1988. The essays are part of an ongoing attempt to integrate feminist theories of representation with methods of cultural history and interpretation. In this regard, they represent a move away from grand generalizations of television and toward the particulars of its reception contexts and representational conventions. Indeed, rather than presenting "big bang" theories of mass culture and its social effects—theories that attempt to explain as much as possible under a single covering law—this volume presents close analyses of television texts and their historical frameworks. This approach, we think, is more apt to explain cultural differences—more apt to tell us something about the variety of ways a mass medium can variously make sense to different people in particular historical situations. In this sense, *Private Screenings* builds on previous feminist scholarship by offering strategies for understanding how sexual and other social differences can proliferate through the technologies and techniques of mass culture.

The authors address these concerns in a variety of ways. Some deal with the relationship between television programs and their sociohistorical context; others consider how television texts offer interpretive strategies to viewers; others look at television audiences; and still others attempt to join these approaches. The first four essays present historical interpretations of television's social and cultural function in the 1950s. Rather than subscribing to a single historical "truth," the authors offer speculative, interpretive, "conjunctural" histories that seek to discover how television might have intersected with other social discourses and practices in the postwar era. Drawing on a wide array of documents from the period—including women's magazines, fanzines, market research, demographic data, films, and television programs—these essays look for clues to the riddle of how women might have interpreted television and its programming in the past.

Lynn Spigel's "Installing the Television Set: Popular Discourses on Television and Domestic Space, 1948–1955" explores how television was introduced to the public in popular media of the postwar era. Using middle-class women's home magazines, advertisements, films, and television sit-coms, Spigel examines how the television set was figured in representations of domestic life and demonstrates how the site of exhibition was transferred from the public space of the movie theater to the private space of the home. In particular, she concentrates on the media's contradictory and ambivalent response to television, relating this to the social transitions that marked postwar life—especially the rise of a new consumer-oriented suburban domesticity. On the one hand, Spigel claims, popular media hailed television as a new democratic "window on the world" that would link the suburban family (especially housewives) to the larger public sphere; on the other hand, the media represented television as a threatening instrument of female social isolation and even a source of social upheaval that would disturb the normative ways of seeing in patriarchal cultures. Thus, Spigel argues, the history of television's innovation should be seen as a set of contradictory responses and expectations, laced with anxieties over the sexual politics of leisure and middle-class domestic ideals.

Denise Mann's "The Spectacularization of Everyday Life: Recycling Hollywood Stars and Fans in Early Television Variety Shows" argues that television, like other forms of mass media, engages its female audiences by enhancing its representation of everyday life. Analyzing 1950s variety shows and their star casts, Mann demonstrates how television capitalized on an earlier generation's libidinally charged, imaginary relationship with Hollywood celebrities—a relationship institutionalized by the studio system's publicity departments. In repackaging Hollywood stars, the variety show often parodied the cinema's glorified portrayals of motion-picture personalities—its representation of stars as upper-class elites. Mann shows how the variety genre borrowed performance techniques from vaudeville, and an ironic perspective from radio, to poke fun at the aristocratic lifestyles of movie stars and to celebrate instead the more middle-class averageness of television celebrities. Using examples from *The Martha Raye Show*, she demonstrates how the variety show mobilized such comparisons between Hollywood and television by casting Raye in skits where she played the role of an "average" woman (a housewife, a waitress, a maid) who fell in love with an aging Hollywood star (Cesar Romero, Douglas Fairbanks, Jr.). The interactions between the "glamorous" movie star and the "everyday" television character encouraged women to rethink beauty and consumer ideals from the 1930s and 1940s, and to adapt them to the new postwar ideals of domesticity and classlessness.

George Lipsitz's "The Meaning of Memory: Family, Class and Ethnicity in Early Network Television Programs" investigates ethnic and working-class family dramas of the 1950s with respect to the wider social and economic history of the times. He argues that nostalgic portrayals of class and ethnic difference in such programs as *Mama* helped ease the transition from World War II to the increasing homogeneity of postwar culture. At a time when Americans were moving to the Levittowns around the nation, these programs helped to legitimate tel-

evision's consumption aesthetic by presenting romanticized visions of
an American past where people still lived in urban neighborhoods
among friends and family. They worked to justify historical changes
by restoring traditional meanings to the often disturbing and confusing
social upheavals of the postwar world.

Mary Beth Haralovich's "Sit-coms and Suburbs: Positioning the
1950s Homemaker" details the ways in which postwar housing design,
suburban development, and consumer product design were premised
on an idealized portrait of a middle-class housewife that was similarly
depicted in popular television sit-coms of the mid-1950s and early
1960s. She shows how this consumer-housewife type was inscribed in
the Federal Housing Administration's zoning practices and loan restrictions designed to produce racial, ethnic, and class barriers to property
and home ownership. Using examples from shows such as *Father
Knows Best* and *Leave It to Beaver*, Haralovich demonstrates how this
goal of enforcing a homogeneous and socially stable community was
naturalized in sit-coms that effaced evidence of alternative class or ethnic groups.

The next three articles chart significant transitions in television history from the late 1960s through the 1980s by looking at how political
movements associated with feminism or civil rights were adapted and
popularized by the programs themselves. The authors draw on existing
archival documents—particularly viewer response mail that was sent
to the producers of prime-time programs—and with these documents
they begin to illuminate the ephemeral and complex processes at work
in women's interpretations of television programs.

Aniko Bodroghkozy's " 'Is This What You Mean by Color TV?'
Race, Gender and Contested Meanings in NBC's *Julia*" discusses the
emergence of the first situation comedy since *Amos 'n' Andy* and *Beulah*
to feature a black star. *Julia* appeared against the backdrop of black
nationalism, civil rights, political activism, and the social unrest of the
1960s. Critics and journalists debated the program in the popular
press, while viewers wrote letters to the network and its producer, Hal
Kanter, criticizing the show's portrayal of blacks for being out of touch
with the real circumstances of black life in 1960s America. By analyzing the popular criticism, as well as the correspondence and scripts in
Kanter's production file, Bodroghkozy works to reconstruct the dialogue that took place among the producers, writers, and audiences. As
the viewer response mail indicates, the meanings of the program were
not entirely determined by the narrative strategies of the text; instead,
Bodroghkozy concludes, interpretations of *Julia* depended in large part
on the social, cultural, and racial backgrounds of particular viewers.

Julie D'Acci's "Defining Women: The Case of *Cagney and Lacey*" also demonstrates how audience interpretations of television programs can exceed those meanings intended by producers, and it further shows how producers in turn try to reassert their authority over interpretation by changing the show's content and form. As a distinctly hard-edged version of the female police genre, known for its tough portrayals of women cops, *Cagney and Lacey* attracted the "new woman audience" that advertisers of the 1980s desired, but it repelled those viewers and critics who preferred to see classically "feminine" cops like Angie Dickinson in *Police Woman* and Farrah Fawcett in *Charlie's Angels*. Through her examination of production files and her personal interviews with producers and writers, D'Acci unravels the intricate process of negotiation among the producers, network, public interest groups, critics, and viewers, and she shows how this was played out in the context of the women's movements of the 1970s and 1980s. In particular, she demonstrates how viewers attempted to enter the debates—already raging in the popular press—over how women should and should not be depicted on network television. Viewers and critics alike contested and helped to shape the network's decision to revamp its female characters so that they would avoid connotations of lesbianism. Meanwhile, the series attracted a large lesbian following who found ways to relate to the show despite the network's attempts to leave them out of it.

Robert H. Deming's "*Kate and Allie*: 'New' Women and the Audience's Television Archives" shares with D'Acci's work a concern for how programs aimed at female audiences responded to the women's movement. Deming considers how feminism was popularized on the situation comedy *Kate and Allie*, which, he argues, recycled images of the "new woman" found in earlier television programs and popular magazines. He claims that female audiences understood the program by drawing on their previous encounters with "new women" that appeared in the mass media of the early 1970s. Thus, according to Deming, interpretation is an intertextual process: the television audience draws on a repertoire of images from previous texts to make sense of any one particular program. Moreover, he claims, because *Kate and Allie* drew on intertextual references from both the "new woman" genre of the 1970s and from the more traditional family and working-girl comedies of previous decades, it offered contradictory positions of identification: ones based on new definitions of femininity found in the women's movements of the 1970s and ones based on more conventional nuclear family models.

The final two articles analyze the cultural significance of contemporary television melodrama, posing questions about television's overdetermined relation to the "feminine" aspects of consumer culture. Both show in close detail how television programs mobilize melodrama's potential for critiquing social norms through the creation of excess in decor, costume, music, and other details of *mise en scène*.

Sandy Flitterman-Lewis's "All's Well That Doesn't End: Soap Operas and the Marriage Motif" examines the quintessential commodity form on television, the daytime soap opera. Using a psychoanalytic/semiotic model of the text, she considers wedding sequences in soap operas, arguing that while the soap opera form departs from the storytelling conventions of the classical Hollywood film, wedding sequences evoke memories of a cinematic past (e.g., editing based on alternation, linear narratives with resolutions based on coupling, and the conflation of women with spectacle). For this reason, Flitterman sees the soap opera marriage as a trace or symptom of the residual influence of Hollywood narrative on contemporary mass-media forms and the kind of feminine desire they elicit. Moreover, by looking closely at one particular sequence in *General Hospital,* Flitterman-Lewis shows how the content of the wedding sequence is symptomatic of a prior event—this time an event embedded in the unconscious of the female character, who on her wedding day reenacts a traumatic scene from the past. The reenactment delays the marriage ceremony and thus works to introduce doubts about romantic coupling and undermine the ceremony's harmonious closure.

In "All That Television Allows: TV Melodrama, Postmodernism and Consumer Culture" Lynne Joyrich takes the links between women, commodities, and melodrama as a central theme. Refuting Laura Mulvey's claim that melodrama's subversive potential ended with the arrival of television, Joyrich argues that melodrama has become the dominant generic form for television programming, extending its focus on domestic life and "women's issues" to a more generalized audience of consumers. Drawing on examples that range from daytime soap operas to postmodernist experiments such as *Max Headroom,* Joyrich claims that melodrama's heightened emotionalism and emphasis on everyday life counteracts the feeling of weightlessness and passivity endemic to an increasingly consumer-oriented society.

The final essay in this collection is a source guide to television family comedy, drama, and serial dramas that lists archival holdings and distributors of programs from 1946 through 1970. Compiled by Dan Einstein, Nina Leibman, Randall Vogt, Sarah Berry, Jillian Steinberger, and William Lafferty, the source guide presents listings of holdings at major archives across the country, and it also lists video distributors and collectors that deal in early television programs. It is intended to give readers ideas for research and thus to spur ongoing analyses of the issues presented in this volume.

Taken together, then, the essays in *Private Screenings* are part of a larger feminist project of close analysis and historical contextualization that serves, we think, as a necessary complement and corrective to the generalizations that mass culture theory has presented in the past. Indeed, whether a democratic "global village" or a ruinous "vast wasteland," television has typically been conceptualized as an amorphous geographical terrain across which people communicate only in the most abstract, reified ways. But such theoretical generalizations have done little to explain television's specific discursive functions as they are played out in different cultural and social contexts. By attending to television's textual systems and to the specific historical frameworks in which television is received, we might better understand how mass media help to produce, transmit, and at times transform the logic of cultural fantasies and practices.

Private Screenings

Better Homes and Gardens 31 (October 1953), p.8

Installing the Television Set: Popular Discourses on Television and Domestic Space, 1948–1955
Lynn Spigel

Between the years 1948 and 1955 more than half of all American homes installed a television set and the basic mechanisms of the network oligopoly were set in motion. Historical studies have concentrated upon the latter half of this problem. That is to say, the history of television has been conceived primarily as a history of the economic, regulatory, and political struggles which gave rise to the network industry.[1] But television histories have only marginally attended to the social and domestic context into which television inserted itself. At most, television histories typically explain the coming of television into the home through a set of economic determinations, including manufacturer and network business strategies and the postwar climate of consumption. But these economic determinations cannot fully comprehend the process by which television came to be a domestic object and entertainment form.

In this paper I look at the coming of television in the context of a history of representation. The years which witnessed television's arrival in domestic space were marked by a vast production of discourses which spoke to the relationship between television, the home and the family. The industry and its advertising campaign, popular magazines, books on interior decor, films, newspapers, and television programming itself spoke in seemingly endless ways about television's place in the home. By looking at these representations and the media institutions from which they were distributed, we can see how the idea of television and its installation in the home was circulated to the public. Furthermore, we can see that even while the industry and its advertising campaign were attempting to promote the purchase and installation of the television set, popular discourses were replete with ambivalence and hesitation.[2] Utopian statements which idealized the new medium as an ultimate expression of technological and social progress were met by equally dystopian discourses which warned of television's devastating effects on family relationships and the efficient functioning of the household. Indeed, television was not simply promoted; rather, it was something which had to be questioned and deliberated upon.[3]

For example, how would television affect romantic relations of the couple? Would it blend with interior decor? Would it cause eyestrain, cancer, or even as one orthodontist suggested in a 1953 issue of *TV Guide,* would television lead to "malocclusion—an abnormal arrangement of the teeth likely to be caused by Junior's cradling his jaw in his hand as he watches television?"[4]

This essay brings together a variety of popular discourses on television and domestic space which were distributed from a number of institutions—including popular books and magazines, especially middle-class women's home magazines, magazine advertisements for television which idealized a middle-class lifestyle, and early television narratives, especially family situation comedies which took the middle-class domestic interior as their principal setting.[5] In examining these discourses in connection with one another, I want to establish the ways in which representations disseminated by different media institutions converge or intersect around questions of television's place in the home. I want to look at the meanings attached to the new object and the modes of use or reception which the media advised. Although these discourses most certainly do not reflect directly the public's response to television in the postwar period, they do begin to reveal the intertextual context through which people (and here especially middle-class women) might have made sense of television and its place in everyday life.

The following pages deal with a specific theme central to these discourses on television and the home—namely, the theatricalization and specularization of domestic space. These representations depicted the home as a theater, and they gave instructions for ways to arrange the home as a space of exhibition. In addition, these discourses deliberated upon ways in which to organize the gaze in the home equipped with television. They suggested ways to maximize visual pleasure in television—both as a household object (as part of the aesthetics of interior decor) and as an entertainment form. Just as importantly, they dramatized television's displeasurable effects and sought ways to manage the new medium. Finally, these discourses help to illuminate the representational conventions established in early television programming because they reveal a set of expectations about what constituted pleasurable or displeasurable narrative modes for home entertainment. Here I address these problems in the following way: First, I focus on the domestic reception context and look at the discursive refiguring of the home as a theater. Next I examine some of the representational strategies used in domestic sit-coms—in particular their theatricality. And finally, I move back to the reception context and look at the organization of the gaze in the home—especially in the light of television's highly disruptive effect on visual pleasure in domestic space.

There are two mechanical contrivances. . . . the talking motion picture and the electric vision apparatus with telephone. Either one will enable millions of people to see and hear the same performance simultaneously, by the 'seeing telephone' and the telephone, or successively from kinetoscopic and photographic records of it . . . . these inventions will become cheap enough to be, like the country telephone, in every home, so that one can go to the theater without leaving the sitting room. From this fact we may call both devices the home theater.

S.C. Gilfillan, "The Future Home Theater,"
in *The Independent*, 1912[6]

Although the idea of home television had been suggested in the popular press by early media prophets like S.C. Gilfillan and also widely discussed in industry trade journals since the 1920s, the actual installation of a television set was still a completely new concept for most Americans in the 1940s. As late as 1939, the year when the New York World's Fair celebrated the technological future with its "World of Tomorrow" (including RCA's debutante ball for TV which took place in its radio tube-shaped building), Gallup polls revealed that only 13% of the public would consider purchasing a television set for their homes.[7] Even so, postwar Americans installed TVs at a speed far surpassing any previous home entertainment medium. In order to understand the phenomenal growth of television, historians have recently begun to consider the social conditions which made the coming of television possible. As both Douglas Gomery and Mary Beth Haralovich have argued, among the most important of these conditions was the construction of a new suburbia in the 1950s.[8]

The suburban housing boom entailed a massive migration from the city into remote farm lands reconstituted by mass-produced housing which offered, primarily to the young adults of the middle class, a new stake in the ideology of privacy and property rights. A severe housing crisis, caused by a decline in residential construction during the Depression that lasted through World War II, was fueled by an increasing demand for housing as marriage and birth rates rose to new heights. Often unable to secure housing in the densely populated urban areas, the middle-class homeless looked to the new pre-fabricated housing built by corporate speculators like Levitt and Sons. With the help of the Federal Housing Association and veteran mortgage loans, these young couples, for the first time in history, found it cheaper to own their own homes than to rent an apartment in the city. One of the prevailing historical descriptions of the ideology which accompanied this move to suburbia emphasizes a generalized sense of isolationism in the postwar years, both at the level of cold war xenophobia and in terms of domestic everyday experiences. From this point of view, the home functioned as a kind of fall-out shelter from the anxieties and uncertainties of public life. According to this argument, the fifties witnessed a nostalgic return to the Victorian cult of domesticity which was predicated upon the clear division between public and private spheres.[9]

The problem with this kind of explanation is that it reifies the very ideology of privacy which it attempts to explain—in other words, it begins by assuming that the home was indeed a retreat and that people understood their domestic lives and social lives to be clear cut and distinct entities. I would argue that the private and public dimensions were experienced in a less distinct fashion. The ideology of privacy was not experienced simply as a retreat from the public sphere; instead it also gave people a sense of belonging to the community. By purchasing their detached suburban homes, the young couples of the middle class were given a new, and flattering, definition of themselves; in newspapers, magazines, advertisements and on the airwaves, these young couples came to be the cultural representatives of the "good life." Furthermore, the rapid growth of family-based community organizations like the PTA suggests that these neo-suburbanites did not barricade their doors, nor did they simply "drop out." Instead, they secured a position of meaning in the *public* sphere through their new found social identities as *private* landowners. In paradoxical terms, then, privacy was something which could be enjoyed only in the company of others. When describing the landscape of the mass-produced suburbs, a 1953 issue of *Harpers* magazine succinctly suggested the new form of social cohesion which allowed people to be alone and together at the same time. The magazine described "monotonous" tract houses "where nothing rises above two stories, and the horizon is an endless picket fence of telephone poles and television aerials."[10] There was an odd sense of connection and disconnection in this new suburbia, an infinite series of separate, but identical homes, strung together like Christmas tree lights on a tract with one central switch. And that central switch was the growing communications complex through which people could keep their distance from the world but at the same time imagine that their domestic spheres were connected to a wider social fabric.

The domestic architecture of the period was itself a discourse on this complex relationship between public and private space. Women's home magazines, manuals on interior decor, and books on housing design all idealized the flowing, continuous spaces of California ranch-style architecture which followed the functionalist design principles of "easy living" by eliminating walls in the central living spaces of the home.[11] Continuous spaces allowed residents to exert a minimum of energy by reducing the need to move from room to room. Beyond the "form follows function" aesthetic, however, this emphasis on continuous space suggested a profound preoccupation with space itself. These rambling domestic interiors appeared not so much as private sanctions which excluded the outside world, but rather as infinite expanses which incorporated that world. The home magazines spoke constantly of the illusion of spaciousness, advising readers on ways to make the home appear as if it included the public domain. Landscape paintings and wallpaper depicting scenes of nature or a foreign city welcomed far-off spaces into the home.[12] Particularly emphasized were large picture windows or a wall of sliding glass doors which, as *Better Homes and Gardens* suggested in 1953, "magnifies [the] room's effect."[13]

Given its ability to bring "another world" into the home, it is not surprising that television was often figured as the ultimate expression of progress in utopian statements concerning man's ability to conquer and to domesticate space. In 1946, Thomas H. Hutchinson, an early experimenter in television programming, published a popular book designed to introduce television to the general public, *Here is Television, Your Window on the World*. In his opening pages, Hutchinson wrote, "Today we stand poised on the threshold of a future for television that no one can begin to comprehend fully. . . . We do know, however, that the outside world can be brought into the home and thus one of mankind's long-standing ambitions has been achieved."[14] And in *Radio, Television and Society*, a general readership book of 1950, Charles Siepmann explained that, "television provides a maximum extension of the perceived environment with a minimum of effort. Television is a form of 'going places' without even the expenditure of movement, to say nothing of money. It is bringing the world to people's doorsteps."[15] Indeed, as this statement suggests, television meshed perfectly with the aesthetics of modern suburban architecture. It brought to the home a grand illusion of space while also fulfilling the "easy living," minimal motion principles of functionalist housing design.

In fact, I would argue that the ideological harmony between utopian dreams for housing design and for technological solutions to distance created a joint leverage for television's rapid growth in the postwar period. Both of these utopias had been on the agenda well before television's arrival in the fifties. As Leo Marx has suggested with reference to nineteenth-century literary utopias, the dream of eradicating distances was a central trope of America's early discourse on technology. Particularly in the post–Civil War years, it was machines of transport (especially the train) which became the rhetorical figure through which this dream was realized in popular discourse and literature.[16] By the end of the nineteenth century, communication technology had supplanted transportation. It was now the telegraph, telephone, radio—and later, television—which promised to conquer space.

In the years following World War II, this technological utopia was joined by a complementary housing utopia which was for the first time mass produced. Although the 1950s witnessed the most extreme preoccupation with the merging of indoor and outdoor space, this ideal had been part of the model for interior design in the first suburban houses of the latter nineteenth century. In their widely read book of 1869, *The American Woman's Home,* Catherine Beecher and Harriet Beecher Stowe suggested, for example, that the thrifty Victorian housewife might fashion a "rustic [picture] frame made of branches . . . and garnish the corners with . . . a cluster of acorns," or else copy their illustration of a large window "ornamented with a variety of these rural economical adornings."[17] For the Beecher sisters the merging of indoor and outdoor worlds was a response to the Victorian cult of domesticity—its separation between private/female and public/male domains. Also concerned with bringing nature into the home, the architects of the late 1870s began to build bay windows or else smaller windows that were grouped together in order to form a composite view for the residents.[18] Here, the natural world was associated with the "true woman" who was to make her home a kind of nature retreat that would counteract the signs of modernity—smokestacks, tenement buildings, crowded streets—found in the urban work centers. As the sharp gender divisions between private and public worlds became increasingly unstable at the end of the nineteenth century, the merging of outside and inside space became more important for domestic architecture, and its meaning was somewhat altered. By the early decades of the twentieth century, the nature ideal still would have been understood in terms of its association with femininity, but it also began to have the more modern meaning of an erasure between separate spheres of public and private life. The bungalow cottages built across the country began to merge inside and outside worlds with their window views and expansive porches.

The most exaggerated effort to erase spatial barriers took place in the modernist architecture movements which emerged in the 1920s in Europe. Architectural modernism, or the "International Style" as it was also called, quickly took root on American soil, and architects working from a variety of traditions developed many of the principles of modernist design, not least of all the erasure between public and private domains. Homes ranging from Richard Neutra's classical modernist Lovell House of 1929 (a machine-like futuristic structure) to Richard Keck's almost-all-glass Crystal Palace of 1934 to Cliff May's rambling ranch-style homes of the 1940s, foregrounded the merging of indoors and outdoors with window walls, continuous living areas, and/or patio areas that appeared to extend into interior space.

Although these "homes of tomorrow" were clearly upper-class dreamhouses—too expensive or too "unhomey" for most Americans—the public was at least to some degree familiar with architectural modernism because it was widely publicized through fairs, museum exhibitions, department stores, home magazines, and the movies.[19] In the years following World War II the spatial aesthetics established by modernists appeared in a watered down, mass-produced version when the Levittowns across the country offered their consumers large picture windows or glass walls and continuous dining-living areas, imitating the principle of merging spaces found in the architectural ideal. That this mass-market realization of utopian dreams for housing was to find its companion in television, modernity's ultimate "space-merging" technology, is a particularly significant historical meeting.

Indeed, the ideological harmony between technological utopias and housing utopias created an ideal nesting ground for television's introduction to the public in the postwar years. Women's home magazines often displayed television sets in decorative settings which created the illusion of spatial conquests. The set was typically placed in rooms with panoramic window views, or else installed next to globes and colorful maps.[20] The image of television as a "global village," which media critic Marshall McLuhan spoke of in the sixties, was already suggested in the popular discourses of the postwar period.

Even the manufacturers seemed to realize the marketing potential of this new global village in a box. Advertisers for television typically used this illusion of the outside world as part of their promotional rhetoric. They placed their TV sets against scenic backgrounds suggestive of the far-off spaces which television promised to make domestic. In 1953, Arvin's advertising campaign used the Eiffel Tower and Big Ben as backdrops for its console models.[21] In that same year, Emerson TV went further than Europe. Its television set, with a picture of New York City on its screen, appeared among the planets (and note that the ad also included a smaller TV with a little girl and her poodle, thereby tying domestic meanings to the sci-fi imagery).[22]

This obsession with a view of far-away places was also registered in family sit-coms. Like the model homes in women's magazines, these TV homes incorporated an illusion of outside spaces which could be seen through large picture windows that often dominated the *mise en scène*. It was not just that these domestic interiors repeated the popular architectural ideal; they also fulfilled the expectations about television which were voiced in popular discourses of the time. That is to say, the depiction of domestic space appears to have been based in part upon those utopian predictions which promised that television would provide for its audiences a view of outside spaces. Thus, the representation of the family's private interior world was often merged with a view of public exteriors, a view which

Better Homes and Gardens 33 (March 1953), p. 130

was typically a fantasy depiction of high-priced neighborhoods not readily accessible to television's less affluent audiences. Beginning with its first episode in 1950, *The Burns and Allen Show* included numerous windows and glass doors through which appeared a painted backdrop depicting George and Gracie's Beverly Hills yard. In *Make Room for Daddy,* a slightly more realistic window view of New York City dominated the *mise en scène* of the Williams's luxury penthouse. Margie Albright, the spoiled rich girl character of *My Little Margie,* was typically depicted lounging in her sprawling New York apartment—complete with a terrace view of the city skyline. In 1955, the most popular show on television, *I Love Lucy,* attempted to give the TV audience a vicarious vacation by moving its characters to Hollywood for the entire season. The Ricardo's hotel suite contained a wall of windows through which audiences were given a panoramic view of the Hollywood Hills. This travelogue motif was to become conventionalized in the sit-com form when, for example, subsequent seasons saw *Burns and Allen*'s move to New York, *I Love Lucy*'s and *The Honeymooners*' season-long European vacations, and *Make Room for Daddy*'s visit to the Grand Canyon.

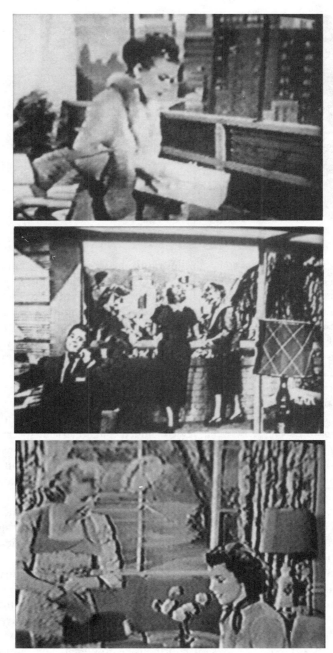

My Little Margie (1952); *I Love Lucy* (1955); *The Burns and Allen Show* (1951)

Make Room for Daddy (1954)

This interest in bringing an illusion of the world into the home can be seen as part of a larger historical process in which the home was designed to incorporate social space. Increasingly in the twentieth century, home appliances and other luxury items replaced community facilities. In the postwar years the community activity most under question was spectatorship. According to a 1955 *Fortune* survey, even while postwar Americans were spending a phenomenal "30 billion dollars for fun" in the prosperous postwar economy, when calculated in terms of disposable income, this figure actually reflected about a 2% decline since 1947. By far, the greatest slump was in the spectator amusements—most strikingly in movie attendance, but also in baseball, hockey, theater, and concert admissions. The *Fortune* survey concluded that American spectators had moved indoors where high fidelity sound and television promised more and better entertainment than in "the golden age of the box-office."[23]

Fortune's analysis indeed describes what happened to spectator amusements during the early fifties. But its conclusion was also typical of a wider discourse which spoke of television as part of a home entertainment center which promised to privatize and domesticate the experience of spectatorship. Moreover, as in the case of the *Fortune* survey, it was primarily the movies and the movie theater which television promised to replace. In 1948, *House Beautiful* told its readers that "looking at a television program is much like going to a movie."[24] Advertisements variously referred to the "family theater," the "video theater," the "chairside theater," the "living room theater," and so forth. A 1953 Emerson ad went one step further by showing an oversized television set which appears on a movie theater stage as a full house views the enormous video screen. The caption reads,

"Now! A TV picture so clear, so sharp . . . you'll think you're at the movies."[25]

The discursive refiguring of the site of theatrical exhibition was by no means a matter of simple substitution. While "going to television" might replace going to the theater, this replacement ushered in a grave spatial problem, primarily stated as a woman's problem of spatial confinement in the home. The movie theater was not just a site of exhibition, it was also an arena in which the housewife was given access to social life in the public sphere. In 1951, a cartoon in *Better Homes and Gardens* stated the problem in graphic terms. On his way home, a husband imagines a night of television viewing while his kitchen-bound wife dreams of a night out at the movies.[26] As this cartoon suggests, the utopian discourses which promised that television would connect the home to outside spaces were met by dystopian counterparts. For even if television offered a grand illusion of the outside world with its panoramic vistas and travelogue plots, it seems likely that women were critical of this illusionism, that they recognized the discrepancy between the everyday experience of domestic isolation perpetuated by television, and the imaginary experiences of social integration which television programming constructed.

Better Homes and Gardens 29 (Nov. 1951), p. 218

Beyond this separation from the public sphere there were other complications for women in their new "family theaters." Although television was often promoted as the great instrument of family togetherness, it was just as often depicted as a divisive force. This was especially true in the case of women, who were typically shown to be isolated from the group watching television. In 1951, *American Home* showed a continuous living and dining room in which a woman supposedly was allowed to accomplish her housework among the group watching television. However, as the graphic representation shows, the woman's table serving chores clearly isolate her from the television crowd which is pictured in the background, as the woman stands to the extreme front-right border of the frame.[27] This problem of female spatial isolation gave way to what can be called a corrective cycle of commodity purchases. Typically here, in 1950, Hotpoint advertised its dishwasher by claiming that the machine would bring the woman into the living room where she could watch television with her family.[28]

American Home 46 (Sept. 1951), p. 27

The television advertisements in women's home magazines (as well as general audience magazines like *Life* and *Look*) also attempted to negotiate this conflict between women's domestic isolation and their integration into social life. Here, the television set itself was figured in the context of a night out on the town. Advertisements typically displayed glamorously dressed husbands and wives whose evenings of television took on, for example, the status of a theater date.[29] According to the logic of such ads, television turned the home into a public meeting hall in which residents could imagine that they were involved in a social occasion.

Indeed, television—at its most ideal—promised to bring to audiences not merely an illusion of reality as in the cinema, but a sense of "being there," a kind of *hyper-realism*. Advertisers repeatedly promised that their sets would deliver picture and sound quality so real that the illusion would come alive. In 1952, Motorola promised that its "new dimension of realism brings action right into the living room."[30] Far exceeding the imagination of Motorola's advertising firm were the advertisers for Sparton television who produced what might be called the emblematic advertisement of this "come to life" genre. The 1953 ad pictured a large full-color photograph of a baseball stadium. On home plate stood a Sparton TV console whose screen showed a picture of a baseball player up at bat. Out in right field (and in the foreground of the composition), stood a modern-style easy chair with baseball bats and catchers mitts placed nearby. In this way Sparton TV literally transported the living room to the baseball field.[31]

Life 34 (April 27, 1953), p. 12

You Are There: Theatricality and the Illusion of Presence

It is in the context of this promise of hyper-realism that we might begin to understand the modes of representation used in many early domestic comedies. Early television drew upon a number of representational and performance traditions, incorporating principles from cinema (such as continuity editing) and radio (such as direct address), as well as vaudeville, burlesque and legitimate theater (such as theatrical scenery flats). In borrowing from and extending upon these traditions, early television was varied in style, and often family comedies mixed various modes of storytelling with musical, dance and stand-up comic-type performances.[32] Given the fact that we do not have a body of literature on the development of representational conventions in television (such as exists for cinema), it is obviously impossible to take on such a task in the space of this article. Here, I want to focus on television's simulation of live performance. By "simulation" I mean a reproduction of a situation through its model, and in this sense, what I have in mind is quite different from mimesis. For more than presenting an illusion of resemblances—the spectator's imaginary sense of being placed in a scene—early television attempted to present a reproduction of the entire situation of being at the theater—the spectator's imaginary sense of being placed on the scene.

This "ideology of liveness" has been noted by television critics and historians who have argued, for example, that TV's illusion of presence is rendered through the real-life appearance of the electronic image and the eternal "flow" of the television text (its sense of an ever-present, simultaneous world). Apart from this, there is very little work done on the specific representational strategies through which the simulation of live performance is accomplished.[33] I would like to argue that early domestic comedies both developed (and borrowed from other media) modes of representation, or what I will call "theatrical" modes of representation, which produced the simulation of live theater. These representational strategies had important connections to the expectations about television and its mode of reception which were voiced in popular discourses in the early period. Theatricality fulfilled the utopian promise that television would present an illusion so compelling that it would be identical to a live performance. This can be seen in sit-coms which were broadcast live, filmed live in front of a studio audience, or filmed in the studio without a live audience. I want now to demonstrate these points through a number of examples.

The first of these is the emblematic example of theatricality in the sitcom form, *The Burns and Allen Show.* At the level of content, this program was based on the premise of a real life couple (George Burns and Gracie Allen) who played themselves playing themselves as real-life performers who had a television show based on their lives as television stars. If this is a bit hard to follow, it should be, because the fundamental principle of this program was a *mise-en-abyme* structure, an endless stage within a stage, a bottomless pit of representation.[34] Gracie Allen's style of humor was also a kind of bottomless pit in which audiences were caught in an endless quagmire of meta-realities. In formal construction this program repeated the *mise-en-abyme* structure because it continually "reframed" the action in two separate, but intricately linked spaces—a stage space and a domestic space. The spatial articulations between the stage and domestic spaces created for the home audience the illusion of being at a live theatrical performance. There were a variety of ways in which this was achieved. In the most simple form, the stage space was shown as a proscenium with drawn curtains, behind which the domestic space was contained. After the initial commercial, we cut to the stage, the curtains opened, the domestic space was revealed, and the evening's story unfolded.

It wasn't simply the image of the stage on the TV screen which gave the illusion of being at the live theater—rather, it was the alternation between the stage space and the domestic space which gave a sense of "being there." Through this alternation, viewers experienced a kind of layered realism in which the stage appeared to contain the domestic space, and thus, the stage appeared spatially closer—or more real—than the domestic space.

This heightened sense of realism on the stage space was further suggested by the shifting forms of address as the program moved from the stage to the domestic space. At various intervals during the program, the diegesis of the sit-com story was frozen and the terms of address were altered. For example, in a 1952 episode[35] George literally walks out of his role as a character in the space of the story, moves up-stage to reveal the entire domestic setting, takes his place in front of the curtain on the right side of the stage and delivers a monologue in direct address to the camera. After the monologue, George walks back across the stage to reveal once more the domestic setting behind him. He arrives at the front porch, knocks on the door, Gracie answers, and George walks into his living room— literally returning to his place in the story.

Obviously, in this example the domestic space is rendered with a high degree of artifice; in fact there is no attempt to sustain the illusion that it is a real space at all. Instead, it is the stage space which is represented through realist conventions. The spatial and temporal unities of the stage space are kept intact, and the actions on the stage always appear to unfold in real time—that is, in the time that it takes the home audience to watch the program. Thus, the stage appears more real than the domestic space, and the home audience is given the sense of watching a live play in the theater.

This heightened sense of realism rendered through the framing of the story also served as an advertising discourse. In a number of episodes the announcer appeared on the stage at the beginning of the story, where he would relate a commercial message and then introduce the program. This stage within a stage device served to represent the idea that it was the advertiser who was responsible for the evening's entertainment. It also had the effect of marking off the sponsor's discourse from the level of story, a point which is further demonstrated in a 1952 episode of *I Love Lucy* ("Lucy Does a Commercial") in which the sponsor's product literally served as the stage of representation for the narrative. In the opening sequence we see a cartoon drawing of an oversized box of Philip Morris cigarettes. This cigarette box turns into a stage when two cartoon figures which represent the real-life stars, Lucille Ball and Desi Arnaz, approach the box. They peel up the cigarette box wrapper (which now looks like a curtain) to reveal a narrative space in which the lead character, Lucy

Ricardo, appears sitting on her living room sofa. The camera then zooms into this narrative space and the sit-com story begins. At the end of the story, an animation sketch representing a theater stage appears, and the two cartoon drawings of the stars draw the curtains over the narrative space of the Ricardo home. Subsequently, the real-life Lucille Ball and Desi Arnaz appear in a heart shaped frame and deliver a commercial for their sponsor. Not only did this framing structure work as a graphic reminder that the story had been brought to our homes through the courtesy of the sponsor, it also served to make the advertiser's discourse appear to be in a world closer to the viewer's real life.

I Love Lucy (1952)

This kind of hyper-realist effect becomes clearest in *The Goldbergs,* a popular Jewish-ethnic family comedy. At the start of each episode, the central character, Molly Goldberg (but ambiguously also the star, Gertrude Berg) leaned out her window and delivered her sponsor's commercial directly into the camera. This served to give the home audience a sense of being Molly's next door neighbor, and the advertising discourse took on a life-like quality. The heightened realism of the commercial message was further constructed through the transition into the domestic space where the story unfolded. In a 1952 episode,[36] for example, the transition from the window frame to the domestic space served to produce an illusion of moving from a level of pure discourse to the level of story, of moving from a kind of unmediated enunciation to a narrative space where the fiction took place.

The episode begins with the usual advertisement delivered by Molly in direct address as she leans out her window. In this particular case, Molly delivers a commercial message for RCA television sets. This leads to another

mise-en-abyme structure when Molly introduces us to an RCA representative who appears in a filmed commercial segment which is demonstrational in nature. The RCA rep shows the home audience a series of TV
monitors which all promise "true tone," and which all picture Molly
leaning out of her window frame. At the end of this demonstrational
narrative we cut back to Molly (live) at her window who continues the
commercial with her neighborly advice. The commercial ends when Molly
turns her back on the window frame (as well as the TV frame) and enters
the Goldberg living room where she now takes her place in the story. This
transition from commercial to story is made absolutely explicit in the
program because Molly literally *turns her back* on the ad's enunciative
system and *takes her position* in the tale as she walks into the living room
where her daughter, Rosalie, now addresses Molly as a character in the
story. In this way, Molly's turn from commercial to fiction dramatizes the
separation of the ad from the program, thus giving the ad a *non-fictional*
status. However, this transition from ad to story also alerts the viewer to
the artifice of the domestic setting, thus making us more aware of the
fictional status of the story itself.

The world that Molly Goldberg's window opened onto was, as in all
television, an alternate view, an endlessly self-referential world as opposed
to a document. The domestic spaces contained within the frame of these
stages were also often represented as stage-like, as prosceniums rather than
real spaces. In some ways, this had to do with technological conditions
and in-studio shooting practices. On the ten and twelve inch television
screen, it was typically difficult to show depth of field, and the even, high
key lighting used for live and live-on-film television gave the picture a kind
of flattened-out quality. In addition, because many of these sit-coms were
broadcast live, or else filmed live in real time, it was impossible to shoot
reverse fields. Finally, sound booms were often rooted in one place at the
front of the stage, so that the principal dialogue usually took place in a
frontal, proscenium position. (Note, however, that many programs did
utilize off-screen sound effects and dialogue which added a more realist
dimension of space.)

Aside from these technological and practical determinations, it appears
that theatricality was also a preferred style for the representation of the
home in early television. Contrary to the notion that these early television
households presented a "mirror" of the audience's life at home, I would
suggest that these early family sit-coms presented the home as a theatrical
stage and thus depicted highly abstract versions of family identity. In *Burns
and Allen,* for example, domestic spaces actually took on the functions of
the stage space. For instance, at the end of the program, George and Gracie
often did a short vaudeville routine on the stage. However, the front porch

of their house was just as typically used as the stage for their final act. In addition, windows, doorways, and passageways between rooms typically became the framing stages for performance segments. Even commercial messages were frequently integrated into the narrative space, so that the home became a stage for product display.

This theatricalization of the domestic world has been a subject of interest for film scholars — in particular, Serafina Bathrick, whose illuminating analysis of *Meet Me In St. Louis* (MGM, 1944) demonstrates the way the Hollywood musical mixed performance and storytelling conventions within the domestic setting.[37] Early TV domestic comedies, I would argue, imported these kind of representational strategies from the cinema, but they developed them in relation to their own broadcast context. Domestic comedies like *Burns and Allen* existed alongside variety-comedy, which had been highly popular on radio since the 1930s and was especially popular in early television. *Burns and Allen* was in many ways a transitional text because it included both elements of domestic comedy (organized around story development and continuing characters) and elements of variety-comedy (organized around vaudeville-type gags, performance, direct address, etc.). In fact, the series' first episodes, which aired in 1950, included variety ensembles that performed song and dance numbers on the stage space between acts of the sit-com story. However, by 1951–1952 these variety acts had been incorporated into the narrative/domestic space, so that now performances were clearly motivated by the story.

This mixture of variety-act performance with story elements is particularly significant when looked at in the context of the popular discourses which promised that watching television would be like going to a live theater. As others have argued, the variety-comedies, with their kinetic acts and studio audiences, produced a sense of live spontaneous action. By incorporating these elements into the diegesis, the domestic comedy was able to produce an illusion of being there — an illusion which must have been particularly compelling considering that some of the most popular programs were organized around these principles.

For example, two of the most acclaimed and highly rated comedies, *Make Room for Daddy* and *I Love Lucy*, each systematically incorporated variety-act performances into their domestic worlds. Like *Burns and Allen*, these latter two were each based upon the alternations between a stage space and a domestic space. But unlike *Burns and Allen*, both the stage and the domestic spaces were part of the story. In these cases the premises of family melodrama were seamlessly joined with the premises of variety-show entertainment through storylines which focused on the domestic lives of "show-biz" families. The male heroes (Danny Williams and Ricky Ricardo) were entertainers who regularly performed on their nightclub stages. However, these performance segments were just as often incorporated into the domestic space where they were integrated with the story.

This sense of the home as a theater was also operative in programs which were based upon more realistic story premises. A good example is *The Adventures of Ozzie and Harriet,* a sit-com of enormous popularity which began on television in 1952. In popular magazines the Nelsons were famous for their typicality, and in many ways the program was constructed on realist codes of representation. The Nelson home was decorated with a warm family feel, and shots of their surrounding neighborhood created a sense of a real space. The stories centered around normal, real-life adventures, so that the program had a general sense of "everydayness" about it.

Even with this "overkill" of realist codes, however, the interior space of the Nelson home was often rendered in a highly theatrical fashion, particularly in the early episodes. In a 1952 episode entitled "The Chairs," the foyer in the Nelson home served as a proscenium on which the events took place in the opening scene. A round white rug which covered the center of the foyer floor functioned as a spotlight for the action. The scene, which lasted for about six minutes of screen time, contained a minimal amount of editing, and the camera moved only in order to follow the principal action or to reframe the action slightly as actors entered or exited the frame. The scene was played almost entirely in long to medium long shot. Given this high degree of stasis, the editing, camera movement, and shot distance variation which was employed tells us something about the rules of representation upon which, I would argue, many of these early sit-coms were based. There are a total of five edits in this lengthy scene. The first is a cinematic form of editing, a match cut on action which is used as Ricky Nelson opens the front door. But mixed with this form of cinematic realism is an editing style based on a theatrical conception of representation—namely, editing on the stage entrances and exits of principal actors. First we get two cut away shots as Ozzie and Harriet each enter the central space of action. Later in the scene, the camera pans to follow Ricky and David as they exit the room, after which we cut back to Ozzie.

The other sense of theatrical representation in this scene stems from the absence of point-of-view editing between characters. Much as in the live theater, the action and dialogue in this scene is played to the audience, a pattern typical of many scenes in early situation comedies. But it wasn't just that these kinds of scenes imitated the theater; they were not simply documents of the performance. Instead, I would suggest that there were camera practices and editing rules for television which proceeded on theatrical assumptions about representation. For example, although this scene in *Ozzie and Harriet* is played almost entirely at a wide camera distance, towards the end of the scene, Ozzie Nelson engages in a long telephone conversation in which the camera first zooms into a close-up and then cuts to an extreme close-up of his facial expressions. Through what logic, if any, do these shots appear?

These close-ups are symptomatic of a more general shot rhetoric of early television. Often the scenes in these sit-coms were shot and edited on principles of distance (close-up, medium shot, long shot) or angle variation. In these kinds of scenes the action is less motivated by story elements (such as character psychology, or even unity of time and space) than it is by the viewer's relationship to the performance of the action. It is the viewer's sight—his/her ability to see an action performed—which becomes the central interest in the scene. In this case, the camera movement and editing are motivated by Ozzie Nelson's facial expression—his face registers exasperation with the party on the other end of the telephone. Ozzie's "be-

The rug works as a spotlight for the action as Ricky and David play football in the Nelson foyer (*The Adventures of Ozzie and Harriet*, 1952)

Ozzie performs his "gag" in a close-up (*The Adventures of Ozzie and Harriet*, 1952)

fuddledness" was a recurring gag on the program, so that this moment would have been particularly meaningful for the viewer who would have understood that Ozzie now was going to "do his gag." Camera movement and editing, then, were often motivated by performance details. While the camera's wide view narrativizes a story played out on the central stage/ foyer of the house, the close-ups of Ozzie's face give us another kind of performance—here what can be called, "mugging for the camera."

This kind of "theatrical" representational strategy was used in the cinema—in particular, film comedies featuring well-known comedians relied heavily on "mugging" close-ups. Television sit-coms developed these kinds of passages with particular force, and within their specific broadcast context. The diegetic universe—in shows ranging from *Burns and Allen* to *Ozzie and Harriet*—was often interrupted by scenes that seemed to be of another order. Here, shooting and editing on distance and angle of view gave sit-coms a sense of immediacy, of "unmediated" action, of performance aimed directly at the spectator at home. Put another way, the action appeared to be less mediated by characters (less based on secondary identification) and more directly addressed to the viewer (or more based on primary identification with the camera).[38]

The surrounding trade and popular discourses on television style help to illuminate the significance which these representational practices held for producers, critics and audiences at the time. According to these discourses, it was not just that television in the home had to approximate the live theater—instead, TV was ideally intended to perfect the experience of watching a live performance. Television was meant to give the home audience not just a view, but rather, a *perfect view*.

This perfect vision was typically discussed in terms of television's ability to depict action at optimum distances and to provide ideal angles of sight. Television was better than the theater because it could give people both a wide view of the action and a sense of intimacy through the close-up— and all within the space of one's private living room theater. Both industry trade journals and the popular press repeatedly debated upon the shot distances through which certain kinds of action were best portrayed. For example, in 1949 *House Beautiful* compared the televised concert to its performance in the concert hall claiming that "Television not only embodies [the concert performance] it . . . adds a dimension not offered to the concert goer." This dimension was the specialized view which could be had in the home—the "close-up" which permitted "the spectator to look at the orchestra and the conductor from every angle, to peer into the faces of the musicians, to note their physical characteristics, and to watch the play of emotion on their patently exposed faces."[39] In 1950, a critic for the same magazine thought it better to present the action in the televised concert from a wider distance, stating that, "all musical talent on TV had to be made to look better," by for example, "the elimination of the close-up of the players sweating."[40]

We might recall here that early discourses on the cinema likewise idealized the notion of a perfect view. But again, this ideal had specific meanings within the context of broadcasting and home reception. The perfect view in the cinema was intended to evoke a state of forgetfulness—to make the spectator feel somehow absent from the space of reception and thus more fully immersed in the fantasmatic illusion of presence rendered by the scene itself. But in the discourses on television, the perfect view was meant to produce a different kind of spectatorial fantasy. Implicit in these discourses was the notion that the television text should address its spectator as an audience member—as someone present on the scene of action. Scenes like the one in *Ozzie and Harriet* helped to create the illusion of "being there" because they acknowledged the viewer's presence—they seemed to say, "We know you are watching . . . you out there in television land!" When the camera moved to a wider angle to show Lucy ride on a trick bicycle, or alternatively when it moved in to show one of her numerous mug shots, the text appeared to acknowledge the spectator's presence because its change in perspective was motivated by the audience's point of view, rather than the point of view of the characters or enunciative agency.

Thus, to recapitulate my earlier remarks, the spectator of domestic comedy was not simply placed in the scene of a story—but also at many points in the text the spectator was placed on the scene of action, addressed as part of an audience watching a play. (And the studio audiences and/or laugh tracks used in the domestic comedies added to the sense of "being there"). This illusion of presence was part and parcel of the surrounding discourses on television, discourses which promised that TV would give its audience a sense of connection to the outside world. In this way the private activity of watching television was made pleasurable precisely because one could remain alone in the living room, but at the same time sustain an illusion of being in the company of others.

The Domestic Gaze

While early television programming attempted to fulfill the utopian promise of bringing the world into the home, popular discourses continually deliberated upon the degree to which this new way of seeing could be enjoyed within the domestic context. In some cases, the home was figured as a kind of "ideal theater" where visual pleasures achieved new heights. In fact, the perfect view in television was not only discussed in terms of representational strategies in programming, but also in the context of the home reception environment. In his book, *The Future of Television*, Orrin

E. Dunlap, Jr. wrote in 1947 that television was "Utopia for the Audience." Appraising an early NBC drama, he claimed, "The view was perfect—no latecomers to disturb the continuity; no heads or bonnets to dodge. . . . In television every seat is in the front row."[41]

The arrangement of the perfect view in the home was constantly discussed in women's home magazines, which advised readers on ways to organize seating and ambient lighting so as to achieve a visually appealing effect for the spectator. In these discussions the television set was figured as a focal point in the home, with all points of vision intersecting at the screen. In 1951, *Good Housekeeping* advised its readers that "television is theatre; and to succeed, theatre requires a comfortably placed audience with a clear view of the stage."[42] Furniture companies like Kroehler "Tele-Vue" advertised living room ensembles which were completely organized around the new TV center. As this focal point of vision, television was often represented in terms of a spatial mathematic (or geometry) complete with charts indicating optimal formulas for visual pleasure. In 1949, *Better Homes and Gardens* suggested, "To get a good view and avoid fatigue, sit on eye level with screen at no more than 30 degrees off to the side of screen."[43] Even the TV networks recognized the significance of this new science. CBS in conjunction with Rutgers University studied 102 television homes in order "to determine the distance and angle from which people watch TV under normal conditions."[44]

This scientific management of the gaze in the home, this desire to control and to construct a perfect view, was met with a series of contradictory discourses which expressed multiple anxieties about the ability of the domestic environment to be made into a site of exhibition. The turning of the home into a theater engendered a profound crisis in vision and the positions of pleasure entailed by the organization of the gaze in domestic space. This crisis was registered on a number of levels.

Perhaps the most practical problem which television was shown to have caused was in its status as furniture. Here, television was no longer a focal point of the room; rather it was a technological eyesore, something which threatened to destabilize the unities of interior decor. Women's magazines sought ways to "master" the machine which, at their most extreme, meant the literal camouflage of the set. In 1951, *American Home* suggested that "television needn't change a room" so long as it was made to "retire at your command." Among the suggestions were hinged panels "faced with dummy book backs so that no one would suspect, when they are closed, that this period room lives a double life with TV."[45] In 1953, *House Beautiful* placed a TV into a cocktail table from which it "rises for use or disappears from sight by simply pushing a button. . . ."[46] These attempts to render the television set invisible are especially interesting in the light of critical and popular memory accounts which argue that the television set was a privileged figure of conspicuous consumption and class status for postwar Americans. This attempt to hide the receiver complicates those historical accounts because it suggests that visual pleasure was at odds with the display of wealth in the home.

It wasn't only that the television set was made inconspicuous within domestic space, it was also made invisible to the outside world. The overwhelming majority of graphics showed the television placed in a spot where it could not be seen through the windows of the room.[47] This was sometimes stated in terms of a solution for lighting and the glare cast over the screen. But there was something more profoundly troubling about being caught in the act of viewing television. The attempt to render television invisible to the outside world was imbricated in a larger obsession with privacy—an obsession which was most typically registered in statements about "problem windows." As discussed earlier, the magazines idealized large picture windows and sliding glass doors for the view of the outside world they provided. At the same time, however, the magazines warned that these windows had to be carefully covered with curtains, venetian blinds, or outdoor shrubbery in order to avoid the "fish bowl" effect. In these terms, the view incorporated in domestic space had to be a one-way view.

Television would seem to hold an ideal place here because it was a "window on the world" which could never look back. Yet, the magazines treated the television set as if it were a problem window through which residents in the home could be seen. In 1951, *American Home* juxtaposed suggestions for covering "problem" windows with a tip on "how to hide a TV screen."[48] Even the design of the early television consoles, with their cabinet doors which covered the TV screen, suggested the fear of being seen by television. Perhaps, this fear was best expressed in 1949 when the *Saturday Evening Post* told its readers, "Be Good! Television's Watching." The article continued, "Comes now another invasion of your privacy. . . . TV's prying eye may well record such personal frailties as the errant husband dining with his secretary. . . ."[49] The fear here was that the television camera might record men and women unawares—and have devastating effects upon their romantic lives.

The theme of surveillance was repeated in a highly self-reflexive episode of the early fifties science fiction anthology, *Tales of Tomorrow*. Entitled "The Window,"[50] the tale begins with a standard sci-fi drama but is soon "interrupted" when the TV camera picks up an alien image, a completely unrelated view of a window through which we see a markedly lower-class and drunken husband, his wife and another man (played by Rod Steiger). After a brief glimpse at this domestic scene, we cut back to the studio where a seemingly confused crew attempts to explain the aberrant image, finally suggesting that it is a picture of a real event occuring simultaneously in the city and possibly "being reflected off an ionized cloud right in the middle of our wavelength, like a mirage." As the episode continues to alternate between the studio and the domestic scene, we learn that the wife and her male friend plan to murder the husband, and we see the lovers' passionate embrace (as well as their violent fantasies). At the end of the episode, after the murder takes place, the wife stares out the window and confesses to her lover that all night she felt as if someone were watching her. As this so well suggests, the new TV eye threatens to turn back on itself, to penetrate the private window and to monitor the eroticized fantasy life of the citizen in his or her home. That this fantasy has attached to it a violent dimension, reminds us of the more sadistic side to television technology as TV now becomes an instrument of surveillance. Indeed, this fear of surveillance was symptomatic of many statements which expressed profound anxieties about television's control over human vision in the home—especially in terms of its disruptive effects on the relationship between the couple.[51]

Television brought to the home a vision of the world which the human eye itself could never see. We might say that in popular culture there was a general obsession with the perfection of human vision through technology. This fascination of course pre-dates the period under question, with the development of machines for vision including telescopes, x-rays, photography and cinema. During the postwar period many of these devices were mass produced in the form of children's toys (including microscopes, 3-D glasses, and telescopes) and household gadgets like gas ranges with window-view ovens.

Television, the ultimate expression of this technologically improved view, was variously referred to as a "hypnotic eye," an "all seeing eye," a "mind's eye," and so forth. But there was something troubling about this television eye. A 1954 documentary produced by RCA and aired on NBC suggests the problem. Entitled *The Story of Television*, this program tells the history of television through a discourse on the gaze. A voice-over narration begins the tale in the following way:

> The human eye is a miraculous instrument. Perceptive, sensitive, forever tuned to the pulsating wavelengths of life. Yet the eye cannot see over a hillside or beyond the haze of distance. To extend the range of human eyesight, man developed miraculous and sensitive instruments.

Most prominent among these instruments was the "electronic eye" of television.

In this RCA documentary, the discourse on the gaze was used to promote the purchase and installation of the TV set. However, even in this industry promo, there is something disturbing about the "electronic eye" of television. For here, television inserts itself precisely at the point of a failure in human vision, a failure which is linked to the sexual relations of the couple. Accompanying this sound track is a visual narrative which represents a young couple. A woman frolics on the hillside and we cut to an extreme close-up of a man's face, a close-up which depicts a set of eyes that appear to be searching for the woman. But the couple are never able to see one another because their meeting is blocked by an alternate, and more technologically perfect view. We are shown instead the "electronic eye" of a TV control tower which promises to see better than the eyes of the young lovers. Thus, the authority of human vision, and the power dynamics attached to the romantic exchange of looks between the couple, is somehow undermined in this technology of vision.

This failure in the authority of human vision was typically related to the man's position of power in domestic space. In 1953, *TV Guide* asked, "What ever happened to men? Once upon a time (Before TV) a girl thought of her boyfriend or husband as her prince charming. Now having watched the antics of Ozzie Nelson and Chester A. Riley, she thinks of her man as a prime idiot." Several paragraphs later the article relates this figure of the ineffectual male to an inability to control vision, or rather television, in the home. As the article suggests, "Men have only a tiny voice in what programs the set is tuned to."[52]

In a 1954 episode of *Fireside Theatre*, a filmed anthology drama, this problem is demonstrated in narrative terms. Entitled "The Grass is Greener," the episode revolves around the purchase of a television set, a purchase which the father in the family, Bruce, adamantly opposes. Going against Bruce's wishes, the wife, Irene, makes use of the local retailer's credit plan and has a television set installed in her home. When Bruce returns home for the evening, he finds himself oddly displaced by the new center of interest. Upon entering the kitchen door, he hears music and gun shots emanating from the den. Curious about the sound source, he enters the den where he sees Irene and the children watching a TV western. Standing in the den doorway, he is literally off-center in the frame, outside the family group clustered around the TV set. When he attempts to get his family's attention, his status as outsider is further suggested. Bruce's son hushes his father with a dismissive "Shh," after which the family resumes its fascination with the television program. Bruce then motions to Irene who finally—with a look of condescension—exits the room to join her husband in the kitchen where the couple argue over the set's installation. In her attempt to convince Bruce to keep the TV, Irene suggests that the children and even she herself will stray from the family home if he refuses to allow them the pleasure of watching TV. Television thus threatens to undermine the masculine position of power in the home to the extent that the father is disenfranchised from his family whose gaze is fastened onto an alternate, and more seductive, authority.

Bruce's son hushes his father as television takes center stage in the home (*Fireside Theatre*, 1954)

This crisis in vision was also registered in terms of female positions of pleasure in television. In fact, for women, pleasure in viewing television appears to have been a "structured absence." These representations almost never show a woman watching television by herself. Typically, the woman lounges on a sofa, perhaps reading a book, while the television remains turned off in the room.[53] Two points emerge. First, for women the continuum, visual pleasure—displeasure, was associated with interior decor and not with viewing television. In 1948, *House Beautiful* made this clear when it claimed, "Most men want only an adequate screen. But women alone with the thing in the house all day, have to eye it as a piece of furniture."[54] Second, while these discussions of television were often directed at women, the continuum, visual pleasure—displeasure, was not associated with her gaze at the set, but rather with her status as representation, as something to be looked at by the gaze of another.

On one level here, television was depicted as a threat to the visual appeal of the female body in domestic space. Specifically, there was something visually displeasurable about the sight of a woman operating the technology of the receiver. In 1955, Sparton Television proclaimed that "the sight of a woman tuning a TV set with dials near the floor" was "most unattractive." The Sparton TV, with its tuning knob located at the top of the set, promised to maintain the visual appeal of the woman.[55] As this ad indicates, the graphic representation of the female body viewing television had to be carefully controlled; it had to be made appealing to the eye of the observer.

Beyond this specific case, there was a distinct set of aesthetic conventions formed in these years for male and female viewing postures. A 1953 advertisement for CBS-Columbia Television illustrates this well. Three alternative viewing postures are taken up by family members. A little boy stretches out on the floor, a father slumps in his easy chair, and the lower portion of a mother's outstretched body is gracefully lifted in a sleek modern chair with a seat which tilts upward.[56] Here as elsewhere, masculine viewing is characterized by a slovenly body posture. Conversely, feminine viewing posture takes on a certain visual appeal even as the female body passively reclines.

This need to maintain the "to-be-looked at" status of the woman's body within the home might be better understood in the context of a second problem which television was shown to bring to women—namely, competition for male attention. Magazines, advertisements and television programming often depicted the figure of a man who was so fascinated with the screen image of a woman that his real life mate remained thoroughly neglected by his gaze. Thus, in terms of this exchange of looks, the television set became the "other woman." Even if the screen image was not literally another woman, the man's visual fascination evoked the structural relations of female competition for male attention, a point well illustrated by a cartoon in a 1952 issue of the fashionable men's magazine, Esquire, which depicted a newly wed couple in their honeymoon suite. The groom, transfixed by the sight of wrestling on TV, completely ignores his wife.[57] This sexual scenario was also taken up by Kotex, a feminine hygiene company with an obvious stake in female sexuality. The 1949 ad shows a woman who, by using the sanitary napkin, is able to distract her man from his TV baseball game.[58] Perhaps, the ultimate expression of female competition with television came in a 1953 episode of *I Love Lucy* entitled, "Ricky and Fred are TV Fans." Lucy and her best friend, Ethel Mertz, are entirely stranded by their husbands as the men watch the fights on the living room console. In a desperate attempt to attract their husbands' attention, Lucy and Ethel stand in front of the TV set, blocking the men's view of the screen. Ricky and Fred Mertz become so enraged that they begin to make violent gestures, upon which Lucy and Ethel retreat into the kitchen. Having lost their husbands to television, the women decide to go to a drugstore/soda shop. However, once in the drugstore they are unable to get service because the proprietor is likewise entranced by the TV boxing match.

Ladies' Home Journal 66 (May 1949), p. 30

But in what way could this sexual/visual competition appeal to women? A 1952 Motorola ad provides some possible answers. The graphic shows a man lounging on a chair and watching a bathing beauty on the TV screen. His wife, dressed in apron, stands in the foreground holding a shovel, and the caption reads, "Let's go, Mr. Dreamer, that television set won't help you shovel the walk." Television's negative effect on household chores was linked to the male's visual fascination in the televised image of another woman. This relationship drawn between the gaze and household chores only seems to underline TV's negative appeal for women; but another aspect of this ad suggests a less "masochistic" inscription of the female consumer. The large window view and the landscape painting hung over the set suggest the illusion of the outside world and the incorporation of that world into the home. In this sense, the ad suggests that the threat of sexuality/infidelity in the outside world can be contained in the home through its representation on television. Even while the husband neglects his wife and household chores to gaze at the screen woman, the housewife is in control of his sexuality insofar as his visual pleasure is circumscribed by domestic space. The housewife's gaze in the foreground and cited commentary further illustrate this position of control.[59]

This competition for male attention between women and television also bears an interesting relationship to the construction of the female image in domestic comedies. Typically the representation of the female body was de-feminized and/or de-eroticized. The programs usually featured heroines who were either non-threatening matronly types like Molly Goldberg, middle-aged, perfect housewife types like Harriet Nelson, or else zany women like Lucy Ricardo who frequently appeared clown-like, and even grotesque.

I Love Lucy (1954)

Popular media of the postwar years illuminate some of the central tensions expressed by the mass culture at a time when spectator amusements were being transported from the public to the private sphere. At least at the level of representation, the installation of the television set was by no means a simple purchase of a pleasure machine. These popular discourses remind us that television's utopian promise was fraught with doubt. Even more importantly, they begin to reveal the complicated processes through which conventions of viewing television in the home environment and conventions of television's representational styles were formed in the early period.

Magazines, advertisements and television programming helped to establish rules for ways in which to achieve pleasure and to avoid displeasure caused by the new TV object/medium. In so doing they constructed a subject position—or a series of subject positions—for family members in the home equipped with television. Certainly, the ways in which the public took up these positions is another question. How women and men achieved pleasure from and avoided the discomforts of television is, it seems to me, an on-going and complicated historiographical problem. The popular media examined here allow us to begin to understand the attitudes and assumptions which informed the reception of television in the early period. In addition, they illustrate the aesthetic ideals of middle-class architecture and interior design into which television was placed.

As historian Carlo Ginzburg has argued, "Reality is opaque; but there are certain points—clues, signs—which allow us to decipher it." It is the seemingly inconsequential trace, Ginzburg claims, through which the most significant patterns of past experiences might be sought.[60] These discourses which spoke of the placement of a chair, or the design of a television set in a room, begin to suggest the details of everyday existence into which television inserted itself. They give us a clue into a history of spectators in the home—a history which is only beginning to be written.

NOTES

1. For the standard three volume text written along these lines see Erik Barnouw, *A History of Broadcasting in the United States*, 3 vols. (New York: Oxford, 1966–70).

2. In fact, even while television manufacturers advertised heavily in women's home magazines and the general slicks like *Life*, the magazines did not simply promote television— rather, as this essay shows, they also spoke of the problems which television brought to the home. This should remind us that the ideological content of consumer magazines is not entirely determined by the sales effort. Rather, women's magazines had, since the nineteenth century, been a site for "women's discourses"—albeit in a mass-produced form. The ad-man had to place his consumer messages in this site in order to appeal to potential female consumers. In this sense, I would argue, we need to give the sales effort a less deterministic role and to remember that while magazines and advertisers might work in mutual relations of support, they are relatively autonomous institutions whose strategies might sometimes be at odds. For more on this see my forthcoming dissertation for UCLA, "Installing the Television Set: The Social Construction of Television's Place in the Home and the Family, 1948–55."

3. The media's ambivalent response to technology pre-dates television. In particular, the innovation of household communication technologies like the radio have been greeted by the popular press with skepticism. See, for example, Catherine Covert, "We May Hear Too Much: American Sensibility and the Response to Radio, 1919–1924," in *Mass Media Between the Wars: Perceptions of Cultural Tension, 1918–1941*, ed. Catherine L. Covert and John D. Stevens (Syracuse, NY: Syracuse University Press, 1984), pp. 199–220. Certainly, then, television's introduction in the early period is part of an entire historical context of technological innovation, and it bears continuity with other technologies in this regard. A comparative study which looks at television with respect to other media might better reveal historical differences between them. My work, which explores the case of television and postwar domestic ideals, is, I think, a necessary first step in answering these larger questions.

4. *TV Guide* 1 (June 5–11, 1953), p. 1.

5. This article is based on the research for my dissertation (see above). Three leading home magazines (*House Beautiful, Better Homes and Gardens* and *American Home*) and one leading women's service magazine which foregrounded home economics (*Ladies' Home Journal*) were examined in entirety for the years under consideration. All of these magazines presented idealized (upper) middle-class depictions of domestic space, and were addressed to a female-housewife, middle-class reader. According to audience research studies conducted at the time, the magazines all attracted a largely female, middle-class readership. See for example, Alfred Politz Research, Inc., *The Audiences of Nine Magazines* (N.p.: Cowles Magazines, Inc., 1955). In addition to examining these publications, I used sampling techniques to analyze leading general magazines, men's magazines, and a leading women's magazine, *Good Housekeeping* (which was directed at a less affluent class). The print advertisements were found in these magazines. Finally, the paper is based upon a large number of programs from the early period including almost all episodes from *Burns and Allen, I Love Lucy*, and *The Honeymooners* as well as numerous episodes from *Ozzie and Harriet, The Goldbergs, Make Room For Daddy*, and *I Married Joan*. I refer to these programs as sit-coms, although it should be noted that at the time the sit-com form for television was not yet fully conventionalized.

6. S.C. Gilfillan, "The Future Home Theater," *The Independent* 73 (October 17, 1912), p. 886.

7. Warren J. Susman, *Culture as History: The Transformation of American Society in the Twentieth Century* (New York: Pantheon, 1984), p. 218.

8. Douglas Gomery, "The Coming of Television and the 'Lost' Motion Picture Audience," *Journal of Film and Video* 38 (Summer 1985), pp. 5–11; and Mary Beth Haralovich, "The Suburban Family Sit-com and Consumer Product Design: Middle-Class Consumption in the 1950s," forthcoming in *Quarterly Review of Film Studies*.

9. See, for example, Douglas T. Miller and Marion Nowak, *The Fifties: The Way We Really Were* (Garden City, NY: Doubleday, 1977), especially Chapter 13; and Clifford E. Clark's recent book, *The American Family Home, 1800–1960* (Chapel Hill and London: University of North Carolina Press, 1986). Clark writes, "Almost without thinking middle-class suburbanites took the protected-home vision of the nineteenth-century reformers and turned it into their central pre-occupation" (p. 236). Clark does acknowledge that the new suburbanites were often involved in community activities, but he maintains that the haven model for the home persisted at the ideological level. My argument, on the other hand, insists that the ideology of suburbanization was not merely a return to a nineteenth-century ideal, but rather it included within it the terms of the contradiction between community involvement and domestic seclusion.

10. Harry Henderson, "The Mass-Produced Suburbs," *Harpers* 207 (November 1953), p. 26.

11. For popular books on architecture and interior decor see, for example, *Sunset Homes for Western Living* (San Francisco: Lane Publishing Co., 1946); Robert Woods Kennedy, *The House and the Art of Its Design* (Huntington, NY: Robert E. Krieger Publishing Company, 1953); Cliff May, *Western Ranch Houses* (Menlo Park, CA: Lane Book Co., 1958); Katherine Murrow Ford and Thomas H. Chrieghton, *The American House Today* (New York: Reinhold Publishing Co., 1951).

12. Mural wallpaper was especially used in the homes of the wealthy as exhibited in the exclusive client-built homes of *Architectural Digest*. See, for example, vols. 12 (June 1948), pp. 47, 90; 14 (circa 1955), p. 23.

13. *Better Homes and Gardens* 31 (December 1953), p. 71.

14. Thomas H. Hutchinson, *Here is Television, Your Window on the World* (1946; New York: Hastings House, 1948), p. ix.

15. Charles Siepmann, *Radio, Television and Society* (New York: Oxford, 1950), p. 340.

16. Leo Marx, *The Machine in the Garden: Technology and the Pastoral Ideal in America* (New York: Oxford, 1964), see especially p. 193.

17. Catherine Beecher and Harriet Beecher Stowe, *The American Woman's Home* (New York: J.B. Ford and Company, 1869), pp. 91, 96.

18. Gwendolyn Wright discusses this in *Building the Dream: A Social History of Housing in America* (Cambridge, MA: MIT Press, 1981), p. 107.

19. For an interesting discussion of how modern architecture was popularized through the cinema see Donald Albrecht, *Designing Dreams: Modern Architecture in the Movies* (New York: Harper & Row, 1986).

20. See, for example, "Home Without Compromises," *American Home* 47 (January 1952), p. 34; *Better Homes and Gardens* 33 (September 1955), p. 59; *Good Housekeeping* 133 (September 1951), p. 106.

21. *Better Homes and Gardens* 31 (October 1953), p. 48; *Better Homes and Gardens* 31 (December 1953), p. 21.

22. *Better Homes and Gardens* 33 (March 1953), p. 130.

23. *Fortune* editors, "$30. Billion for Fun," reprinted in *Mass Leisure,* ed. Eric Larrabee and Rolf Meyersohn (1955; Glencoe, IL: The Free Press, 1958), pp. 162–168.

24. *House Beautiful* 90 (November 1948), p. 230.

25. *Better Homes and Gardens* 31 (October 1953), p. 8.

26. *Better Homes and Gardens* 29 (November 1951), p. 218.

27. *American Home* 46 (September 1951), p. 27.

28. *House Beautiful* 92 (December 1950), p. 77.

29. See, for example, *Ladies' Home Journal* 67 (May 1950), p. 6; *American Home* 46 (October 1951), p. 8; *House Beautiful* 97 (November 1955), p. 126; *Colliers* 126 (December 9, 1950), p. 58.

30. *Better Homes and Gardens* 30 (October 1952), p. 215. For other examples see, *Life* 34 (October 26, 1953), p. 53; *Life* 35 (October 5, 1953), p. 87; *House Beautiful* 91 (November 1949), p. 77.

31. *Life* 34 (April 27, 1953), p. 12.

32. Early television borrowed this mixed style from popular radio shows of the forties like *The Aldrich Family* which also blended conventions of live vaudeville performance (such as the studio audience and the variety act) with classical storytelling conventions (such as temporal and spatial continuities).

33. For an interesting discussion of the aesthetics and ideology of "liveness" in contemporary TV programming see Jane Feuer, "The Concept of Live Television: Ontology as Ideology," in *Regarding Television,* ed. E. Ann Kaplan (Los Angeles: University Publications of America, Inc., 1983), pp. 12–22.

34. In fact, in the 1956–7 season, the *mise-en-abyme* became literal when George's magic TV was incorporated into the story. George replayed the story on his magic TV and commented upon the narrative events.

35. This episode, for which I have no title, was broadcast live on June 23, 1952.

36. The episode, for which I have no title, deals with a spat between Uncle David and his brother.

37. Serafina Kent Bathrick, *The True Woman and the Family Film: The Industrial Production of Memory,* diss.; University of Wisconsin–Madison, 1981.

38. The fact that many of the early domestic comedies featured characters who were named for real-life stars (like George and Gracie, Lucy, or the entire Nelson family) and whose roles as characters often directly corresponded to real-life events in the lives of the stars, added to this sense of immediacy.

Patricia Mellencamp discusses this conflation of fiction and reality with respect to *I Love Lucy* in her article, "Situation Comedy, Feminism, and Freud: Discourses of Gracie and Lucy," in *Studies in Entertainment: Critical Approaches to Mass Culture,* ed. Tania Modleksi (Bloomington: Indiana University Press, 1986), see especially pp. 87–88.

39. Samuel Chotzinoff, "The Future of Music on Television," *House Beautiful* 91 (August 1949), p. 113.

40. Henry W. Simon, "The Charm of Music Seen," *House Beautiful* 92 (August 1950), p. 97.

41. Orrin E. Dunlap, Jr., *The Future of Television* (New York: Harper and Brothers, 1947), p. 87.

42. "Where Shall We Put the Television Set?" *Good Housekeeping* 133 (August 1951), p. 107.

43. Walter Adams and E.A. Hunferford, Jr., "Television: Buying and Installing It is Fun; These Ideas Will Help," *Better Homes and Gardens* 28 (September 1949), p. 38.

44. Cited in "With an Eye . . . On the Viewer," *Televiser* 7 (April 1950), p. 16.

45. "Now You See It . . . Now You Don't" *American Home* 46 (September 1951), p. 49.

46. *House Beautiful* 95 (December 1953), p. 145.

47. See, for example, *House Beautiful* 91 (October 1949), p. 167; *Better Homes and Gardens* 30 (March 1952), p. 68; *Better Homes and Gardens* 31 (December 1953), p. 71.

48. *American Home* 45 (January 1951), p. 89.

49. Robert M. Yoder, "Be Good! Television's Watching," *Saturday Evening Post* 221 (May 14, 1949), p. 29.

50. Circa 1951–1953.

51. We might also imagine that television's previous use as a surveillance medium in World War II and the early plans to monitor factory workers with television sets, helped to create this fear of being seen by TV. For an interesting discussion of these early surveillance uses, and the way in which this was discussed in the popular and industry press, see Jeanne Allen, "The Social Matrix of Television: Invention in the United States," in *Regarding Television,* ed. E. Ann Kaplan (Los Angeles: University Publications of America, Inc., 1983), pp. 109–119.

52. Bob Taylor, "What is TV Doing to MEN?" *TV Guide* 1 (June 26—July 2, 1953), p. 15.

53. See, for example, *Better Homes and Gardens* 33 (September 1955), p. 59; *Better Homes and Gardens* 31 (April 1953), p. 263; *Popular Science* 164 (February 1954), p. 211; *Ladies' Home Journal* (May 1953), p. 11.

54. W.W. Ward, "Is It Time to Buy Television?" *House Beautiful* 90 (October 1948), p. 172.

55. *House Beautiful* 97 (May 1955), p. 131.

56. *Better Homes and Gardens* 31 (October 1953), p. 151.

57. *Esquire* 38 (July 1952), p. 87.

58. *Ladies' Home Journal* 66 (May 1949), p. 30.

59. *Better Homes and Gardens* 30 (February 1952), p. 154.

60. Carlo Ginzburg, "Morelli, Freud and Sherlock Holmes: Clues and Scientific Method," *History Workshop* 9 (Spring 1980), p. 27.

House Beautiful 91 (Nov. 1949), p.1.

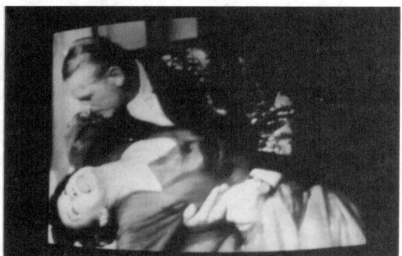

The Martha Raye Show

The Spectacularization of Everyday Life: Recycling Hollywood Stars and Fans in Early Television Variety Shows
Denise Mann

> Many advertisements took their place alongside other mass diversions—the amusement park, the slick-paper romance, the movies. None demanded to be taken literally or even all that seriously; yet all promised intense "real life" to their clientele, and all implicitly defined "real life" as something outside the individual's everyday experience.
>
> Jackson Lears[1]

At the turn of the century in America, the burgeoning field of mass amusement institutionalized the promise that "real life" was just around the corner. Hollywood, with its charged overpresence of stars, glitter and glamor, went on to institutionalize the idea that "real life" was to be found in the movie theater. Studio publicity departments singled out female fans, in particular, for their devoted attention to Hollywood stars and product tie-ins through fan magazines and mass circulation magazines.[2]

Hollywood Stars and Female Fans

The privileged relationship between the motion picture industry and the female fan at the turn of the century has been charted in several social histories as well as in theoretical studies such as Miriam Hansen's recent analysis of the Valentino case and its relationship to female viewer habits.[3] Little attention has been given to the transformation that takes place in this impassioned relationship some thirty years later once Hollywood stars and stories are received in the mundane circumstances of women's everyday lives—the domestic setting of television. The transfer of Hollywood stars to the home via television during the transitional period from 1946 to 1956 shifts the viewing context not just from a public, community event to a private, isolated experience, but also restructures the spectator's fantasy engagement with the movies. This change constitutes a radical transformation in the social imaginary that had previously bound Hollywood

41

stars to their fans. Television representations of the Hollywood star as well as radio's representations before them, reflect a decay in aura[4] once they have been transferred to the new broadcast media.

This study focuses on the television comedy variety show and musical variety show which featured guest stars from Hollywood. These formats represent two arenas of nostalgic return, not only to earlier entertainment traditions (to vaudeville, burlesque, minstrel, etc.), but to strategies adopted by Hollywood films and by their publicity departments to engage women as the most devoted audience of Hollywood stars. The fan and mass-circulation magazines surrounding Hollywood and its star system marked women spectators as an economically and socially viable group—one which the broadcast industry sought to incorporate as an audience for its own mass-media forms.[5]

The Hollywood star offered a potent connection with the fascination of Hollywood cinema—invoking not only the cinema's "cult of subjectivity" but also the star's association with a charged "otherness"; alternatively, the Hollywood star's association with consumer excesses and ostentatious behavior ran counter to fifties ideals of homogeneity and equal opportunity for all.[6] The Hollywood studio publicity departments in previous decades had devised various techniques to negotiate the contrasts in lifestyle and appearance between the Hollywood star and the average working-class or middle-class woman. Contradictory representations of women in the films themselves—as glamorous "screen sirens" and average housewives or working women—do not begin in the postwar period but can be traced to an earlier period. For instance, Mary Ann Doane discusses this phenomenon in the woman's films of the forties using the example of Bette Davis as the twin sisters in *A Stolen Life*.[7] She notes that these oppositional roles are recapitulated in the advertiser's address to female audiences which claim "Every Woman Plays a Double Role . . . [as] Secretary and Siren. . . . " In addition, Jane Gaines's analysis of the forties "pin-up" demonstrates how easily this standardized icon of eroticism was adapted to conform to the more conventional female social roles of wife and mother.[8]

While these studies indicate that contradictory representations of women exist prior to the period under examination, television substantially alters the spectator's relation to these conflicting beauty ideals and social roles for women. In particular, the television variety show helped arbitrate the contrasts in lifestyle between the Hollywood screen siren and the average woman by bringing the performative aspects of vaudeville (its direct address and mugging for the camera) into conflict with the cinema's "illusionist" conventions, challenging as well, the passivity inherent in the cinema's representation of the woman in her object-like-ness.

Early television variety shows adopted a complex set of narrative strategies to produce a "marriage of spectacle and intimacy."[9] This integration of opposing tendencies is based, on the one hand, on television's self-conscious attempts to duplicate vaudeville, burlesque and Broadway theater, entertainment forms which took place in communities bound by ethnic and class alliances.[10] On the other hand, TV variety shows retained ties to the "intimacy" of the classical Hollywood cinema in narrative skits which took place in domestic settings (and which reproduced the illusion of centered subjectivity); this continuity was produced in part by borrowing stylistic elements from the cinema (e.g., close-ups to convey interiority and point-of-view editing).

Recycling the Movie Star as Individual

For working-class and middle-class women of postwar America, the home no longer constituted a sanctuary from the forces of consumer culture—despite efforts of popular culture to convey the contrary through nostalgic references to the past; for instance, Serafina Bathrick's analysis of nostalgic family-musicals from the forties demonstrates how these films cultivated a female audience of consumer allies by translating the more traditional values of home and family to contemporary products of the culture industry.[11] National advertising, network corporations and their bureaucratic agencies had penetrated the daily lives of the family at home with their magazine and radio commercial messages by the 1930s. These and related advertising and network corporate structures were responsible for relaying Hollywood stars and stories to female fans via television—institutions whose presence was foregrounded by means of the various mediating figures of network announcer, product announcer and, in the case of the variety show, the TV show host. The illusion of "centeredness" which the classical codes had insured, mobilizing individual desire through elaborate fantasy scenarios, had been substituted in the television setting by a complex organization composed of anonymous institutions which "made it possible" for these stars to appear on television.

This changed circumstance of spectatorship meant a decentered relation between star and fan. In turn, this decenteredness altered the previous terms of the bond, throwing into jeopardy the apparent "autonomy" and "individualism" of the media celebrity. Richard deCordova's work on the early manifestations of the star system has demonstrated how star discourses work to suggest the marks of enunciation, contradicting Metz's claim that the classical Hollywood film effaces this discursive register.[12] The emphasis on the performative activities of movie stars coupled with a studio star system which promotes the illusion of "individualism" surrounding its stars through its publicity and press releases, makes these performers appear to subsume the category of enunciative address.

This institutionalization of the cult of the individual by the studio star system and studio publicity departments underwent a series of decisive changes in the postwar period. In the midst of the CBS talent raids in 1948, the broadcast star was legally reconfigured to adapt to the new capital gains tax structure.[13] Star names were reconstituted as "property" to be administered primarily by the celebrity rather than by the studio or network. These highly publicized negotiations over star properties in popular press and trade discourses regulated knowledge of these celebrities[14] — emphasizing their status as property over their status as private persons.[15] In the fifties, Hollywood actors began renegotiating their contracts as well, setting up independent companies and demanding control over their image, their roles, and their own advertising and publicity, even in those instances when they made studio films.[16] Ironically, even though motion picture actors were taking charge of their own image, this radically undermined their status as individuals—an image that studio publicity departments began carefully monitoring as early as 1909.[17]

During this transitional period, one means of reengaging the public's imaginary relation to movie stars on television was to enact a nostalgic return to their earlier careers and to the popular discourses surrounding these stars. For instance, there were prime-time variety shows and family sit-coms which targeted the whole family and featured the regular appearance of movie stars as guests. Programs such as *I Love Lucy, The Jack Benny Show* and *The Martha Raye Show* contained narratives which reworked the middle-class housewife's relationship to these celebrated figures from Hollywood by foregrounding the position of the female fan. In addition, in the mid-fifties, a series of "tributes to Hollywood" emerged. One of the first of these appeared in 1952 when Ed Sullivan saluted the career of producer Samuel Goldwyn. This was followed by several movie tie-ins produced by the studios which provided ten to fifteen minute "trailers" of recent Hollywood releases, including *MGM Parade, Warner Brothers Presents* and 20th Century–Fox's *Front Row Center* (for General Electric) as well as Disney's *Disneyland* and *The Mickey Mouse Club*. In addition, Paramount Pictures's interest in York Productions, which it jointly owned with Dean Martin and Jerry Lewis, resulted in *The Colgate Sunday Hour* and *The Colgate Comedy*. The latter show followed Ed Sullivan's lead in "saluting" new feature pictures through talent tie-ups.

These movie talent tie-ins on television proliferated into publicity campaigns, talent promotional tours and sundry merchandising activities which resulted in an almost seamless penetration of Hollywood's consumer appeals into the interstices of the family's everyday life.[18] Daniel Boorstin characterized this tendency in postwar America as television's capacity to create a bond among viewers which constitutes a false community of consumers: "never before had so many individuals been so dependent on material goods for their identity."[19] This community of consumer citizens produced a radical break from the individual spectator's personal past and the community's shared historical past. One of the ways in which television variety shows and other products of fifties culture industry helped negotiate entry into the modern era for middle-class viewers was by adapting the now devalued Hollywood "cult of subjectivity" to more longstanding traditions and values from the past—in particular by wedding the fifties version of the "nineteenth-century True Woman and the twentieth-century movie star."[20]

For instance, *Look* magazine featured a fashion article on the "back button" dress which conflates the fifties nostalgia for the past with the vogue for leveling class differences between stars and fans. This complex advertising strategy is accomplished by featuring movie star Charlton Heston helping his wife, Lydia Clarke, into a "recycled" fashion concept— the back button dress.[21] By conveying the idea that women are helpless, the fashion feature does not just sell women on a "new" style, but reinforces cultural stereotypes of the "True Woman" and the caretaker husband, and promotes the institution of marriage as well: these dresses require "a husband's helping hand" to allow the woman to get dressed in the morning. The article notes the ironies of this fashion design for "America's 14 million unmarried women," but celebrates nonetheless, this "impractical throwback to the 19th century. . . . " The writer notes the contradictions for modern women who "breathed a sigh of relief with the passing of the unwieldy back-laced corset . . . but now, down their backs [find] not only

The dress that needs a man

back buttons are back again and so are men-in-waiting

Look 20 (Feb. 7, 1956), p. 82

buttons, but snaps, hooks and slide fasteners to harness the girls again and put a high premium on a man—personal maids being even harder to come by."[22] The feature encourages fashion-conscious modern women to take up these impractical designs by conflating the traditional values of home and marriage with the image of the Hollywood star as domestic homebody. Charlton Heston's function is thereby split between that of husband and "auratic star"—between attending to the "homey" task of helping his wife get dressed in the morning, *and* introducing "romantic" fantasy associations into an otherwise banal activity.

Recycling Middle-Aged Stars on TV

In a 1955 article, "Old Film Stars Never Die—Just Keep B.O. Rolling Along," *Variety* states that the box office draw of current stars doesn't match that of stars nurtured under the star system of previous decades.[23] The article claims that "audiences today apparently are much slower to 'make' a star . . . [hence] the studios are competing energetically for men and women who played their first lead parts in the middle 30s." *Variety*'s list of durable "glam personalities" includes Clark Gable, Bette Davis, John Wayne, Betty Grable, Spencer Tracy, Ginger Rogers. . . . " According to *Variety*, the only newcomers who command the same box office stature as these older stars are Marilyn Monroe and Marlon Brando. The disadvantages of relying on the older stars, of course, is "that the passage of years is beginning to whittle away at the appeal of the stars of yesteryear."

Variety's comments reiterate the popular view that the old stars and the old Hollywood represented a "glamour" and "extravagance" that was no longer valid in 1950s America—except, that is, through nostalgic recyclings of the star's previous persona in new formats. Popular culture forms which recycled stars in this way include, for instance, the "self-reflexive" musicals of the fifties (Fred Astaire in *Bandwagon,* Judy Garland in *A Star is Born*); middle-class magazine photo essays featuring star biographies which chart the career of the star in pictures; advertising for contemporary beauty and fashion ideals associated with Hollywood stars; and variety shows "saluting" the stars and their careers.

The success of each of these popular culture strategies depended on their ability to trigger the audience's memory of details from the star's personal life and screen persona. Much of early television programming, then, consisted of "simulations" of popular culture traditions from the past. Many of these fragments of past performances emerged out of ethnic theater—leisure practices which took place in communities defined by ethnic, class and gender specificities; however, once these forms were transposed to television, they were stripped of any previous associations with the community. These nostalgic images from the past appeared on early television variety shows in an abstracted, fragmented form, borrowing elements from vaudeville and burlesque; taking scenes from already self-reflexive Hollywood stories (e.g., Gloria Swanson's spoof on her role in *Sunset Boulevard* on *The Texaco Star Theater*); or in caricatures of famous performers from the past (e.g. Milton Berle's drag impersonation of Carmen Miranda).[24] This postmodernist impulse—the creation of a new television spectacle out of the fragments and reworkings of the original spectacular, public event—invoked "simulated" emotions and produced a synthetic sense of community, united by its shared memory of previous media contexts. This is nowhere more evident than in early television variety shows which restaged Hollywood stories and recycled stars. Hollywood's penetration into the television industry provided a means of spectacularizing the everyday. By evoking memories of intensely felt emotions and an opulent world that existed outside the home, these programs provided a much needed antidote to the homogenizing tendencies of so much of the popular culture imagery of the postwar period. One movie producer summed up popular assumptions about the differences between Hollywood stars and TV stars: "TV can give them stories about frustrated butchers and homely aunts . . . but we can take an audience into Vesuvius or plunk them headfirst into the China Sea."[25]

The movies in postwar America promoted themselves by holding onto their associations with aristocratic behavior and conspicuous consumption. Television variety shows featuring Hollywood stars as guests were capitalizing on the lingering appeal of these idols of consumption. On the other hand, these same TV shows contained skits which made Hollywood stars appear as intruding figures, threatening the positive values and associations of domesticity and family life maintained by the television star, week after week.[26] According to Jane Gaines, audiences were more likely to direct their bitterness and envy toward Hollywood stars during the Depression, or in war-torn America "because they were visible and identifiable whereas institutions are anonymous."[27] A brief examination of popular discourses on Hollywood stars reveals strategies which may have helped audiences negotiate their contradictory responses to Hollywood stars during the period of vast social and economic upheaval that followed WWII. Many of these same techniques are taken up by the TV variety show.

Hollywood/Television: A Period of Consolidation

According to Roland Marchand, in postwar America the popular press conveyed an image of average Americans as being more affluent, having more leisure time and more opportunity to improve their standard of living.[28] But in point of fact, only those in the very top income bracket were noticeably affected by the postwar boom.[29] The 1950s saw a 26% rise in average income with credit and installment buying providing more possibility for more families to duplicate the portrait of the affluent suburban family being promoted by advertisers. But most lower-to-middle-class families had to struggle to meet this ideal image.

In response to perceived changes in the public's attitude toward these idols of consumption in an era which valued equality of opportunity, in 1956 *Look* featured an article called "Hollywood Revisited: A Psychological X-Ray of the Movie Colony Today—its Manners, its Conflicts, its Morals—Where Television, Wide-screen and Middle-age Have Forever Changed the Life and Work of the Glamorous."[30] Charting the lives of Hollywood stars in 1956, the article proclaims: "they are less carefree, less reckless, less extravagant. Today it's chic to be simple."[31] The article is meant to demonstrate how "toned down" Hollywood stars have become, and yet photos of the stars convey the opposite impression. One shows Susan Hayward wearing an "odd getup" consisting of harem pants, halter top and what look like police boots, an outfit designed to "beguile the blasé." Another features Sonja Henie's flamboyant arrival at a party at Ciros. She wears a sequined trapeze artist costume and rides a baby elephant. The article conveys the ambivalence fifties fans felt toward Hollywood, their dissatisfaction with its class pretensions and also their ongoing fascination with its sensual excesses. This provided women at home with an imaginary link to a charged "real life" outside their everyday life in the domestic sphere.

On the other hand, the animosity expressed in this article toward Hollywood stars' aristocratic sensibilities can be traced to the forties, when studio publicity efforts downplayed certain stars in order to militate against what the studios perceived as reader hostility toward the stars' "upper class" lifestyles. For instance, in her analysis of fan magazines in the forties, Jane Gaines says Lana Turner was brought down to earth in a report which told readers that "she returned her rented sable to the furrier after every party . . . [while] Joan Crawford was described as a homebody who preferred listening to Bing Crosby or Dinah Shore to listening to opera."[32] Radio (and later television) stars such as Bing Crosby and Dinah Shore came to embody the "down to earth" qualities favored by the popular press in the postwar period. Studio press releases began to emphasize those qualities which made movie stars appear to be "homebodies." By deemphasizing class distinctions, representations of Hollywood stars in fan and mass circulation magazines during the forties and increasingly during the fifties served a therapeutic function, helping the housewife or working woman overcome feelings of powerlessness and the inability to rise above her current social role or class standing.[33]

Postwar Fashion and Beauty Ideals for the Average Housewife

By the 1950s, popular ideals regarding women's bodies and clothes were in transition. *Look* and *Life* began featuring articles on fashion and body types that emphasized comfort and uniformity in contrast to Hollywood's often unwieldy and extravagant designs. For instance, when Gregory Peck and 20th Century–Fox star, Maris Pavan, appeared in *The Man in the Gray Flannel Suit, Look* carried a series of ads and fashion spreads which showed the stars sporting ubiquitous gray flannel suits.[34] "Gray flannel is in the limelight from Hollywood to the Eastern suburbs," *Look* claims. "Whether a girl is a movie star, advertising executive or housewife, gray flannel's appeal to her is limitless." To convey this "classless, ageless fashion," *Look* features a suburban wife meeting her husband in gray flannel slacks (by Evan-Picone) at the Pelham, N.Y. railroad station in a photograph which is not only larger, but dominant on the page, placed above the photo of the movie stars wearing gray flannel.[35] Another example promoted by *Look* magazine is the "strapless apron [which] shows your shoulders."[36] The caption explains that "it goes on in a jiffy over strapless dresses—and still keeps you looking beautifully bare." For fashions that extend "classlessness" in the opposite direction, *Look* magazine in 1948 offers ranch clothes that take clothing previously designed for the "hard-working" ranch life to the "vacation-minded" American from Portland, Maine, to Portland, Oregon.[37]

As these features suggest, postwar fashion tastes reflect a composite of opposing ideals—a conflation of the star's wardrobe with that of the average suburban housewife, or alternatively, the conflation of working man's clothes with the middle-class leisure set. The "leveling" effect of these outfits is overdetermined in the fashion feature on gray flannel suits which explains: for the "huckster," gray flannel conveys "sincerity," and for the average woman it conveys "slickness."[38] While this ad expresses the mistrust and skepticism which underlies the public's reading of visual images and consumer appeals in the media, it also produces a compensatory image of social relations in postwar America.

The superficial appearance of equal opportunity for all underlying these complex popular culture strategies—their purportedly neutral goal of "classlessness"—can in point of fact be seen to reinforce an ideology of political indifference which diffuses whatever class consciousness had been prompted by studio releases foregrounding class distinctions between the stars and their fans in the thirties and forties. In her analysis of fan magazines, Jane Gaines indicated the extent of this class awareness which prompted readers to express anger toward press releases which tried to downplay the celebrity's obvious advantages over their working-class counterparts.[39] A series of ads for Auto-Lite Spark Plugs which appeared in *Look* magazine in 1948 epitomize this superficial homogenizing process. These ads emphasize the crossover between movie stars and average housewives by featuring "lookalikes." In one of these ads, a housewife from Brooklyn, N.Y., who "looks so much like Miss [Dorothy] Lamour that strangers frequently ask her for her autograph on the street . . . " is pictured side by side with a photograph of the "real" Dorothy Lamour. The ad asks the reader to guess which is the movie star.[40]

Look 12 (March 30, 1948), p. 15

In the same year, *Look* offers a feature asking average citizens "How has having a movie star's name affected you?" Average men and women with stars' names are interviewed—including a beautician named Anne Sheridan, a cafeteria helper named Esther Williams, and a truck driver named Harold Lloyd.[41] Photos of the average citizen are produced, but none are provided of the stars to whom they are compared. If the reader had been allowed to scrutinize one photograph next to the other, it would have introduced an uncomfortable "class awareness," reminding the reader of the material discrepancies dividing the two groups. The subtlety of this rhetorical strategy serves two ends: it preserves the auratic qualities of the stars (by invoking in the reader memories of some previous experience of a fantasy engagement with a favorite star at the movies, or in a fan magazine); secondly, it neutralizes any evidence of the material class distinctions separating stars and fans. This double-edged strategy plays an important role in the development of early television variety programming which introduced Hollywood stars into their shows. By dividing the auratic from the class-defined characteristics of the Hollywood star, early television programs were able to exorcise any lingering associations of Hollywood stars with aristocratic behavior.

TV Stars: Frustrated Butchers, Homely Aunts and Obsessive Fans

The previous discussion indicates that popular attitudes toward Hollywood stars were in a process of transition in postwar America. Visual representations of TV stars as ordinary individuals—frustrated butchers and homely aunts—can be seen as a compensatory gesture designed to counteract the celebrity's status as either upper class, *or* as corporate property. However, a brief look at the popular discourse on television stars and radio stars before them reveals the contradictions which were exposed in trying to portray these "corporate salesman" as authentic individuals. For instance, *Look* magazine's 1949 spread on Arthur Godfrey lauded him for his "honest, plain common-sense approach."[42] In the following month, several viewers wrote letters to the editor expressing their mixed feelings about Godfrey's supposed sincerity.[43] These readers challenged the popular press' image of Godfrey as natural and spontaneous, pointing out his ultimate responsibility to sponsors. For instance, reader R.L. Morrisey notes: "this guy Godfrey has the formula, all right. He slouches down in an easy chair, takes off his tie, rolls up his sleeves and convinces 40,000,000 radio listeners that he's just like good ol' Uncle Fred. Like Uncle Fred, he spins salty yarns and leads the group singing. But unlike Uncle Fred, Godfrey's payoff is of strictly big business proportions. . . . "[44]

This letter and others like it evoke the contradictions attending reception of radio's purportedly authentic stars. On the other hand, despite the unmistakable hostility of this letter, Morrisey closes by conceding that Godfrey satisfies a "social need" for the majority of viewers. This therapeutic mode points to the conflicting needs which media celebrities satisfied in postwar America. Morrisey concludes: "More power to Godfrey . . . because he's a daily tonic to so many people."[45]

In the early thirties Jack Benny's radio show produced a separation of star functions by displacing the role of the "glamorous star" onto his Hollywood guest stars, making Benny himself their dupe or fool. (This separation was already in place in his vaudeville persona—his ironic presentation of himself as an arrogant, pretentious concert violinist who plays the violin badly.) In his radio and television programs Benny undermined his own status as star by pitting himself against glamorous movie stars like Marilyn Monroe, Claudette Colbert or Ronald Colman. By coveting their Oscars, their film roles, and their co-stars, he was openly acknowledging his "difference" from the Hollywood star, a difference which audiences no doubt recognized when they compared themselves to Hollywood stars. By contrasting the TV stars to their Hollywood counterparts, the believability and trustworthiness of the former were reinforced. This split in function attributed to each set of stars—the broadcast vs. the Hollywood—provided a means of rechanneling the libidinal attachment fans felt for Hollywood stars, and at the same time encouraged women to empathize with TV stars as sincere product salespersons.

One of the rhetorical strategies used in variety show skits to integrate these two arenas was to nest one audience/text relation within the other: in other words, the Hollywood star/fan relation was framed in the context of the broadcast star/audience relation. This narratological structure is apparent when Marilyn Monroe makes her first television appearance on Benny's show. Benny holds the position both of movie star fan *and* TV star/host. As TV star/host, Benny introduces Marilyn Monroe as his guest star. However, once he steps into character in the skit that follows, he maintains his character role of movie star fan and he also plays himself— Jack Benny, the TV star.

In the skit, his imaginary relation to the auratic star is constructed *in her absence*: he imagines that he is pursuing Marilyn Monroe; in fact, he is pursuing an ordinary-looking woman. Like Benny's character, this woman is imaginatively tied to Hollywood's romantic fantasies—she reads a Hollywood fan magazine. When Benny confuses her with Marilyn Monroe, she adapts herself immediately to the fantasy scenario. In contrast, once he realizes she's not Marilyn Monroe, he pulls away. She testily reminds him that he's not Errol Flynn either. The exchange is symptomatic

The Jack Benny Show

of the contrast in popular attitudes toward Hollywood vs. TV stars. In addition, the skit characterizes popular assumptions about female spectators—that they have a more active imaginary—allowing them to participate more fully in the Hollywood romance scenario. But, it is suggestive that in this instance the male TV star is being put in the "feminized" position of the fan.

This strategy informs other comedy variety shows which place the TV star in the powerless, "feminized" role of the movie star fan. These rhetorical strategies can be seen as a way of arbitrating the contrasts between the movie star and the home audience via the TV star. Benny's power and autonomy vanish once he adopts the "feminized" position of the adoring fan in the narrative skit. It returns once he reappears on stage as the star of his own show and speaks to the audience in "direct address." These changing power dynamics are the result of shifting rhetorical positionings rather than some essentially "female" characteristic of desire. By having TV stars (both male and female) function in this intermediary role of "feminized" spectator (conforming to popular assumptions about female fans), these TV variety shows may have helped produce alternative and multiple positions of identification and so helped mediate the public's receptivity to Hollywood stars. However, this case requires further exploration.

The TV Star/Host as Authentic Individual

After the skit, Benny comes out on stage to thank Fox Studios for allowing him to "dream" about Marilyn Monroe on his show. The irony implicit in Benny's statement is that while the sponsor has made a contractual agreement with the studio to have one of its stars appear on television, what has in fact been purchased is the imaginary affect or aura linking Hollywood stars to their fans. This imaginary relation is the result of the star's pictures, publicity and fan materials—synthesizing aspects of the actor's public and private life. As a result, stars like Marilyn Monroe appear out of place in the overtly commercial context of television, unless that presentation is negotiated—in this case by the split roles of the TV star as star/host and fan. When Marilyn does finally appear on stage at the end of the show, plugging her recent film, wearing a glamorous evening gown and adopting her often photographed "open mouthed smile," her Hollywood star persona remains intact. Her appearance on Benny's show functions much like the traditional product testimonial for shampoo and other beauty products—an accepted formula for linking the female star's image to consumer products while at the same time providing promotional tie-ins to the star's recent pictures.[46]

The Jack Benny Show

The Hollywood star persona from the past projected a cohesive portrait of an individual—a synthesis of the various elements of the star's career and home-life, all engineered by the studio publicity department. Even overt product tie-ins had to refer the viewer to the star's glamorous persona. In contrast, the radio and television host's star persona is radically split between his or her function as autonomous individual and as corporate spokesperson. In order to systematize the heterogeneity underlying this "direct address" to the audience, Benny, along with Ed Wynn and several other performers, began incorporating an ironic perspective into their speech. The radio star could reengage listener trust by calling attention to the commercial structure of the television address. For instance, in 1931, Benny began substituting his opening line, "Hello, again" with "Jello, again."[47] In addition, Benny expresses the irony of trying his "direct sell" techniques on audiences who were immune to sales pitches: "Gee, I thought I did that pretty well for a new salesman. I suppose nobody will drink it [Canada Dry] now."[48] Irony allows the radio host to expose the materiality underlying his or her speech—its commercial context in the sponsored program. By giving viewers the impression that advertisers and their stars had placed all their cards on the table, viewer skepticism was partially circumvented.[49]

Benny's ironic speech may have distanced him in part from the advertising context, however, it produced a tenuous "individuality" against the overbearing commodification of his broadcast star persona. The instability of the TV star image as a coherent originator of the TV show's enunciative address is further complicated once that position is held by a woman in view of the spectator's memory of the patriarchal bias underlying the Hollywood cinema and its typical portrayal of women as spectacle of a male gaze.

The Everyday Female TV Star vs. The Glamorous Hollywood Star

Alongside the development described above, the TV star's "divided" and hence unstable position of enunciative address, is another set of discourses about female TV stars and female product announcers. These emphasize their "naturalness" in contrast to Hollywood's elaborate machinery for deception. A 1954 article, "Claws Out!—Glamor Girls vs. TV Actresses," graphically outlines the opposition by stating that Hollywood stars are the product of Hollywood's massive publicity techniques, their glamour the result of Hollywood's extensive costume, makeup and lighting.[50] Television advertisers perpetuated this image of the TV star's naturalness in their appeals to women. *Television Magazine,* for instance, advised advertisers not to use overly glamorous stars to advertise their products because women don't like to see a glamorous woman washing dishes or scrubbing floors.[51] When asked about Kate Smith selling products on the air, a viewer says ". . . I don't see how Kate Smith would have too much time to use a sewing machine. And . . . I don't think she herself puts it [floor wax] on or knows anything about it." When asked if that bothered her, the viewer said: "No, I just don't think about it because I love to hear Kate Smith talk and sing, she's a wonderful woman."[52] These advertising claims reinforced the view that mass media images of housewives were "natural" and images of glamorous Hollywood stars were unnatural. These popular assumptions intervene in the spectator's reception of Hollywood stars on television variety programming in the early period.

Martha Raye—Recasting The Movie Star as Television Star

These contradictory attitudes toward female media celebrities in the postwar period frame the following discussion of *The Martha Raye Show.* Martha Raye's address to women at home—as herself (presumed to be an authentic individual) and as a product spokesperson (for Hazel Bishop cosmetics)—is complicated by her previous Hollywood persona. The remainder of this study is devoted to the Martha Raye case in view of the relationship between her film and television roles. Her contradictory representations of femininity from films made in the thirties and forties figure significantly into television's negotiated portraits of feminine ideals for the postwar period.

From 1936–1938 Raye appeared in a series of Paramount films playing various "trouble-prone secretaries" and "boy-mad coeds."[53] In 1938 Paramount decided to change her image as slapstick comedienne and feature her in a series of glamour girl roles, including *Give Me a Sailor* (1938) in which she won not only a legs contest against Betty Grable but the leading man as well. This was followed by several other films which adapted Raye's image to suit more conventional standards of feminine behavior and beauty from the forties. The contradictions inherent in Raye's movie career are restaged in her 1950s television show. Opposing representations of women are structurally woven into the variety format. The program alternated between staged spectacles featuring Raye in elaborate gowns and glamorous lighting and narrative skits in which Raye plays average working-class and middle-class women.

Raye's suitability for sincere product testimonials was jeopardized by the instability of her image. For instance, *The Martha Raye Show* opened with Raye demonstrating Hazel Bishop cosmetics while "mugging" in front of the camera, mocking traditional cosmetic ads which used glamorous models or movie stars. The second and third ads in the program returned to a more conventional ad structure (and notably excluded Raye). These ads took place in Hollywood, a shift in location that did not in fact take place but was indicated by an announcer and by showing filmed scenes of familiar Hollywood locales. These techniques were designed to transform the "live" New York stage into Hollywood for the benefit of the home audience. Lesser known female stars were brought onto the stage to demonstrate the glamorizing effects of these cosmetics. Despite these efforts to reproduce the typical association of Hollywood and glamour (a standard technique borrowed from magazine advertising), Hazel Bishop spokesperson, Raymond Spector, repeatedly voiced his dissatisfaction with his company's sponsorship of Raye's show and eventually dropped the show in the 1955 season.[54]

The Martha Raye Show

This shift in locations—from filmed sequences to the television stage—has other implications beyond the advertiser's cooption of Hollywood's glamour for product demonstrations. Spatial continuity between TV's "live" sets and filmed exteriors appear in other portions of the "live" variety show and demonstrate television's debt to classical Hollywood conventions on a number of fronts. Typically, these two "spaces" are brought together by means of conventions borrowed from classical Hollywood films; for instance, in an episode which shows Martha leaving her apartment and entering the street, the transfer from the staged, domestic setting to the filmed exterior is produced by having her neighbor look out the apartment window and wave to Martha below. The second (filmed) shot shows Martha looking back up from the street. The sequence perpetuates this alternation of staged and filmed views, culminating in an automobile crash (which is simulated by intercutting filmed long-shots of Martha, driving her antiquated car in busy city streets, and close-ups of Martha inside the car, shot on a stage). When Martha collides with a Rolls Royce belonging to a glamorous Hollywood starlet, the sequence that follows highlights the striking contrast between Martha and the movie star. This is conveyed by returning to a "staged" version of the street scene and by shooting the scene in a frontal long-shot: Martha's austere clothes and old car are juxtaposed to the glamorous movie star's furs, jewels and Rolls Royce. The overt class dimensions of this scene are commingled with questions of preferred beauty standards for women. The sequence overtly parodies the convention of the male gaze at the female-as-object: several male bystanders "reconstruct" the accident in favor of the glamorous movie star, pretending not to see Martha, focusing their attention instead on the starlet. On the other hand, the audience is able to see both women side by side, as well as the inequity of the social dynamics at play, and is encouraged, thereby, to empathize with Martha.

These reconstructed views, depending on the audience's familiarity with Hollywood conventions—the object/glance structure in this case—would *not* be enacted for the studio audience. In order to overcome this lapse in

The Martha Raye Show

the variety show's "marriage of spectacle and intimacy," large monitors were placed above the stage for the benefit of the studio audience.[55] This addition of a frame or screen to the "live" television event undermines statements made by critics of the period who criticized TV for enacting a simple return to vaudeville and other forms of ethnic theater.[56] TV producers may have been responding in part to these critics when they adapted these theatrical stage traditions by incorporating alternative forms of representation. In particular, the presence of a screen, necessary to mediate the studio audience's reading of the "live" theatrical event, reveals the extent to which variety shows abstracted elements from these earlier forms of stage entertainment and adapted them to contemporary tastes by incorporating conventions inherited from the classical Hollywood film.

TV Retraces the Past: Adapting Hollywood Conventions to Postwar Ideals—The Case of Martha Raye

In previous sections I examined strategies taken up by the popular press both to preserve the star's auratic properties and efface the troubling question of class underlying the star/fan relation through visual representations which leveled material differences separating these two social groups. To this set of contingencies, *The Martha Raye Show* contributes yet another dimension—the need to adapt her unstable femininity to contemporary ideals of domesticity and feminine behavior. Her TV variety show made use of a complex series of narrative strategies to realign contemporary social roles for women with representations of women institutionalized by the Hollywood cinema. As described above, several episodes of *The Martha Raye Show* undermine the Hollywood convention of the male gaze at the female-as-object as men avert their eyes from Martha and stare at attractive Hollywood starlets. These scenes are invariably shot in television's predominantly-used frontal long-shot and *not* according to the Hollywood convention of the object/glance structure which tends to naturalize gendered hierarchies. In these instances, using theatrical staging helped negotiate viewers' responses to Raye's unstable image: female spectators were more likely to align themselves with Raye's social circumstances rather than identify with the glamorous Hollywood starlet if allowed to scrutinize the material discrepancies between the two women in the tableau shot. The shot reveals class dimensions which had been effaced in the example cited earlier—*Look*'s editorial feature, "How Has Having a Star's Name Affected You?" Rather than suppress the class dimensions of the movie star/female fan relation, *The Martha Raye Show* produces hyperbolic versions of this power relation. Martha Raye's guest stars appeared variously as a king, a movie mogul, a director, a famous celebrity (Liberace), a millionaire son of a corporate president, and an advertising executive. In each case, Raye plays an "average girl." (She is identified as such by newspaper headlines, radio announcers and an advertising accountant). Raye plays a maid, a waitress, a manicurist.

In most episodes of *The Martha Raye Show,* Raye plays the role of the female fan in love with her Hollywood guest stars. Mary Ann Doane has described several Hollywood melodramas, such as *Stella Dallas* and *The Spiral Staircase,* which also incorporate scenes of female viewers at the movies.[57] These women are typically portrayed as victims in narrative trajectories which make the cinematic apparatus appear "to be mobilized against the woman."[58] By fixing her as object of another's gaze, she loses the capacity to see and hence to act on her desires. In contrast, the television variety show's representation of female fans produces a different result. While Raye is often "caught" by the gaze of the camera, her status as object-of-the-look is undermined when she stares back, mugging for the camera. In addition, her aggressive pursuit of her male guest stars from Hollywood overturns the Hollywood trope of the powerless woman "caught" by the male gaze. Raye and other "average-looking" female fans who appear on the show tend to stare at, chase and throw themselves at Raye's male guest stars. *The Martha Raye Show,* then, reframes the TV spectator's role—making it into a more complex, contradictory engagement on several fronts: first, by subverting Hollywood's representation of the woman as erotic spectacle of the male gaze; second, by challenging the one-sidedness and passivity of the object/glance structure; and finally, by challenging preconceptions about the acceptable limits of female expressions of desire.

On those occasions when other "average" women appear on *The Martha Raye Show* alongside Raye, she mediates between these women and the Hollywood star (just as she mediates between the home audience and the guest star). In one case, Martha appears on stage with Gordon McRae to negotiate the exchange between him and his fan club. In another episode, Raye is the only woman who is *not* in love with Cesaroni (Cesar Romero parodying Liberace, a fifties sex symbol). The latter show opens in a flashback to Martha being tried by a courtroom full of angry, vengeful female fans for having disfigured their beloved object of desire. (Raye accidentally knocked out his teeth, ruining his "perfect smile.") These episodes provide unflattering portraits of female fans, producing an imperceptible negotiation for viewers at home—one which encourages them to change the imaginary bond between themselves and their favorite Hollywood star. Invariably, these scenes invite viewers to dissociate themselves from empathetic identification by breaking down the Hollywood convention of the "fourth wall." By having the voice-over announcer speak directly to Raye or to the fans who in turn stare into the camera, the possibility of identification with these women is complicated.

The Martha Raye Show

The typical skit in *The Martha Raye Show* encourages the home viewer to observe critically Martha's one-sided love affair with her rich and famous Hollywood guest star. (The male movie star always has ulterior motives for seducing Martha which are revealed to the audience but not to Martha.) For instance, in one skit, Douglas Fairbanks, Jr. plays a corporate executive in charge of the Fizzo Soft Drink account. He is searching for the perfect woman to advertise his product. He conducts his search by compiling a composite photograph from "the best parts" of seven beautiful women; the final portrait results, ironically, in a photograph of Martha Raye's face. This hyperbolic parody of advertisers' objectification and commercialization of the female image produces contradictory readings. The scene denounces the advertiser's objectification of the female image; however, when Martha eagerly takes up the position of the new Fizzo Girl, the criticism is diffused. The home audience is encouraged to identify with Martha's newly-won position of power and fame as a media star, despite the fact that she plays only a "pitchgirl."

The latter skit reinforces a contemporary trend in the popular press surrounding television—one which encourages women at home to identify with "pitchgirls" who look like housewives.[59] This viewpoint is maintained by having the Fizzo agency receive thousands of letters from female spectators reassuring them that they prefer product spokespersons to be "average" women like Raye rather than glamorous stars. By encouraging women at home to identify with media celebrities whose lives mirror their own, a new form of celebrity worship is invoked and a new form of cultural hegemony is validated—one which constructs women as "consumer allies" by aligning the values of home and family with popular media representations of celebrities. On the other hand, Raye's slapstick performances undermine these same ideals of domesticity and femininity: Raye "washes" the piano with a squeegee and serves cake to her future in-laws using her hands. Once again, her mugging for the camera challenges the stability and passivity invoked in Hollywood representations of women-as-objects. During her performance as the Fizzo Girl she becomes drunk and unruly, making a mockery of the fifties popular ideal of the happy housewife as product spokesperson.

In these episodes, the dominant values of domesticity and femininity are thrown back into a state of flux. The variety show's veneer of ironic self-awareness waylays viewer skepticism. But, by undermining the stability of the woman's image (her object-like-ness in the Hollywood object/glance structure), it also induces an arena of liminality between the old and new sets of values, between the gendered power relations typically associated with the classical Hollywood film (a set of assumptions which inevitably lead one back to Mulvey) and the as yet unformulated power relations being set forth in television's address to women.

The Martha Raye Show challenges the naturalization of gendered power relations learned from the typical Hollywood text in part by exposing conventions such as the object/glance structure. These television shows function as oppositional texts to the extent that they respond to perceived changes in the values and attitudes of the public in the midst of a period of vast social and economic change. *The Martha Raye Show* tends to intercede in conventional narrative trajectories of identification (such as that produced in *Now Voyager,* for instance, which encourages viewers to identify with the homely girl only insofar as she learns how to adopt forties standards of feminine beauty by the end of the film). This is accomplished in *The Martha Raye Show* by introducing alternative views of femininity—in particular, by incorporating negotiated (i.e., oppositional, carnivalesque, slapstick) portraits of the middle-class housewife from fifties popular culture. Ultimately, these compensatory images of femininity from the fifties can be seen to serve a conservative function by helping the home viewer arbitrate the contrast between the Hollywood glamour girl and their own lives.

Another means by which the variety show responded to conflicting representations of female behavior and female desire was by offering alternative conceptual frameworks from which to derive pleasure from the typical Hollywood romance scenario. For instance, when Fairbanks seduces Martha in his apartment, the scene is a parodic inversion of a Hollywood love scene. As Raye sits on the sofa, the lights dim, the music goes up and the bar emerges from the wall, but, in spite of her awareness of the "mechanics" underlying his seduction, Raye falls in love with Fairbanks anyway. The female audience at home, although perhaps aware of the deception inherent in the seduction, is encouraged to identify with Raye's romantic conquest of Fairbanks.

The Martha Raye Show

Raye's internal state of mind is conveyed by the changes in lighting and the shift to soft focus. The scene therefore retains a certain continuity with classical Hollywood conventions used to express interiority and encourage identification. On the other hand, Martha's excessive mugging for the camera calls attention to the overly present technology: stage hands appear from behind pictures hanging on the wall, throwing blossoms and squirting perfume on Martha to signify her euphoric state. The audience's focus is split between acknowledging the artificiality of the romantic scenario (the result of technology's intrusion into the domestic setting) and being imaginatively tied to Raye through identification with her interior state of mind. These structural oppositions are welded together in away that goes beyond Hollywood's typical forms of "self-reflexivity" in backstage musicals which take place in a theatrical setting (as in Gene Kelly's seduction of Debbie Reynolds on the studio lot in *Singin' in the Rain*). These early TV texts refer to a spectator "outside" of the staged scene, challenging thereby, the narrow fictional world of the typical Hollywood film—a strategy designed to make the viewer feel like a participant in the construction of the televised scene.[60]

Because they expose techniques by which Hollywood engages its audience, it is tempting to assign these television texts a subversive or critical role. The television variety show encourages oppositional readings by structurally opposing diverse representational practices (alternating between vaudeville's direct address and proscenium space and the Hollywood film's close-up, closed fiction, and framed view). On the other hand, these oppositional practices can be seen as consistent with rhetorical strategies initiated in the radio period—techniques designed to divert viewer skepticism by exposing the corporate structure and commercial logic underlying the production of these imaginary scenarios. These strategies can be seen to perpetuate the radio star's ironic perspective (described earlier in terms of Jack Benny and Arthur Godfrey). Only now the irony has penetrated the entire fabric of the variety show structure by means of a systematic deconstruction of Hollywood codes responsible for making women passive participants in a libidinally charged, imaginary relationship with Hollywood's stars.

The variety show host, by mediating the Hollywood star/fan relation *for* the television audience, provided the foundation upon which the Hollywood/network interaction was built in the years to come.[61] Previously, female fans at the movies, who were engaged in an unspoken social contract with Hollywood stars, were encouraged to suppress their awareness of the institutionalized mechanisms underlying that relationship. But female spectators of television variety shows were encouraged to reengage in fantasy relationships with Hollywood stars, knowing all the while that they were corporate-produced, commercially-sponsored, consumer-dependent romances.

Conclusion

The variety show contributed to the negotiation of Hollywood's participation in television and to the public's receptiveness to its stars. The "presentational mode" of the variety show abstracted elements from vaudeville's theatrical setting to provide a space in which to transpose the auratic qualities of the Hollywood star to the new mundane setting of the family living room. However, once the transfer of the glamorous into the everyday had been negotiated (preserving women's imaginary relationship to Hollywood's stars and fantasy scenarios), this popular format began to wane by the late fifties. Its restaging of Hollywood's stars and stories pointed up the schizophrenic underside of the Hollywood star/fan relation—its commercial logic and corporate structure.

On the other hand, during this transitional period of negotiation between the two industries, TV's recycled images of Hollywood glamour and glitter encouraged women at home to access the imaginary fantasy world and self-contained moments of pleasure which average women could achieve as fans sitting in front of their TV sets in their own homes. By foregrounding the power relations organizing the Hollywood star/fan encounter (through techniques of ironic reversal and parody of classical Hollywood conventions) viewers were asked to recognize the practical limits of these imaginary scenarios—pleasurable fantasies which could *not* be extended to women's actual social circumstances. Ultimately these television tributes to Hollywood served both the interests of the network hegemony and consumer culture by diverting viewer skepticism away from the anonymous corporate institutions and reasserting media celebrities as the focal point of the public's combined hostility and admiration.

NOTES

1. T.J. Jackson Lears, "From Salvation to Self-Realization: Advertising and the Therapeutic Roots of Consumer Culture, 1880–1930," in *The Culture of Consumption: Critical Essays in American History, 1880–1980*, ed. Richard Wightman Fox and T. J. Jackson Lears (New York: Pantheon Books, 1983), pp. 1–38.

2. Charles Eckert, "The Carole Lombard in Macy's Window," *Quarterly Review of Film Studies* 3:1 (Winter 1978), pp. 1–22; Maria La Place, "Bette Davis and the Ideal of Consumption," *Wide Angle* 6:4 (1985), pp. 34–43; Jane Gaines, "The Popular Icon as Commodity and Sign: The Circulation of Betty Grable, 1941–55." Diss. Northwestern University, 1982.

3. Judith Mayne, "Immigrants and Spectators," *Wide Angle* 5:2 (1982), pp. 32–41; Elizabeth Ewen, *Immigrant Women in the Land of Dollars: Life and Culture on the Lower East Side, 1890–1925* (New York: Monthly Review Press, 1985); Miriam Hansen, "Pleasure, Ambivalence, Identification: Val-

entino and Female Spectatorship," *Cinema Journal* 25:4 (Summer 1986), pp. 6–32.

4. Walter Benjamin, "The Work of Art in the Age of Mechanical Reproduction," in *Illuminations*. Reprinted from the French, 1936; ed. Hannah Arendt (New York: Schocken, 1969), pp. 217–352. In adapting Benjamin's concept to the Hollywood star, I depart slightly from its original meaning—used to describe mass produced products of the culture industry which have lost their uniqueness and claims to autonomy. The changed status of Hollywood stars in the postwar era is a function of popular discourses regulating knowledge of these individuals. These discourses emphasize the stars as institutional products and de-emphasize their status as private persons. John Viera details the modern day legal ramifications of this change—which require legal protections for individual claims on such abstract "properties" as celebrity names and images, both during the individual's lifetime and posthumously in "The Law of Star Images, Media Images and Personal Images: Personality as Property." Diss. University of Southern California, 1985.

5. "The Audience—A Profile of TV Owners, Their Habits and Preferences," *Television Magazine* (November 1953), pp. 19–21. According to this survey, "the highest number of women before the TV receiver [in 1953] is earned by comedy variety shows, with quiz-audience participation, drama and musical variety close behind."

6. Mary Ann Doane, *The Desire to Desire: The Woman's Film of the 1940s* (Bloomington & Indianapolis: Indiana University Press, 1987), p. 26. Doane discusses the ramifications of this association of Hollywood stars and con-sumerism for women: "the glamour, sheen and fascination attached to the movie screen seemed most appropriate for the marketing of a certain feminine self-image."

7. Mary Ann Doane, p. 29.

8. Jane Gaines, p. 16.

9. Sylvester "Pat" Weaver, cited in Judine Mayerle, "The Development of the Television Variety Show as a Major Program Genre at the National Broad-casting Company: 1946–1956." Diss. Northwestern University, 1983, p. 217.

10. Judine Mayerle discusses this continuity in great detail; for example, she notes: "In order to have as much of an old-time vaudeville flavor as possible, NBC/Kudner/Texaco considered renting a vaudeville house and broadcasting the show from there. . . . " p. 87.

11. For a complete discussion of this phenomenon, see Serafina Kent Bathrick, "The True Woman and the Family-Film: The Industrial Production of Memory." Diss. University of Wisconsin-Madison, 1981.

12. Richard deCordova, "The Emergence of the Star System in America: An Examination of the Institutional and Ideological Function of the Star: 1907–1922." Diss. University of California, Los Angeles, 1986, p. 120.

13. Robert Metz, *CBS: Reflections in a Bloodshot Eye* (Chicago: Playboy Press, 1975), pp. 137–145; Irving A. Fein, *Jack Benny: An Intimate Biography* (New York: G.P. Putnam's Sons, 1976), pp. 121–124. Also see Arthur Frank Wertheim, *Radio Comedy* (New York: Oxford University Press, 1979).

14. Richard deCordova. My use of this concept follows from deCordova's analysis of the early star system using an historical methodology informed by Foucault.

15. "Talent Agents: Have They Won Control over TV Costs?" *Sponsor* 9:1 (January 24, 1955), pp. 35–37, 116, 119–120. "Should You Hire Your Competitor's Star?" *Sponsor* 7:1 (June 15, 1953), pp. 32–33, 82. "Tips on Using Your Film Show Talent in Ads," *Sponsor* 7:1 (June 15, 1953), p. 36. "Five Ways to Promote Your Program," *Sponsor* 6:2 (October 20, 1952), pp. 40–41, 64–72.

16. "Stars Now Experts on Ads, Too," *Variety* 200 (October 12, 1955), p. 5.

17. Richard deCordova, pp. 116–17.

18. Charles Sinclair, "Should Hollywood Get it for Free?" *Sponsor* 9:2 (August 8, 1955), p. 102. Every kind of plug imaginable has been used to boost the new Disneyland amusement park. As one ABC TV official in New York network headquarters likes to paraphrase Churchill: "Never have so many people made so little objection to so much selling."

19. Daniel Boorstin cited in Marty Jezer, *The Dark Ages: Life in the United States 1945–1960* (Boston: South End Press, 1982), p. 133.

20. Serafina Bathrick, p. 5. Bathrick's analysis demonstrates how nostalgic family-musicals sought ". . . to remake and so to naturalize the history of the relationship between the nineteenth century True Woman and the twentieth century movie star." I have extrapolated from her analysis a model for analyzing how other fifties products of the culture industry made this transition into the postwar era.

21. Marjorie Schlesinger Deane, "The Dress That Needs a Man," *Look* 20 (February 7, 1956), pp. 80, 82–85.

22. Marjorie Schlesinger Deane, p. 80. The pages of *Look* in the fifties have numerous references to recycled "old-fashioned fashions;" for instance "a return of 'buckles, buttons and bows to modern shoes, and the 1956 version of the hobble-skirt as briskly modern.'" *Look* 20 (July 24, 1956), pp. 58–59.

23. Fred Hift, "Old Film Stars Never Die—Just Keep B.O. Rolling Along," *Variety* 200 (September 7, 1955), p. 7. Also see "Is TV a Haven for Hollywood Has-Beens?" *TV Guide* 2:3 (August 21–27, 1954), p. 22.

24. Arthur Frank Wertheim, "The Rise and Fall of Milton Berle," *American History/American Television: Interpreting the Video Past,* ed. John E. O'Connor (New York: Frederick Ungar Publishing Co., 1983), pp. 55–78. Wertheim argues that Berle's ethnically derived vaudeville humor was no longer responsive to changing tastes in view of the altered demographics of the audience—

from urban metropolitan areas, expanding in 1952–1954 to small town and rural regions with the addition of coaxial cable and national hookup. Various strategies taken up by *The Martha Raye Show* and *The Buick-Berle Show* in the mid-fifties reflect this process of adaptation to a program format stripped of its association with an ethnic and class-defined community.

25. Leo Rosten, "Hollywood Revisited: A Psychological X-Ray of the Movie Colony Today—its Manners, its Conflicts, its Morals—Where Television, Wide-screen and Middle-age Have Forever Changed the Life and Work of the Glamorous," *Look* 20 (January 10, 1956), pp. 17–30.

26. "How Can Prominent TV Entertainers Best Avoid a 'Boom and Bust' in Their Popularity on Video?" *Sponsor* 9:1 (June 27, 1955), pp. 54–55. Charles B. Ripin says: ". . . material taken from real life situations . . . [allows] the audience to project itself into the skit and participate with the entertainer." "Sid Caesar has recently shown an appreciation of this thinking by inserting his 'family type' sketches." Lefebvre, cited in Bathrick (p. 4), remarks that everyday life "evades the grip of form," and "eludes all attempts at institutionalization." However, as Bathrick demonstrates, the family-musical [and by extension, the television variety show] are culture industry products which make female audiences believe they have participated in the construction of the film's spectacle of everyday life.

27. Jane Gaines, p. 475. Gaines's remarks refer to the thirties and forties but may be seen as true of the fifties as well.

28. Roland Marchand, "Visions of Classlessness, Quests for Dominion: American Popular Culture, 1945–1960" in *Reshaping America: Society and Institutions, 1945–1960*, eds. Robert H. Bremner and Gary W. Reichard (Columbus: Ohio University Press, 1982), pp. 163–192.

29. Richard Parker cited in Marchand, p. 170.

30. Leo Rosten, pp. 17–28.

31. Leo Rosten, p. 21.

32. Jane Gaines, p. 471.

33. In a four page photo essay on Gregory Peck with his new wife at home, he is described as a star who "disdains the noisy trappings of 'star stuff.'" Stanley Gordon, "Tall, dark and dignified . . . Gregory Peck," *Look* 20 (July 24, 1956), p. 82; another article says Gable, "unlike other stars . . . likes to hang around and talk with 'lower echelons.'" Joe McCarthy, "Clark Gable: How He Became King of Hollywood," *Look* 19 (November 1, 1955), p. 104.

34. "The Girl in the Gray Flannel Suit," *Look* 20 (April 3, 1956), pp. 59–61; Ad for *The Man in the Gray Flannel Suit*, *Look* 20 (April 3, 1956), p. 83.

35. *Look* 20 (April 13, 1956), p. 61.

36. "*Look*'s Strapless Apron Shows Your Shoulders," *Look* 12 (March 2, 1948), p. 49.

37. "Ranch Clothes Craze," *Look* 12 (March 2, 1948), pp. 55–56.

38. *Look* 20 (April 3, 1956), p. 59.

39. Jane Gaines, p. 443. Gaines has demonstrated the type of class backlash that occurred in the forties; for instance, when working class women objected to the unlikely press depiction of Lana Turner as ". . . a lonely, almost friendless beauty. . . ." In another case, a black college girl wrote to Bette Davis in a question and answer feature of *Photoplay-Movie Mirror Magazine*. She told Davis that she felt she shared with the stars the ability to make a success of herself, although she admits that "it is a little more difficult for her than for a white girl." Davis's response effaced the race issue altogether by saying "God helps those who help themselves" (p. 420).

40. Auto-Lite Spark Plugs ad. "Which is *Really* Dorothy Lamour?" *Look* 12 (March 30, 1948), p. 15.

41. "How Has Having a Movie Star's Name Affected You?" *Look* 12 (March 16, 1948), pp. 14, 16.

42. Jonathan Kilbourne, "America's Man Godfrey," *Look* 13 (February 1, 1949), pp. 28–29, 32.

43. "Letters and Pictures: Whose Man Godfrey Is He, Anyhow?" *Look* 13 (March 4, 1949), p. 8. The public's mistrust of Godfrey culminates when Godfrey publicly fires Julia La Rosa for his "loss of humility." Fans and critics question his actions in a series of editorials, articles and interviews; see for instance, Bob Stahl, "Godfrey Snaps Back at 'Untruths,' " *TV Guide* 2:28 (July 7–14, 1954), pp. 13–14.

44. *Look* 13 (March 4, 1949), p. 8.

45. *Look* 13 (March 4, 1949), p. 8.

46. Atwan, R., D. McQuade and J. Wright, *Edsels, Luckies, and Frigidaires: Advertising the American Way* (New York, Dell, 1979), p. 312. "Familiar movie formula of planting guest stars in exchange for movie credits has been brought to a new high polish on tv, as in Marilyn Monroe's visit to CBS TV's 'Person to Person,'" *Sponsor* 9:2 (August 8, 1955), p. 33.

47. Wertheim, *Radio Comedy* (New York: Oxford University Press, 1979), p. 141.

48. Wertheim, p. 141.

49. ". . . the effective use of humor and ridicule involving the sponsor and his product can actually enhance the value of the testimonial." "Pitfalls in Commercial Techniques," *Television Magazine* 10 (November 1953), p. 36.

50. "Claws Out! Movie Glamor Girls vs. TV Actresses," *TV Guide* 2:11 (March 12–18, 1954), pp. 5–7. "Hollywood bigwigs are backed by tremendous glamor buildup that TV players can only envy."

51. Joseph C. Franklin and G. Maxwell Ule, "Is Your Brand Showing?" *Television Magazine* 10 (July 1953), p. 24. "Housewives don't want to see anything that's

not so. . . . Now we all know how to wash dishes, and if we're looking at television and we see somebody come on, she's got diamonds on her hands, she's all dressed up, and she's in the height of fasion—you know, a model."

52. Joseph C. Franklin and G. Maxwell Ule, "Who Speaks for You?" *Television Magazine* 10 (September 1953), pp. 49–50.

53. Tom O'Malley, "Raucous Raye: Martha's Clicking Again Without Hollywood's Glamor Treatment," *TV Guide* 2:3 (January 15–21, 1954), pp. 15–17. James Robert Parish and William T. Leonard, *The Funsters* (New Rochelle: Arlington House Publishers, 1979), pp. 519–527.

54. "Why I'm Through with Big TV Shows," *Sponsor* 9:1 (May 2, 1955), pp. 31–32, 93–95. Raymond Spector, head of both Hazel Bishop, Inc., and the Raymond Spector Agency, says: "He is not renewing the spectaculars or NBC TV's *The Martha Raye Show*. He states that he is not interested in Martha Raye's high ratings but the question of "intensity of viewing . . . [i.e.,] whether the loyalty and affection which a star generates flows over to the commercials" (p. 94). Spector favors "sentimental and heavily emotional" melodramatic over spectacular shows; for instance, he prefers *This is Your Life*, a program which engages members of the studio audience in tearful reunions with individuals from their past.

55. Sylvester "Pat" Weaver cited in Judine Mayerle, p. 217.

56. "Fred Allen Speaks Out on Television," *Television Magazine* 6 (December 1949), p. 27. "Everything is for the eye these days—'Life,' 'Look,' the picture business. Nothing is for the mind . . . Berle isn't doing anything for television. He's photographing a vaudeville act."

57. Doane, p. 37.

58. Doane, p. 37.

59. "They've Got Sales Appeal: In TV It's No Longer a Man's World," *TV Guide* 1:35 (November 27–December 3, 1953), pp. 10–11. "Dorothy Collins' Success Key: Listen for Opportunity's Knock," *TV Guide* 1:3 (April 17–23, 1953), pp. 16–19.

60. See for instance, "I'm on Your Side: Ken Murray Finds it Safer to String Along with the Audience," *TV Guide* 1:10 (June 5–12, 1954), pp. 16–18. "I become the liaison between the show and the audience. . . . I represent you, the audience. For example, I'll just stand at one end of the stage and look at the girls performing. If they tell a bum joke I'll turn and shrug: 'They're pretty bad, but what can I do. You see, I'm on your side.'"

61. "Glamor that sells merchandise is the television order of the day. That's why Gloria Swanson was selected mistress of ceremonies of the *Crown Theater* series of telefilms. . . . " *TV Guide* 1:8 (May 22–28, 1954), pp. 10–12. During the mid-fifties with the "rise of the telefilm," the smooth penetration of movie stars into television is institutionalized.

Mama

The Goldbergs

The Meaning of Memory: Family, Class, and Ethnicity in Early Network Television Programs
George Lipsitz

Almost every Friday night between 1949 and 1956, millions of Americans watched Rosemary Rice turn the pages of an old photograph album. With music from Edvard Grieg's "Holverg Suite" playing in the background, and with pictures of turn-of-the-century San Francisco displayed on the album pages, Rice assumed the identity of her television character, Katrin Hansen, on the CBS network program *Mama*. She told the audience about her memories of her girlhood, her family's house on Steiner Street, and her experiences there with her big brother Nels, her little sister Dagmar, her Papa, and her Mama—"most of all," she said, "when I remember that San Francisco of so long ago, I remember Mama."

Katrin Hansen's memories of her Norwegian immigrant working-class family had powerful appeal for viewers in the early years of commercial network broadcasting. *Mama* established itself as one of CBS's most popular programs during its first season on the air, and it retained high ratings for the duration of its prime-time run.[1] The show's popularity coincided with that of other situation comedies based on ethnic working-class family life— *The Goldbergs*, depicting the experiences of Jews in the Bronx; *Amos 'n' Andy*, blacks in Harlem; *The Honeymooners* and *Hey Jeannie*, Irish working-class families in Brooklyn; *Life with Luigi*, Italian immigrants in Chicago; and *The Life of Riley*, working-class migrants to Los Angeles during and after World War II.[2]

The presence of this subgenre of ethnic, working-class situation comedies on television network schedules seems to run contrary to the commercial and artistic properties of the medium. Television delivers audiences to advertisers by glorifying consumption, not only during commercial breaks but in the programs themselves.[3] The relative economic deprivation of ethnic working-class households would seem to provide an inappropriate setting for the display and promotion of commodities as desired by the networks and their commercial sponsors. Furthermore, the mass audience required to repay the expense of network programming encourages the depiction of a homogenized mass society, not the particularities and peculiarities of working-class communities. As an artistic medium, television's capacity for simultaneity conveys a sense of living in an infinitely renewable present—a quality inimical to the sense of history permeating shows about working-class life. Yet whether set in the distant past like *Mama*, or located in the contemporaneous present, the subgenre of ethnic working-class situation comedies in early network television evoked concrete historical associations and memories in their audiences.[4]

Anomalous to the commercial and artistic properties of television, these programs also ran counter to the dominant social trends in the era in which they were made. They presented ethnic families in working-class urban neighborhoods at the precise historical moment when a rising standard of living, urban renewal, and suburbanization contributed to declines in ethnic and class identity.[5] They showed working-class families struggling for material satisfaction and advancement under conditions far removed from the *embourgeoisement* of the working class celebrated in popular literature about the postwar era. They displayed value conflicts about family identity, consumer spending, ethnicity, class, and gender roles that would appear to be disruptive and dysfunctional within a communications medium primarily devoted to stimulating commodity purchases (see Table 1).

The dissonance between ethnic working-class situation comedies and their artistic, commercial, and historical surroundings might be explained by the persistence of artistic clichés and the conservatism of the entertainment business. Though four of these seven television programs previously existed as radio serials, radio popularity did not guarantee adaptation to television: many successful radio series never made that transition, and television networks actually made more profit from productions specially created for the new medium.[6] Even when radio programs did become television shows, they underwent significant changes in plot and premise. Television versions of urban, ethnic working-class situation comedies placed more emphasis on nuclear families and less on extended kinship relations and ethnicity than did their radio predecessors.[7] Those changes reflect more than the differences between television and radio as media: they illuminate as well significant transformations in U.S. society during the 1950s, and they underscore the important role played by television in explaining and legitimizing those transitions to a mass audience.

More than their shared history in radio or their reliance on common theatrical traditions from vaudeville and ethnic theater unites the subgenre of urban ethnic working-class situation comedies. Through indirect but powerful demonstrations, all of these shows arbitrated complex tensions caused by economic and social change in postwar America. They evoked the experiences of the past to lend legitimacy to the dominant ideology of the present. In the process they served important social and cultural functions, not just in returning profits to investors or attracting audiences for advertisers, but most significantly as a means of ideological legitimation for a fundamental revolution in economic, social, and cultural life.

Table 1.

Program	Ethnicity	Occupations	Location	Dwelling
Mama	Norwegian	Carpenter	San Francisco	House
The Goldbergs	Jewish	Tailor/Small Business	Bronx/Long Island	Apartment/House
Amos 'n' Andy	Black	Cab Driver/Hustler	Harlem	Apartment
The Honeymooners	Irish	Bus Driver/Sewer Worker	Brooklyn	Apartment
Life with Luigi	Italian	Shopkeeper	Chicago	Apartment
Life of Riley	Irish	Machinist	Los Angeles	Duplex/cottage
Hey Jeannie	Scottish/Irish	Cab Driver	Brooklyn	Apartment

The Meaning of Memory

In the midst of extraordinary social change, television became the most important discursive medium in American culture. As such, it was charged with special responsibilities for making new economic and social relations credible and legitimate to audiences haunted by ghosts from the past. Urban, ethnic working-class situation comedies provided one means of addressing the anxieties and contradictions emanating from the clash between the consumer present of the 1950s and collective social memory about the 1930s and 1940s.

The consumer consciousness emerging from economic and social change in postwar America conflicted with the lessons of historical experience for many middle and working-class American families. The Great Depression of the 1930s had not only damaged the economy, it also undercut the political and cultural legitimacy of American capitalism. Herbert Hoover had been a national hero in the 1920s, with his credo of "rugged individualism" forming the basis for a widely shared cultural ideal. But the Depression discredited Hoover's philosophy and made him a symbol of yesterday's blasted hopes to millions of Americans. In the 1930s, cultural ideals based on mutuality and collectivity eclipsed the previous decade's "rugged individualism" and helped propel massive union organizing drives, anti-eviction movements, and general strikes. President Roosevelt's New Deal tried to harness and co-opt the grass roots mass activity in an attempt to restore social order and recapture credibility and legitimacy for the capitalist system.[8] The social welfare legislation of the "Second New Deal" in 1935 went far beyond any measures previously favored by Roosevelt and most of his advisors, but radical action proved necessary for the Administration to contain the upsurge of activism that characterized the decade. Even in the private sector, industrial corporations made more concessions to workers than naked power realities necessitated because they feared the political consequences of mass disillusionment with the system.[9]

World War II ended the Depression and brought prosperity, but it did so on a basis even more collective than the New Deal of the 1930s. Government intervention in the wartime economy reached unprecedented levels, bringing material reward and shared purpose to a generation raised on the deprivation and sacrifice of the depression. In the postwar years, the largest and most disruptive strike wave in American history won major improvements in the standard of living for the average worker, both through wage increases and through government commitments to insure full employment, decent housing, and expanded educational opportunities. Grass roots militancy and working-class direct action wrested concessions from a reluctant government and business elite—mostly because the public at large viewed workers' demands as more legitimate than the desires of capital.[10]

Yet the collective nature of working-class mass activity in the postwar era posed severe problems for capital. In sympathy strikes and secondary boycotts, workers placed the interests of their class ahead of their own individual material aspirations. Strikes over safety and job control far outnumbered wage strikes, revealing aspirations to control the process of production that conflicted with capitalist labor-management relations. Mass demonstrations demanding government employment and housing programs indicated a collective political response to problems previously adjudicated on a personal level. Radical challenges to the authority of capital (like the 1946 Auto Workers' strike demand that wage increases come out of corporate profits rather than from price hikes passed on to consumers), demonstrated a social responsibility and a commitment toward redistributing wealth, rare in the history of American labor.[11]

Capital attempted to regain the initiative in the postwar years by making qualified concessions to working-class pressures for redistribution of wealth and power. Rather than paying wage increases out of corporate profits, business leaders instead worked to expand the economy through increases in government spending, foreign trade, and consumer debt. Such expansion could meet the demands of workers and consumers without undermining capital's dominant role in the economy. On the presumption that "a rising tide lifts all boats," business leaders sought to connect working-class aspirations for a better life to policies that insured a commensurate rise in corporate profits, thereby leaving the distribution of wealth unaffected. Federal defense spending, highway construction programs, and home loan policies expanded the economy at home in a manner conducive to the interests of capital, while the Truman Doctrine and Marshall Plan provided models for enhanced access to foreign markets and raw materials for American corporations. The Taft-Hartley Act of 1947 banned the class-conscious collective activities most threatening to capital (mass strikes, sympathy strikes, secondary boycotts): the leaders of labor, government, and business accepted as necessity the practice of paying wage hikes for organized workers out of the pockets of consumers and unorganized workers, in the form of higher prices.[12]

Commercial network television played an important role in this emerging economy, functioning as a significant object of consumer purchases as well as an important marketing medium. Sales of sets jumped from three million during the entire decade of the 1940s to over five million *a year* during the 1950s.[13] But television's most important economic function came from its role as an instrument of legitimation for transformations in values initiated by the new economic imperatives of postwar America. For Americans to accept the new world of 1950s' consumerism, they had to make a break with the past. The depression years had helped generate fears about installment buying and excessive materialism, while the New Deal and wartime mobilization had provoked suspicions about individual acquisitiveness and upward mobility. Depression era and wartime scarcities of consumer goods had led workers to internalize discipline and frugality while nurturing networks of mutual support through family, ethnic, and class associations. Government policies after the war encouraged an atomized acquisitive consumerism at odds with the lessons of the past. At the same time, federal home loan policies stimulated migrations to the suburbs from traditional, urban, ethnic working-class neighborhoods. The entry of television into the American home disrupted previous patterns of family life and encouraged fragmentation of the family into separate segments of the consumer market.[14] The priority of consumerism in the economy at large and on television may have seemed organic and unplanned, but conscious policy decisions by officials from both private and public sectors shaped the contours of the consumer economy and television's role within it.

Commercial Television and Economic Change

Government policies during and after World War II shaped the basic contours of home television as an advertising medium. Government-sponsored research and development during the war perfected the technology of home television while federal tax policies solidified its economic base. The government allowed corporations to deduct the cost of advertising from their taxable incomes during the war, despite the fact that rationing and defense production left business with few products to market. Consequently, manufacturers kept the names of their products before the public while lowering their tax obligations on high wartime profits. Their advertising expenditures supplied radio networks and advertising agencies with the capital reserves and business infrastructure that enabled them to dominate the television industry in the postwar era. After the war, federal antitrust action against the motion picture studios broke up the "network" system in movies, while the FCC sanctioned the network system in television. In addition, FCC decisions to allocate stations on the narrow VHF band, to grant the networks ownership and operation rights over stations in prime markets, and to place a freeze on the licensing of new stations during the important years between 1948 and 1952 all combined to guarantee that advertising-oriented programming based on the model of radio would triumph over theater TV, educational TV, or any other form.[15] Government decisions, not market forces, established the dominance of commercial television, but these decisions reflected a view of the American economy and its needs which had become so well accepted at the top levels of business and government that it had virtually become the official state economic policy.

Fearing both renewed depression and awakened militancy among workers, influential corporate and business leaders considered increases in consumer spending—increases of 30% to 50%—to be necessary to perpetuate prosperity in the postwar era.[16] Defense spending for the Cold War and Korean Conflict had complemented an aggressive trade policy to improve the state of the economy, but it appeared that the key to an expanding economy rested in increased consumer spending fueled by an expansion of credit.[17] Here too, government policies led the way, especially with regard to stimulating credit purchases of homes and automobiles. During World War II, the marginal tax rate for most wage earners jumped from 4% to 25%, making the home ownership deduction more desirable. Federal housing loan policies favored construction of new single-family, detached suburban housing over renovation or construction of central city multi-family units. Debt-encumbered home ownership in accord with these policies stimulated construction of thirty million new housing units in just twenty years, bringing the percentage of home-owning Americans from below 40% in 1940 to more than 60% by 1960. Mortgage policies encouraging long term debt and low down payments freed capital for other consumer purchases, while government highway building policies undermined mass transit systems and contributed to increased demand for automobiles.[18] Partly as a result of these policies, consumer spending on private cars averaged $7.5 billion per year in the 1930s and 1940s, but grew to $22 billion per year in 1950 and almost $30 billion by 1955.[19]

For the first time in U.S. history, middle-class and working-class families could routinely expect to own homes or buy new cars every few years. Between 1946 and 1965 residential mortgage debt rose three times as fast as the gross national product and disposable income. Mortgage debt accounted for just under 18% of disposable income in 1946, but it grew to almost 55% by 1965.[20] In order to insure eventual payment of current debts, the economy had to generate tremendous expansion and growth, further stimulating the need to increase consumer spending. Manufacturers had to find new ways of motivating consumers to buy ever increasing amounts of commodities, and television provided an important means of accomplishing that end.

Television advertised individual products, but it also provided a relentless flow of information and persuasion that placed acts of consumption at the core of everyday life. The physical fragmentation of suburban growth and declines in motion picture attendance created an audience more likely to stay at home and receive entertainment there than ever before. But television also provided a locus redefining American ethnic, class, and family identities into consumer identities. In order to accomplish this task effectively, television programs had to address some of the psychic, moral, and political obstacles to consumption among the public at large.

The television and advertising industries knew that they had to overcome these obstacles. Marketing expert and motivational specialist Ernest Dichter stated that "one of the basic problems of this prosperity is to give people that sanction and justification to enjoy it and to demonstrate that the hedonistic approach to life is a moral one, not an immoral one."[21] Dichter went on to note the many barriers that inhibited consumer acceptance of unrestrained hedonism, and he called on advertisers "to train the average citizen to accept growth of his country and its economy as *his* growth rather than as a strange and frightening event."[22] One method of encouraging that acceptance, according to Dichter, consisted of identifying new products and styles of consumption with traditional, historically sanctioned practices and behavior. He noted that such an approach held particular relevance in addressing consumers who had only recently acquired the means to spend freely and who might harbor a lingering conservatism based on their previous experience.[23]

Insecurities and anxieties among consumers compelled network television to address the complex legacies of the 1930s and 1940s in order to promote consumption in the 1950s. In the middle of its appeals to change the world in the present through purchase of the appropriate commodities, commercial network television in its early years also presented programs rooted in the historical experiences and aspirations of diverse working-class traditions. From the evocations of the Depression era that permeated the world of *The Honeymooners,* to the recycled minstrel show stereotypes of *Amos 'n' Andy,* from the textured layers of immigrant experience underpinning the drama and the charm of *The Goldbergs* and *Mama,* to the reenactment of immigration in contemporaneous circumstances in *The Life of Riley, Life with Luigi,* and *Hey Jeannie,* the medium of the infinitely renewable present turned to past traditions and practices in order to explain and legitimate fundamentally new social relations in the present.

Family Formation and the Economy—The Television View

Advertisers incorporated their messages into urban ethnic working-class comedies through indirect and direct means. Tensions developed in the programs often found indirect resolution in commercials. Thus Jeannie MacClennan's search for an American sweetheart in one episode of *Hey Jeannie* set up commercials proclaiming the abilities of Drene shampoo to keep one prepared to accept last minute dates and of Crest toothpaste to produce an attractive smile (*Hey Jeannie:* "The Rock 'n Roll Kid"). Conversations about shopping for new furniture in an episode of *The Goldbergs* directed viewers' attention to furnishings in the Goldberg home provided for the show by Macy's department store in exchange for a commercial acknowledgement (*The Goldbergs:* "The In-laws").

But the content of the shows themselves offered even more direct emphasis on consumer spending. In one episode of *The Goldbergs,* Molly expresses disapproval of her future daughter-in-law's plan to buy a washing machine on the installment plan. "I know Papa and me never bought anything unless we had the money to pay for it," she intones with logic familiar to a generation with memories of the Great Depression. Her son, Sammy, confronts this "deviance" by saying, "Listen, Ma, almost everybody in this country lives above their means—and everybody enjoys it." Doubtful at first, Molly eventually learns from her children and announces her conversion to the legitimacy of installment buying by proposing that the family buy two cars so as to "live above our means—the American way" (*The Goldbergs:* "The In-laws"). In the subsequent episode, Molly's daughter, Rosalie, assumes the role of ideological tutor to her mother. When planning a move out of their Bronx apartment to a new house in the suburbs, Molly ruminates about where to place her furniture in the new home. "You don't mean we're going to take all this junk with us into a brand new house?" asks an exasperated Rosalie. With traditionalist sentiment Molly answers, "Junk? My furniture's junk? My furniture that I lived with and loved for twenty years is junk?" But in the end she accepts Rosalie's argument—even selling off all her old furniture to help meet the down payment on the new house, and deciding to buy new furniture on the installment plan (*The Goldbergs*: "Moving Day").

Chester A. Riley confronts similar choices about family and commodities in *The Life of Riley*. His wife complains that he takes her out only to the neighborhood bowling alley and restaurant, not to "interesting places." Riley searches for ways to impress her and discovers from a friend that a waiter at the fancy Club Morambo will let them eat first and pay later, at a dollar a week plus ten percent interest. "Ain't that dishonest?" asks Riley. "No, it's usury," his friend replies. Riley does not borrow the money, but he impresses his wife anyway by taking the family out to dinner on the proceeds of a prize that he received for being the one-thousandth customer in a local flower shop. Though we eventually learn that Peg Riley only wanted attention, not an expensive meal, the happy ending of the episode hinges totally on Riley's prestige, restored when he demonstrates his ability to provide a luxury outing for the family.

Life of Riley

The same episode of *The Life of Riley* reveals another consumerist element common to this subgenre. When Riley protests that he lacks the money needed to fulfill Peg's desires, she answers that he would have plenty if he didn't spend so much on "needless gadgets." His shortage of cash becomes a personal failing caused by incompetent behavior as a consumer. Nowhere do we hear about the size of his paycheck, relations between his union and his employer, or, for that matter, the relationship between the value of his labor and the wages paid to him by the Stevenson Aircraft Company. Like Uncle David in *The Goldbergs*—who buys a statue of Hamlet shaking hands with Shakespeare and an elk's tooth with the Gettysburg Address carved on it—Riley's comic character stems in part from a flaw which in theory could be attributed to the entire consumer economy: a preoccupation with "needless gadgets" (*The Goldbergs*: "Bad Companions"). By contrast, Peg Riley's desire for an evening out is portrayed as reasonable and modest—as reparation due her for the inevitable tedium of housework. The solution to her unhappiness, of course, comes from an evening out rather than from a change in her own work circumstances. Even within the home, television elevates consumption over production: production is assumed to be a constant—only consumption can be varied. But more than enjoyment is at stake: unless Riley can provide her with the desired night on the town, he will fail in his obligations as a husband.

A similar theme provides the crisis in an episode of *Mama*. Dagmar, the youngest child, "innocently" expresses envy of a friend whose father received a promotion and consequently put up new wallpaper in his house. "Why doesn't Papa get promoted?" Dagmar chirps. "Everyone else does." When Mama explains that a carpenter makes less money than other fathers, Dagmar asks if it wouldn't be smarter for Papa to work in a bank. Overhearing this dialogue, Papa decides to accept his boss's offer to promote him to foreman, even though he knows it will ruin his friendships with the other workers. The logic of the episode instructs us that fathers will lose their standing if they disappoint their families' desires for new commodities (*Mama*: "Mama and the Carpenter"). Shows exploring tensions between family obligations and commodity purchases routinely assert that money cannot *buy* love, but they seem less clear about whether one can trade material wealth for affection. Even the usually self-absorbed Kingfish on *Amos 'n' Andy* gives in to his nephew Stanley's wish for "a birthday party with lots of expensive presents," while Jeannie MacClennan's search for romance suffers a setback when a prospective suitor sees her shabby apartment with its antiquated furniture (*Amos 'n Andy*: "Andy the Godfather"; and *Hey Jeannie*: "The Rock 'n Roll Kid"). On *The Goldbergs*, a young woman is forbidden to marry the man she loves because, her mother says, "I didn't raise my daughter to be a butcher's wife" (*The Goldbergs*: "Die Fledermaus"); and Alice Kramden in *The Honeymooners* can always gain the upper hand in arguments with her husband by pointing to his inadequacies as a provider. In each of these programs, consumer choices close the ruptures in personal relations, enabling the episode to reach narrative and ideological closure.

One episode of *Mama* typifies the confusion between consumer purchases and family happiness pervading urban, ethnic working-class situation comedies in early television. "Mama's Birthday," broadcast in 1954, delineated the tensions between family loyalty and consumer desire endemic to modern capitalist society. The show begins with Mama teaching Katrin to make Norwegian potato balls, the kind she used long ago to "catch" Papa. Unimpressed by this accomplishment, Katrin changes the subject and asks Mama what she wants for her upcoming birthday. In an answer that locates Mama within the gender roles of the 1950s she replies, "Well, I think a fine new job for your Papa. You and Dagmar to marry nice young men and have a lot of wonderful children—just like I have. And Nels, well, Nels to become President of the United States".[24] In one sentence Mama has summed up the dominant culture's version of legitimate female expectations: success at work for her husband, marriage and child-rearing for her daughters, the presidency for her son—and nothing for herself.

But we learn that Mama does have some needs, although we do not hear it from her lips. Her sister, Jenny, asks Mama to attend a fashion show, but Mama cannot leave the house because she has to cook a roast for a guest whom Papa has invited to dinner. Jenny comments that Mama never seems to get out of the kitchen, adding that "it's a disgrace when a woman can't call her soul her own," and "it's a shame that a married woman can't have some time to herself." The complaint is a valid one, and we can imagine how it might have resonated for women in the 1950s. The increased availability of household appliances and the use of synthetic fibers and commercially processed food should have decreased the amount of time women spent in housework, but surveys showed that homemakers spent the same number of hours per week (51 to 56) doing housework as they had done in the 1920s. Advertising and marketing strategies undermined the potential of technological changes by upgrading standards of cleanliness in the home and expanding desires for more varied wardrobes and menus for the average family.[25] In that context, Aunt Jenny would have been justified in launching into a tirade about the division of labor within the Hansen household or about the possibilities for cooperative housework, but network television specializes in a less social and more commodified dialogue about problems like housework: Aunt Jenny suggests that her sister's family buy her a "fireless cooker"—a cast iron stove—for her birthday. "They're wonderful," she tells them in language borrowed from the rhetoric of advertising. "You just put your dinner inside them, close 'em up, and go where you please. When you come back your dinner is all cooked."[26] Papa protests that Mama likes to cook on her woodburning stove, but Jenny dismisses that objection with an insinuation about his motive, when she replies, "Well, I suppose it would cost a little more than you could afford, Hansen."[27]

By identifying a commodity as the solution to Mama's problem, Aunt Jenny unites the inner voice of Mama with the outer voice of the sponsors of television programs. Mama's utility as an icon of maternal selflessness would be compromised if she asked for the stove herself, but Aunt Jenny's role in suggesting the gift removes that taint of selfishness while adding the authority of an outside expert. Aunt Jenny's suggestion of hypocrisy in Papa's reluctance to buy the stove encourages the audience to resent him for not making enough money and even to see his poverty as a form of selfishness—denying his wife the comforts due her. In reality, we know that Aunt Jenny's advice probably contains the usual distortions of advertising claims, that even if the fireless cooker enabled Mama to go where she pleased while dinner cooked, it would bring with it different kinds of tasks and escalating demands. But in the fantasy world of television, such considerations do not intervene. Prodded by their aunt, the Hansen children go shopping and purchase the fireless cooker from a storekeeper who calls the product "the new Emancipation Proclamation—setting housewives free from their old kitchen range."[28] Our exposure to advertising hyperbole should not lead us to miss the analogy here: housework is compared to slavery, and the commercial product takes on the aura of Abraham Lincoln. The shopkeeper's appeal convinces the children to pool their resources and buy the stove for Mama. But we soon learn that Papa plans to make a fireless cooker for Mama with his tools. When Mama discovers Papa's intentions she persuades the children to buy her another gift. Even Papa admits that his stove will not be as efficient as the one made in a factory, but Mama nobly affirms that she will like his better because he made it himself. The children use their money to buy dishes for Mama, and Katrin remembers the episode as Mama's happiest birthday ever.[29]

The stated resolution of "Mama's Birthday" favors traditional values. Mama prefers to protect Papa's feelings rather than to have a better stove, and the product built by a family member has more value than one sold as a commodity. Yet the entire development of the plot leads in the opposite direction. The "fireless cooker" is the star of the episode, setting in motion all the other characters, and it has unquestioned value even in the face of Jenny's meddlesome brashness, Papa's insensitivity, and Mama's old-fash-

ioned ideals. Buying a product is unchallenged as the true means of changing the unpleasant realities or low status of women's work in the home.

This resolution of the conflict between consumer desires and family roles
reflected television's social function as mediator between the family and
the economy. Surveys of set ownership showed no pronounced stratifi-
cation by class, but a clear correlation between family size and television
purchase: households with three to five people were most likely to own
television sets, while those with only one person were least likely to own
them.[30] The television industry recognized and promoted its privileged
place within families in advertisements like the one in *The New York Times*
in 1950 that proclaimed, "Youngsters today need television for their morale
as much as they need fresh air and sunshine for their health."[31] Like
previous communications media, television sets occupied honored places
in family living rooms, and helped structure family time; unlike other
previous communications media, they displayed available commodities in
a way that transformed all their entertainment into a glorified shopping
catalogue.

Publicity about television programs also stressed the interconnections
between family and economy. Viewers took the portrayals of motherhood
on these shows so seriously that when Peggy Wood of *Mama* appeared
on the *Garry Moore Show* and asked for questions from the audience,
women asked for advice about raising their families, as if she were actually
Mama, rather than an actress playing that role.[32] The *Ladies' Home Journal* printed an article containing "Mama's Recipes," featuring photographs
of Peggy Wood, while Gertrude Berg wrote an article as Molly Goldberg
for *TV Guide* that contained her recipes for borscht and blintzes. "Your
meal should suit the mood of your husband," Berg explained. "If he's
nervous give him a heavy meal. If he's happy a salad will do." Actors on
the shows also ignored the contradictions between their on-stage and off-
stage roles. Actress Marjorie Reynolds told *TV Guide* that she enjoyed
playing Mrs. Chester A. Riley, because "I've done just about everything
in films from westerns to no-voice musicals, and now with the Riley show,
I'm back in the kitchen. Where every wife belongs."[34]

The focus on the family in early network television situation comedies
involved a special emphasis on mothers. Images of long-suffering but loving
mothers pervaded these programs and publicity about them. Ostensibly
representations of "tradition," these images actually spoke to a radical
rupture with the past: the establishment of the isolated nuclear family of
the 1950s with its attendant changes in family gender roles. The wartime
economic mobilization that ended the Depression stimulated an extraordinary period of family formation that was in sharp contrast to the experience of preceding decades. Americans married more frequently, formed

families at a younger age, and had more children in the 1940s than they had in the 1920s and 1930s.[35] The combination of permissive recommendations for childrearing and social changes attendant to increases in consumer spending isolated mothers as never before. Work previously shared with extended kinship and neighbor networks now had to be done by machines, at home in isolation. Childrearing took up more time and responsibility, but inflation and expanded consumer desires encouraged women to work outside the home for pay. When the conflicting demands of permissivism created guilt and feelings of inadequacy, outside authorities—from child psychologists to television programs—stood ready to provide "therapeutic" images of desired maternal behavior.

Mama

While placing special burdens on women, changes in family identity in the postwar era transformed the roles of all family members. As psychoanalyst Joel Kovel demonstrates, the decomposition of extended kinship networks made the nuclear family the center of the personal world, "a location of desire and intimacy not previously conceptualized."[36] Kovel argues that participation in civil society can keep individuals from sliding back into total narcissism, but that separation of family from society in modern capitalism blocks access to the public realm. The family becomes the locus of all social demands, lauded all the more in theory as its traditional social function disappears in practice. The family appears to be private and voluntary, yet its isolation from neighborhood and class networks leave it subject to extraordinary regulation and manipulation by outside authorities like psychologists and advertisers. The family appears to be the repository of mutuality and affection, but commodity society has truncated its traditional functions into the egoism of possession. The family appears to maintain the privileges and authority of patriarchy, but "like a house nibbled by termites," the outwardly strong appearance of patriarchy masks a collapsing infrastructure no longer capable of wielding authority in an increasingly administered and institutionalized society. According to Kovel, the demise of the traditional family creates a need for authority that becomes filled by the"administrative mode"—the structure of domination that offers commodities as the key to solving personal problems.[37] Sociologist Nancy Chodorow draws a similar formulation in her observation that "the decline of the oedipal father creates an orientation to external authority and behavioral obedience."[38] Chodorow also points out that the idealization of masculinity inherent in the "distant father" role in the nuclear family gives ideological priority to men, while channeling rebellion and resentment against the power wielded by the accessible and proximate mother. Kovel and Chodorow both stress that these patterns are neither natural nor inevitable: they emerge in concrete social circumstances where the nuclear family serves as the main base of support for consumer society.[39]

Commercial network television emerged as the primary discursive medium in American society at the precise historical moment that the isolated nuclear family and its concerns eclipsed previous ethnic, class, and political forces as the crucible of personal identity. Television programs both reflected and shaped that translation, defining the good life in family-centric, asocial, and commodity-oriented ways. As Todd Gitlin argues, "What is hegemonic in consumer capitalist ideology is precisely the notion that happiness, or liberty, or equality, or fraternity can be affirmed through existing private commodity forms, under the benign protective eye of the national security state."[40] Yet the denigration of public issues and the resulting overemphasis on the home contained contradictions of their own. If the harmonious and mutually supportive family of the past granted moral legitimacy to the consumer dilemmas of urban, ethnic working-class families, the tensions of the modern nuclear household revealed the emerging nuclear family to be a contested terrain of competing needs and desires.

The structural tensions basic to the "father absent-mother present" gender roles of the nuclear family identified by Chodorow pervaded television portrayals of urban, ethnic working-class life in the 1950s. Peg Riley, Alice Kramden, and Sapphire Stevens heroically endure their husbands' failures to deliver on promises of wealth and upward mobility, and they earn the sympathy of the audience by compensating for the incompetent social performance of their spouses. Yet their nagging insistence on practical reason also marks them as "shrews," out to undercut male authority. Male insensitivity to female needs forms the focal point of humor and sardonic commentary—as in the episode of *The Life of Riley* where Riley can't understand Peg's complaints about staying home all the time. "I can't figure her out," he tells his son. "She's got a home to clean, meals to cook, dishes to wash, you two kids to look after, floors to scrub—what more does she want?" Few shows displayed hostility between husbands and wives as openly as *The Honeymooners*. (Even the title functioned as bitter irony.) When Alice employs sarcasm in response to Ralph's "get rich quick" schemes and his neglect of her needs, Ralph invariably clenches his fist and says, "One of these days, Alice, one of these days, pow! Right in the kisser!" Coupled with his threats to send her "to the moon," the intimation of wife-beating remains a recurring "comic" premise in the show. Jackie Gleason told one interviewer that he thought many husbands felt the way Ralph did about their wives. And an article in *TV Guide* quoted an unnamed "famous" psychiatrist who contended that the program's popularity rested on male perceptions that women had too much power, and on female perceptions that male immaturity demonstrated the superiority of women.[41] *The Honeymooners* might end with a humbled Ralph Kramden telling Alice, "Baby, you're the greatest," but the show clearly "worked" because tensions between men and women spoke to the experiences and fears of the audience (see Table 2).

Table 2.

Program	Star's Gender	Children	Father or Male Lead	Mother or Female Lead	Extended Family
Mama	Female	Three	Distant but warm	Competent	Relatives neighbors
The Goldbergs	Female	Two	Distant but warm	Competent	Relatives neighbors
Amos 'n' Andy	Male	None	Irresponsible	Hostile	Lodge brother-in-laws
The Honeymooners	Male	None	Irresponsible	Hostile	Neighbors
Life with Luigi	Male	None	Irresponsible	Warm	Neighbors
Life of Riley	Male	Two	Incompetent	Warm	Neighbors
Hey Jeannie	Female	None	Irresponsible	Competent	Neighbors boarder

Structural tensions within families, women betrayed by irresponsible and incompetent husbands, and men chafing under the domination of their wives: hardly an ideal portrait of family life. These depictions reflected the fissures in a fundamentally new form of family, a form which increasingly dominated the world of television viewers. One might expect commercial television programs to ignore the problems of the nuclear family, but the industry's imperial ambition—the desire to have all households watching at all times—encouraged exploitation of the real problems confronting viewers. Censorship ruled out treatment of many subjects, but family tensions offered legitimate and fertile ground for television programs. Individuals cut off from previous forms of self-definition and assaulted by media images encouraging narcissistic anxieties had insatiable needs to survey the terrain of family problems, to seek relief from current tensions and assurance of the legitimacy of current social relations. In order to create subjects receptive to the appeals of advertisers and to achieve ideological and narrative closure for their own stories, the creators of television programs had to touch on real issues, albeit in a truncated and an idealized form. While they unfailingly offered only individual and codified solutions to those problems, the mere act of exposing the contradictions of the nuclear family created the structural potential for oppositional readings. Representation of generational and gender tensions undercut the legitimating authority of the televised traditional working-class family by demonstrating the chasm between memories of yesterday and realities of today. If the programs remained true to the past, they lost their relevance to current tensions. Yet when they successfully addressed contemporary problems, they forfeited the legitimacy offered by the past and made it easier for their viewers to escape the pull of parochialism and paternal authority embedded in the traditional family form. This clash between the legitimizing promise of urban, ethnic working-class shows and their propensity for exposing the shortcomings of both past and present social relations went beyond their treatment of family issues and extended as well to matters of work, class, and ethnicity.

Work, Class, and Ethnicity

In addition to consumer issues, the changing nature of working-class identity also influenced the collective memory of viewers of urban, ethnic working-class situation comedies in the 1950s. The decade of the 1940s not only witnessed an unprecedented transformation in the nature of the American family, but it also saw an extraordinary social upheaval among workers, which labor historian Stanley Aronowitz has characterized as "incipient class formation."[42] War mobilization reindustrialized the sagging U.S. economy, but also reconstituted the working class. Migrations to defense production centers and breakthroughs by women and blacks in securing industrial employment changed the composition of the work force. Traditional parochial loyalties waned as mass production and full employment created new work groups on the shop floor and new working-class communities outside the factory gates. Mass strikes and demonstrations united workers from diverse backgrounds into a polity capable of sustained collective action. Of course, racism and sexism remained pervasive on both institutional and grass roots levels, but the mass activity of the postwar era represented the stirrings of a class consciousness previously unknown in a proletariat deeply divided by ethnicity, race, and gender. By the 1950s, expanded consumer opportunities, suburbanization, and access to education offered positive inducements away from that class consciousness, while anti-Communism, purges, and restrictions on rank and file activism acted negatively to undercut trade unions as crucibles of class consciousness. Yet retentions of the incipient class formation of the 1940s percolated throughout the urban, ethnic working-class situation comedies of the 1950s.

Jeannie Carson, the star of *Hey Jeannie,* began her career in show business by singing to Welsh miners as they came out of the pits. Appropriately enough, her U.S. television series adopted a working-class locale—the home of Al Murray, a Brooklyn cab driver, and his sister Liz.[43] The setting imposed certain structural directions on the program's humor—directions that gave voice to sharp class resentments. One episode concerns Al Murray's efforts to hide his cab in a neighbor's garage so that he can take the day off from work to see his beloved Dodgers play baseball at Ebbetts Field. Sensing Murray's dereliction of duty, the cab company president delivers a self-righteous harangue about the evils of such behavior to his secretary. Pontificating on the social responsibilities of a taxicab company, "a public utility," he asks his secretary if she knows what happens when one of his cabs is not in operation. "No, what?" she inquires. "It cuts into my profits," he responds (*Hey Jeannie*: "The Cab Driver"). Humor based on such hypocrisy by employers has a long history in working-class culture, but it is rarely the subject of mass-media comedy. As the episode continues, the boss's secretary (in an act of solidarity) calls Liz and Jeannie to warn them that the boss is out on the streets looking for Al's cab. Jeannie takes the taxi out of the garage to prevent Al's boss from finding it there, but accustomed to driving in her native Scotland, she drives on the left side of the street and gets stopped by a police officer. The policeman discovers that she is an immigrant and lets her off with a warning, remembering his own days as a newly arrived immigrant from

Ireland. The resolution of the show finds Jeannie getting to the ballpark in time to get Al back to the cab where his boss finds him and apologizes for even suspecting his employee of misconduct. The episode vibrates with class consciousness, from the many acts of solidarity that get Al off the hook to the final victory over the boss—a victory gained by turning work time into play time, and getting away with it. That kind of collective activity in pursuit of common goals appears frequently in the urban, ethnic working-class situation comedies of the 1950s, in incidents ranging from a rent strike by tenants in *The Goldbergs* to community protest against destruction of a favorite neighborhood tree in *Life With Luigi (The Goldbergs*: "The Rent Strike"; and *Life with Luigi*: "The Power Line").

Even though the workplace rarely appears in television comedies about working-class life, when it does provide a focus for comic or dramatic tensions, it also seethes with class resentments. On one episode of *Mama*, Lars Hansen tells another worker that he prefers working for Mr. Jenkins to working for Mr. Kingsley because "Mr. Jenkins doesn't lose his temper so much." Mr. Kingsley also demands speed-ups from the men and tries to pressure Papa into making the other workers produce at a faster pace (*Mama*: "Mama and the Carpenter"). In this episode, the workplace appears as a place where workers with common interests experience fragmentation. Even after Jake Goldberg graduates from his job as a tailor to become owner of a small dressmaking firm, work prevents him from enjoying life. Business pressures take him away from his family and prevent him from developing recreational interests. When Molly's Uncle David starts playing pool, Jake confides that he never learned to play because "pool is a game that requires leisure." However, his business sense causes him to lean over the table, touch it, and murmur with admiration, "nice quality felt, though" (*The Goldbergs*: "Bad Companions"). Jake's work brings in a bigger financial reward than Al Murray's cab driving or Lars Hansen's carpentry, but it still compels him to trade the precious minutes and hours of his life for commodities that he hardly has time to enjoy. Work as a noble end in itself is almost entirely absent from these shows. No work ethic or pride in labor motivates these workers. In fact, Ed Norton's pride in his job as a sewer worker provides a recurrent comic premise in *The Honeymooners*. The object of work in these programs consists of material reward to enhance one's family status or to obtain some leisure-time commodity.

Work not only appears infrequently in 1950s comedies about working-class life, but blue-collar labor often appears as a stigma—a condition that retards the acquisition of desired goods. But even demeaning portrayals of working-class people contain contradictions, allowing for negotiated or oppositional readings. Advertisers and network officials pointed to

Chester A. Riley's "magnificent stupidity" as the key to the big ratings garnered by *The Life of Riley,* but that "stupidity" sometimes masked other qualities. At a fancy dinner where the Rileys are clearly out of place, they meet a blue blood named Cecil Spencer Kendrick III. "You mean there's two more of you inside?" Riley asks. The audience laughter at his gaffe comes in part from resentment against the antidemocratic pretensions of Kendrick and his associates. Similarly, when Riley's neighbor, Jim Gillis, tries to impress him with tales about the fancy food at an expensive restaurant, Riley gets Gillis to admit that crepes suzette are nothing more than "pancakes soaked in kerosene and then set on fire." That sense of the unintentional insight also propels the malaprop-laden humor of Molly Goldberg. Who could dispute her self-sacrificing virtue when Molly vows to save money by getting old furniture: "I don't care how old, even antique furniture would be fine"? She complains that her cousin has been gone for two weeks and that she hasn't seen "hide nor seek of him," and she warns her uncle that she will give him only one word of advice, and that word is "be sure" (*The Goldbergs*: "Is There a Doctor in the House?" and "Bogie Comes Home"). When Molly says that "patience is a vulture," or that "it never rains until it pours," her misstatements carry wisdom (*The Goldbergs*: "Moving Day" and "Is There a Doctor in the House?").

Resentments about work, refusal to acknowledge the legitimacy of the upper classes, and creative word play abound in these programs, transmitting the texture of decades of working-class experience. Similarly, comedy about fraternal orders and ethnic lodges appear in television shows of the 1950s as a reflection of real historical experience. In history, fraternal orders and mutual aid societies comprised essential resources for working-class immigrants, often providing insurance, burial expenses, recreational facilities, and adult education at a time when the state accepted none of those responsibilities. In the urban, ethnic working-class situation comedies of the early 1950s, the fraternal lodge appears as an archaic and anachronistic institution, a remnant of the past at odds with the needs of the family. Lars Hansen brings home officials of the Sons of Norway for dinner, thereby creating more work for Mama.[44] Chester A. Riley wastes his time and money on the Brooklyn Patriots of Los Angeles, an organization set up to revere the world he left behind when he moved his family west. The Mystic Knights of the Sea provide Kingfish with a theater of operations for bilking his "brothers" out of their money, and for indulging his inflated sense of self-importance. The Royal Order of Raccoons keep Ralph Kramden from spending time with Alice, and they divert his paycheck away from the family budget toward lodge dues. In one show Alice asks Ralph what benefit she derives from his lodge activities. He proudly informs her that his membership entitles both of them to free burial in the Raccoon

National Cemetery in Bismark, North Dakota. With appropriate sarcasm, Alice replies that the prospect of burial in North Dakota makes her wonder why she should go on living (*The Honeymooners*: "The Loudspeaker").

In organic popular memory, lodges retained legitimacy as sources of mutuality and friendship. But in an age when suburban tract housing replaced the ethnic neighborhood, when the state took on welfare functions previously carried out by voluntary associations, and when the home sphere became increasingly isolated from the community around it, the lodge hall became a premise for comic ridicule. In television programs, the interests of the family took precedence over those of the fraternal lodge, and a binary opposition between the two seemed inevitable. Yet the very inclusion of lodges in these programs demonstrates the power of the past in the discourse of the present. Television programs validated the atomized nuclear family at the expense of the extended kinship and class relations manifested in the fraternal order. When successful, these shows undercut the ability of the past to provide legitimacy for contemporary social relations. When unsuccessful, these shows called attention to the possibility of other forms of community and culture than those that dominated the present.

Cultural specificity about working-class life provided credibility for early network television programs, but at the same time created problems for advertisers. Erik Barnouw points out that sponsors hardly relished the prospect of shows situated in lower-class environments—like the enormously successful teleplay, *Marty*—because "Sponsors were meanwhile trying to 'upgrade' the consumer and persuade him to 'move up to a Chrysler,' and 'live better electrically' in a suburban home, with help from 'a friend at Chase Manhattan.' The sponsors preferred beautiful people in mouth-watering decor to convey what it meant to climb the socioeconomic ladder. The commercials looked out of place in Bronx settings."[45] When advertisers coasted on the borrowed legitimacy of working-class history to lend sincerity and authenticity to their appeals to buy coffee and soap, they also ran the risk of exposing contradictions between the past and present. Author Kathryn Forbes, who wrote the book on which *Mama* was based, complained that the television Hansen family had too much wealth to present accurately the circumstances she had written about. Forbes's book portrays the Hansen family with four children in a house shared with relatives and boarders; on television they have three children in a house to themselves. In the Forbes book, Mama represents a traditional mother raising independent daughters—using her traditional cooking skills to make social connections that allow Katrin to pursue an untraditional career as a writer. On television, tradition reigns as Mama instructs Katrin about cooking to help her land a husband, and Katrin becomes a secretary rather than a writer. Other shows made similar adaptations to the ideological norms of the 1950s. On radio and for most of their years on television, the Goldbergs lived in a multifamily Bronx dwelling where neighbors and relatives blended together to form an extended community. By the time the television show reached its last year of production in 1955–1956, the Goldbergs moved to a suburban house in a Long Island subdivision where physical and emotional distances constituted the norm. The radio version of *Amos 'n' Andy* began to neglect the solid family man and independent businessman Amos as early as the 1940s; but the television show which began in 1951 pushed Amos even farther into the background in order to zero in on the marital problems and home life of the shiftless and irresponsible Kingfish. In each of these shows, television versions tended to accentuate the dilemmas of atomized nuclear families and to downplay the dramas emanating from extended class and ethnic associations.

Amos 'n' Andy

The working class depicted in urban, ethnic working class situation comedies of the 1950s bore only a superficial resemblance to the historical American working class. Stripped of essential elements of ethnic and class identity, interpreted through perspectives most relevant to a consumer middle class, and pictured in isolation from the social connections that gave purpose and meaning to working-class lives, the televised working-class family summoned up only the vaguest contours of its historical counterpart. Even in comparison to depictions of class in other forms of communication, like folklore, theater, music, literature, or radio, television presented a desiccated and eviscerated version of working-class life. Yet the legitimizing functions served by locating programs in working-class environments caused some attempts at authenticity that brought sedimented class tensions to the surface. While the producers of these television shows hardly intended to direct viewers' attentions toward real ethnic and class conflicts, the social location of the writers and actors most knowledgeable about working-class life served to make some of these programs focal points for social issues. When producers took on working-class settings as a form of local color, they burdened themselves with the contradictions of the communities that provided the color, as evidenced by public controversies over *The Goldbergs* and *Amos 'n' Andy*.

Part of the convincing authenticity of *The Goldbergs* came from actors and writers who developed their skills within the Yiddish theater and the culture that supported it. An organic part of that culture included political activists, including Communists, socialists, and antifascists whose concerns found expression in a variety of community activities including theater. Philip Loeb, who played Jake Goldberg, became the center of controversy when an anti-Communist right-wing publication accused him of subversive connections arising from his appearance at antifascist rallies and his having signed a petition calling for the admission of blacks into professional baseball. Nervous sponsors and advertising representatives, afraid of threatened boycotts by the anti-Communists, dropped their support of the show and demanded that its producer and star, Gertrude Berg, fire Loeb. At first she refused, pointing out that Loeb had never been a Communist, but ultimately Berg gave in to the pressure and fired her co-star in order to keep her show on the air. Sponsors resumed their support after Loeb left the program 1952, and *The Goldbergs* ran for four more years. Loeb received a $45,000 settlement in exchange for dropping any legal actions against the show, but he never worked again as an actor because producers viewed him as "controversial." In 1956, Loeb committed suicide.[46] Similarly, Mady Christians played Mama in the Broadway play *I Remember Mama,* but could not play that role on television: anti-Communist pressure groups questioned her loyalty because she had worked on behalf of refugees from fascism in the 1930s and 1940s with individuals accused of subversion. Blacklisted from her profession, Christians sank into a severe depression that friends felt sapped her strength and made her unable to overcome health problems that led to her death in 1951. Loeb and Christians dismayed advertisers, not because of their political views, but because their presence provoked political controversy and interfered with the illusions created by their programs of a world without politics. Like the real Goldbergs and Hansens in American history, Philip Loeb and Mady Christians lived in a world where ethnicity connected them to complicated political issues. The controversy over their views and the public attention directed toward them threatened to unmask the world of *Mama* and *The Goldbergs* as a created artifact—depriving it of legitimating power.

Amos 'n' Andy contained similar, but more culturally explosive, connections. Stereotyped and demeaning portrayals of black people have long constituted an obsessive theme in American theater, and for that matter, in American life. Historian Nathan Irvin Huggins points out that the minstrel show stereotypes enabled white society at the turn of the twentieth century to attribute to black people the characteristics that it feared most in itself. At a time when industrialization demanded a revolutionary transformation in behavior that compelled Americans to accept Victorian standards about thrift, sobriety, abstinence, and restraint, the minstrel show emerged to present laziness, greed, gluttony, and licentiousness as traits singularly associated with black people. These images worked to legitimate the emerging Victorian code by associating opposition to the dominant ideology with the despised culture of Afro-Americans. The minstrel show "Negro" presented white society with a representation of the natural self at odds with the normative self of industrial culture. Uninhibited behavior could be savored by the ego during the minstrel performance, but overruled afterwards by the superego. The viewer could release tension by pointing to the minstrel show "darkie" and saying "It's him, not me." But the viewer came back, again and again. The desire to subjugate and degrade black people had political and economic imperatives of its own, but emotional and psychic reinforcement for that exploitation came from the ways in which racist stereotypes enabled whites to accept the suppression of their natural selves.

The centrality of racist images to white culture presented peculiar problems for Afro-Americans. Entry into white society meant entry into its values, and those values included hatred of blacks. In order to participate in the white world, blacks had to make concessions to white America's fantasy images. As Huggins notes, black people found it dangerous to step out of character, either on or off stage. The great black vaudeville entertainer Bert Williams demonstrated the absurd contradictions of this process: he donned blackface makeup to perform on stage—a black man imitating white men imitating black men. William's artistic genius and stubborn self-respect led him to inject subtle elements of social criticism into his act, but for most spectators, he merely reinforced their a priori conclusions about the stage black.[47]

The black cast of *Amos 'n' Andy* came out of the theatrical traditions that spawned Williams, and they perpetuated many of his contradictions. As a successful radio program, the all-black world of *Amos 'n' Andy* had been performed mostly by its white creators (Freeman Gosden and Charles Correll). With the move to television, Gosden and Correll hired an all-black cast, but they nonetheless faced protests from community groups. The National Association for the Advancement of Colored People and black actor James Edwards campaigned to have the program taken off the air because they felt that it made the only televised presentation of Afro-American life an insulting one. The NAACP complained in federal court that black citizens routinely suffered abuse from whites addressing them as "Amos" or "Andy," and that the program defamed black professionals by presenting them as liars and cheats. In response, black actors employed on the program and a few black intellectuals defended *Amos 'n' Andy* as a harmless satire and an important vehicle for bringing much needed exposure to black actors.[48]

Placed in historical context, *Amos 'n' Andy* did for the values of the 1950s what the minstrel show accomplished for previous generations. Everything considered precious but contested in white society—like the family or the work ethic—became violated in the world of Kingfish. Ambition and upward mobility drew ridicule when pursued by blacks. In a society nurtured on Horatio Alger stories about rising from rags to riches, this lampooning of a black man's aspirations could function to release tensions about the fear of failure. It could redirect hostility away from the elite toward those on the bottom of society. When Kingfish pretends to be educated and uses grandiose language, the audience can howl derisively at his pretensions, but the same audience could glow with warm recognition when Mama Hansen uses her broken English to express her dreams for her son to grow up to be president. Ambition viewed as worthy and realistic for the Hansens becomes a symbol of weak character on the part of Kingfish.

Consistent with the values of the 1950s as mediated through popular culture, family responsibilities—or neglect of them—define Kingfish even more than does his work. The glorification of motherhood pervading psychological and popular literature of the 1950s becomes comedy in *Amos 'n' Andy*. Wives named for precious stones (Ruby and Sapphire) appear anything but precious, and "Mama" in this show appears as a nagging harpy screaming at the cowering—and emasculated—black man. Kingfish shares Ralph Kramden's dream of overnight success, but his transgressions against bourgeois morality are more serious. Kingfish has no job, his late night revelries and lascivious grins hint at marital infidelity, and he resorts to criminal behavior to avoid what he calls "the horrors of employment."[42]

He betrays his family and cheats his lodge brothers (and by implication the "brothers" of his race) with no remorse. But his most serious flaws stem from his neglect of the proper role of husband and father. In one episode, Kingfish's late night excursions cause his wife, Sapphire, to leave home and live with her mother. Kingfish misses her and orders one of his lackeys to find out where she has gone. When the report comes back that Sapphire has been seen entering an obstetrician's office, Kingfish assumes that he is about to become a father. In reality, Sapphire has simply taken a job as the doctor's receptionist, but the misunderstanding leads Kingfish to tell Amos how much fun he plans to have as a father. When Amos warns him that fatherhood involves serious responsibilities, Kingfish replies, "What you mean serious? All you gotta do is keep 'em filled up wid milk an' pablum and keep chuckin' em under de chin" (*Amos 'n' Andy*: "Kingfish Has a Baby"). Kingfish's ignorance plays out the worst fears of people in a society with a burgeoning obsession with family. By representing the possibility of incompetent parenting, Kingfish provides the audience with a sense of superiority, but one that can be maintained only by embracing parental responsibilities. Lest we miss the point of the show, when Kingfish and his friend Andy go to a clinic for prospective fathers, where they learn to bathe a baby by practicing with a doll, Kingfish lets his slip under the water and "drown."

Black protest made *Amos 'n' Andy* a much debated phenomenon, unmasking the calculation that went into its creation. In the context of the 1950s, when migration to industrial cities created greater concentrations of black political and economic power, these protests could not be dismissed casually by advertisers or the networks. Blatz Beer decided to drop its sponsorship of *Amos 'n' Andy* in 1954, knocking the show off prime-time schedules and into syndication until 1966, when another wave of protests made it untenable even in reruns. As the program most thoroughly grounded in ideologically charged historical material, *Amos 'n' Andy* lent itself most easily to critical historical interpretation and action, a capacity at odds with the interests of advertisers. But like shows rooted in white working-class histories, structural contradictions in black working-class life also held open the possibility for oppositional readings of the program's content. Black activist and author Julius Lester recalls his own formative experiences with *Amos 'n' Andy* in his autobiography in a way that provides the quintessential act of reinterpreting hierarchically prepared and distributed mass culture. Ruminating on the seeming paradox of a home life that installed black pride into him but that also encouraged him to listen to the antics of the Kingfish, Lester recalls that:

> In the character of Kingfish, the creators of *Amos and Andy* may have thought they were ridiculing blacks as lazy, shiftless, scheming and conniving, but to us

Kingfish was a paradigm of virtue, and alternative to the work ethic. Kingfish lived: Amos made a living. It did not matter that my parents lived by and indoctrinated me with the Puritan work ethic. Kingfish has a *joie de vivre* no white person could poison, and we knew that whites ridiculed us because they were incapable of such elan. I was proud to belong to the same race as Kingfish.[50]

Whether through the careful decoding exemplified by Julius Lester, or through the politicization of *Amos 'n' Andy* by mass protest, audience response to the program in some cases focused on the show's artifice and distortions of history. As was the case with *The Goldbergs,* the traditions needed to provide legitimacy for advertising messages surrounding *Amos 'n Andy* contained sedimented contestation that undermined their effectiveness, and instead provoked negotiated or oppositional readings. Dominant ideology triumphed on television in the 1950s, just as it did in political life, but historically grounded opposition remained possible and necessary for at least part of the audience.

The realism that made urban, ethnic working-class situation comedies convincing conduits for consumer ideology also compelled them to present alienations and aspirations subversive to the legitimacy of consumer capitalism. As Antonio Gramsci insists, ideological hegemony stems from the ability of those in power to make their own interests appear to be synonymous with the interests of society at large. But appeals for legitimacy always take place within concrete historical circumstances, in contested societies with competing interests. In a consumer capitalist economy where unmet needs and individual isolation provide the impetus for commodity desires, legitimation is always incomplete. Even while establishing dominance, those in power must borrow from the ideas, actions, and experiences of the past, all of which contain a potential for informing a radical critique of the present.

Dialogue, Negotiation, and Legitimation: Method and Theory

Recent scholarship in literary criticism, cultural studies, and sociology offers investigative methods and theoretical frameworks essential to understanding the historical dialogue about family, class, and ethnicity in early network television. The literary criticism of and "dialogic imagination" proposed by Mikhail Bakhtin demonstrates how all texts inherit part of the historical consciousness of their authors and audience.[51] Cultural studies theorist Stuart Hall notes that commercial mass media seek legitimacy with the audience by effectively representing diverse aspects of social life, including memories of past experiences, current contradictions, and potential sources of division and opposition.[52] Sociologist Jürgen Habermas observes that contemporary capitalist culture destroys the very motivations that it needs to function effectively, such as the work ethic or the willingness to defer gratification. Consequently, capitalist societies draw upon the borrowed legitimacy of cultural values and beliefs from the past, like religion or the patriarchal family, in order to provide the appearance of moral grounding for contemporary forces inimical to the interests of tradition.[53] Taken collectively, these approaches to culture provide a useful context for understanding the persistence of seemingly outdated and dysfunctional elements in early network television.

Bakhtin's analysis of text construction argues that communication does not begin in the present with a speaker or story; but rather that both speech and narrative come from a social matrix that is, at least in part, historical. Each speaker enters a dialogue already in progress; every work of art contains within it past, present, and future struggles over culture and power. Terms and forms of communication from the past not only make current discourse comprehensible and legitimate, but they also imbed within the present a collective historical experience rich with contradictions. The producers of early network television worked in a new medium, but they addressed an audience acclimated to specific forms of comedy and drama that reflected, however indirectly, the real texture of past struggles and present hopes.[54]

Structural unities underlie the seemingly divergent stories of different urban, ethnic working-class situation comedies. Viewers rarely saw Ralph Kramden's bus or Jake Goldberg's dressmaking shop, but the cameras introduced them to every detail of furnishing in the Kramden and Goldberg households. Difficulties encountered in the aircraft factory assembly line by Chester A. Riley or at the construction site by Lars Hansen paled in significance in contrast to the dilemmas of consumption faced in the Riley and Hansen families. The texture and tone of *Life with Luigi* and *Amos 'n' Andy* came from the ethnic worlds they depicted, but the plots of those shows dealt with the aspirations of individuals as if ethnic rivalries and discrimination did not exist. Instead, ethnics attain a false unity through consumption of commodities: Jeannie MacClennan learns to "be an American" by dressing fashionably and wearing the right makeup; Luigi Basco hopes to prove himself a worthy candidate for citizenship by opening a checking account and purchasing an insurance policy; Molly Goldberg overcomes her fears of installment buying and vows to live above her means—which she describes as "the American way" (*Hey, Jeannie*: "The Rock 'n Roll Kid"; *Life with Luigi*: "The Insurance Policy"; *The Goldbergs*: "The In-Laws"). Comedies in this subgenre are clearly cases where, as Stuart Hall points out, the commercial mass media tend to direct popular consciousness toward consumption and away from production. They present social actions and experiences as atomized individual events in order to fragment groups into isolated consumers, and they resolve the tensions confronting their audiences by binding them together in false unities and collectivities defined for the convenience of capital accumulation.[55]

But Hall also shows that the imperial aspirations of the mass media, their imperative to attract as large an audience as possible, lead to a disclosure of contradictions that allows cultural consumers to fashion oppositional or negotiated readings of mass culture. In order to make their dramas compelling and their narrative resolutions dynamic, the media also reflect the plurality of consumer experiences. A system that seeks to enlist everyone in the role of consumer must appear to be addressing all possible circumstances: a system that proclaims consensus and unanimity must acknowledge and explain obvious differences within the polity, if for no other reason than to co-opt or trivialize potential opposition. Television and other forms of commercial electronic media so effectively recapitulate the ideology of the "historical bloc" in which they operate that they touch on all aspects of social life—even its antagonistic contradictions.[56] While the media serve to displace, fragment, and atomize real experiences, they also generate and circulate a critical dialogue as an unintended consequence of their efforts to expose the inventory of social practice.

Of course, mere disclosure of opposition does not guarantee emancipatory practice: ruling elites routinely call attention to "deviant" subcultures in order to draw a clear distinction between permitted and forbidden behavior. In urban, ethnic working-class situation comedies in the 1950s, "deviant" traits—like Kingfish's aversion to work in *Amos 'n' Andy* and Lars Hansen's lack of ambition in *Mama*—taught object lessons about the perils of unconventional behavior. Yet the operative premises and enduring tensions of each of these shows revolved around the "otherness" of the lead characters. The "old-world" attitudes of newly arrived immigrants in *Hey, Jeannie* and *Life with Luigi* or the proletarian cultural innocence manifested in *Life with Luigi* or *The Honeymooners* lead to comedic clashes that exposed the inadequacies and deficiencies of those on the margins of society. But at the same time, these clashes counterposed the conformity and materialism of the mainstream to the narratively privileged moral superiority of those with connections to the past. Traditional values and beliefs prevented protagonists in these shows from achieving success and happiness as defined by society, but those values and beliefs also facilitated a critical distance from the false premises of the present. As Gertrude Berg noted in explaining the popularity of her character Molly Goldberg, Molly "lived in the world of today but kept many of the values of yesterday."[57]

The narrative sequence that framed every episode of *Mama* demonstrates the centrality of this dialogue between the past and present in early network television programs. As soon as Katrin Hansen introduced the show with the words "I remember Mama," a male narrator announced, "Yes, here's Mama, brought to you by Maxwell House Coffee." The camera then panned away from the photograph album to show Mama (played by Peggy Wood) making coffee for the Hansen family in their turn-of-the-century kitchen. The authority of the male narrator's voice established a connection between the continuity of family experience and the sponsor's product, between warm memories of the past and Mama in the kitchen making coffee. In this progression, the product becomes a member of the Hansen family, while tradition and emotional support become commodities to be secured through the purchase of Maxwell House Coffee. The sponsor's introduction announced ownership of the television show, but it also laid claim to the moral authority and warmth generated by the concept of motherhood itself.[58]

Katrin Hansen's retrospective narrative and the pictures from the family album reassured viewers by depicting events that had already happened in the emotionally secure confines of the audience's collective childhood. This false authenticity encouraged viewers to think of the program as the kind of history that might be created in their own homes. A CBS press release during the program's first broadcast season proclaimed, "On 'Mama' we try to give the impression that nobody is acting," and went on to claim success for that effort, quoting an unnamed viewer's contention that the show depicted a real family because "nobody but members of a real family could talk like that."[59] Free from the real history of ethnic, class, and gender experience, the history presented on *Mama* located its action within the personal spheres of family and consumer choices. Within these areas, realism could be put to the service of commodity purchases, as when the narrator followed his opening introduction with a discourse about how Mama in her day "had none of the conveniences of today's modern products" like Minute Rice, Jello, or instant coffee (*Mama*: "T.R.'s New Home"). Thus the morally sanctioned traditions of hearth and home could be put to the service of products that revolutionized those very traditions — all in keeping with Ernest Dichter's advice to his fellow advertising executives: "Do not assert that the new product breaks with traditional values, but on the contrary, that it fulfills its traditional functions better than any of its predecessors."[60]

Every episode of *Mama* began and ended with Mama making coffee in the kitchen — but to very different effects. The opening sequence, with the announcer's statement about Maxwell House Coffee, validates commodities; the ending sequence, however, validates both moralities and commodities. There Katrin, in the kitchen or as a voice-over, summarizes the meaning of that week's story for the audience by relating the lesson that she learned from it. Invariably these lessons belonged to the sphere of old-fashioned values, elevating human creations over commodities and privileging commitment to others over concern with self. In these lessons, the audience discovered that the toys Papa made with his hands meant more to the children than the fancy ones they saw in stores, or that loyalty to family and friends brought more rewards than upward mobility. These resolutions often directly contradicted the narratives that preceded them: after twenty-five minutes of struggle for happiness through commodity acquisition, the characters engaged in a one-minute homily about the superiority of moral goals over material ones. Then, with the high moral ground established, a voice-over by the announcer reminded viewers of the wonderful products that the sponsor of *Mama* had to offer.

The complicated dialogue in the opening and closing segments of *Mama* illumines the complex role played by historical referents in early network television. The past that brought credibility and reassurance to family dramas also contained the potential for undermining the commodified social relations of the present. The Hansen family interested advertisers because audiences identified their story as part of a precious collective memory resonating with the actual experiences and lessons of the past. The Hansens could not be credible representatives of that past if they appeared to live among the plethora of consumer goods that dominated the commercials, or of they appeared uncritical of the consumer world of the present that made such a sharp break with the values of the past. Yet the Hansen family had little value to advertisers unless their experiences sanctioned pursuit of commodities in the present. The creators of the program—like those engaged in production of the other urban, ethnic working-class comedies on television—resolved this potential contradiction by putting the borrowed moral capital of the past at the service of the values of the present. They acknowledged the critique of materialism and upward mobility sedimented within the experiences of working-class families, but they demonstrated over and over again how wise choices enabled consumers to have both moral and material rewards. By positing the nuclear family as a transhistorical "natural" locus for the arbitration of consumer desires, television portrayed the value crises of the 1950s as eternal and recurrent. By collapsing the distinction between family as consumer unit and family as part of neighborhood, ethnic, and class networks, television programs in the early 1950s connected the most personal and intimate needs of individuals to commodity purchases. They implied that the past sanctioned rather than contradicted the ever-increasing orientation toward shopping as the cornerstone of social life, an orientation that characterized media discourse in the postwar era.

The reliance on the past to sanction controversial changes in present behavior forms the core of Jürgen Habermas's analysis of contemporary capitalism's "legitimation crisis." According to Habermas, the consumer consciousness required by modern capitalism revolves around "civil and familial-vocational privatism" — a syndrome that elevates private consumer decisions over social relations and public responsibility.[61] Individuals see families as centers of consumption and leisure, while they regard employment as primarily a means of engaging in status competition. Instead of the rooted independence demanded by traditional family and community life, contemporary capitalist society encourages an atomized dependence on outside authorities — advertisers, self-help experts, and psychiatric, educational, and political authorities. Clearly useful for purposes of capital accumulation, this process undermines traditional motivations for work, patriotism, and personal relations, causing real crises in social relations. In addition, the infantile narcissism nurtured by this consumer consciousness encourages a search for validation from outside authorities — for communication which assures people that the impoverishment of work, family, and public life characteristic of late capitalism constitutes a legitimate and necessary part of progress toward a better life as defined by opportunities for more acquisition and more status.

For Habermas, the mass media play a crucial role in legitimation, but they do so imperfectly. The new forms of family and vocational consciousness cannot be justified on their own, but can be validated by invoking the moral authority of past forms of family and work identity. Thus the "work ethic" is summoned to justify a system based on commodified leisure, while mutual love and affection are called on to sanction families that exist primarily as consumer units. The social relations of the past are used to legitimate a system that in reality works to destroy the world that created those relations in the first place. Consequently, the invocation of the past in the service of the present is a precarious undertaking. Tradition used to legitimate untraditional behavior may instead call attention to the disparity between the past and the present; collective popular memory may see the manipulative use of tradition by advertisers as a conscious strategy, as an attempt to create artifacts that conflict with actual memory and experiences. As Habermas cautions, "traditions can retain legitimizing force only as long as they are not torn out of interpretive systems that guarantee continuity and identity."[62]

Habermas provides us with a framework capable of explaining both the presence of historical elements in early network television shows and their limitations. In conjunction with Bakhtin's emphasis on dialogue and Hall's delineation of negotiation, Habermas's analysis explains how portrayals of traditional, ethnic, working-class families might have been essential for legitimizing social forces that undermined the very values that made those families respected icons in popular consciousness. At the same time, Habermas directs our attention to the fundamental instability of this legitimation process, to the ways in which audiences might come to see manipulative uses of the past as prepared and created artifacts at war with the lessons of history as preserved in collective popular memory.

After 1958, network television eliminated urban, ethnic working-class programs from the schedule. Marc Daniels, who directed *The Goldbergs,* recalls that a changing society less tied to class and ethnicity demanded different kinds of entertainment, and certainly the emergence of ethnically neutral, middle-class situation comedies between 1958 and 1970 lends credence to that view.[63] The entry of major film studios into television production in the mid 1950s also had an impact, since the working-class shows tended to be produced by small companies like Hal Roach Studios. Major studio involvement in television production increased the propor-tion of action/adventure shows with production values ill-suited to the realism of urban, ethnic working-class programs. In action and adventure shows, no embarrassing retentions of class consciousness compromised the sponsors' messages, and no social associations with ethnic life brought up disturbing issues that made them susceptible to protests and boycotts.

One might conclude that television and American society had no need for urban, ethnic working-class programs after 1958 because tensions between consumerist pressures and historical memories had been resolved. But the reappearance of race, class, and ethnicity in the situation comedies of the 1970s like *All in the Family, Chico and the Man,* and *Sanford and Son* testifies to the ongoing relevance of such tensions as existed in the 1950s to subsequent mass-media dialogue. The programs of the 1970s reprised both aspects of the 1950s shows—legitimation through repre-sentation of the texture of working-class life, and commodification of all human relationships, especially within families. Like their predecessors, urban, ethnic working-class shows of the 1970s mixed their commercial and consumerist messages with visions of connection to others that tran-scended the limits of civil and familial vocational privatism. They held open possibilities for transcending the parochialisms of traditional ethnicity and for challenging the patriarchal assumptions of both extended and nuclear families. The same communications apparatus that presented con-sumerism as the heir to the moral legacy of the working-class past also legitimized aspirations for happiness and community too grand to be satisfied by the lame realities of the commodity-centered world.[64]

In the early 1950s, an advertising instrument under the control of pow-erful monopolists established itself as the central discursive medium in American culture. With its penetration of the family and its incessant propaganda for commodity purchases, television helped erode the social base for challenges to authority manifest in the mass political activity among American workers in the 1940s. Yet television did not so much insure the supremacy of new values as it transformed the terms of social contestation. When mass culture gained in importance as an instrument of legitimation, oppositional messages filtered into even hierarchically controlled media constructions like network television programs. The internal contradictions of capitalism fueled this process by generating anxieties in need of legitimation, and by turning for legitimation to the very beliefs and practices most threatened by emerging social relations. Thus every victory for the ideology of civil and familial vocational privatism can also constitute a defeat. Every search for legitimacy can end in the dilution of legitimacy by unmasking media messages as prepared and fabricated ideological artifices. Even successful legitimation fails to a degree because the new social relations destroy their own source of legitimacy.

This is not to assume that the final outcome of television's ideological imperatives must be emancipatory. Inculcation of narcissistic desire coupled with destruction of traditional sources of moral restraint might well suit the needs of capital and produce a population eager for fascist authority. But structural conditions exist for an alternative future. As Joel Kovel argues, "The point is not that people desire the administrative mode, it is rather that administration protects them against the desires they can not stand, while it serves out, in the form of diluted rationalization, a hint of the desire and power lost to them."[65] The separation of individuals from political and community life, combined with the destruction of cultural traditions that previously gave direction and purpose to individuals, might make status competition and "possession" of a secure family role all that much more attractive. Certainly the neo-conservatism of the 1980s seems to hinge upon "protecting" the family from the increasing barbarism of society, and upon shifting the blame for the social disintegration caused by civil and familial vocational privatism onto the opposition movements formed to combat it.[66] But the sleight of hand inherent in the neo-conservative position allows for other possibilities. Reconnection to history and to motivational structures rooted within it is both desirable and possible. More than ever before, communication and criticism can help determine whether people accept the commodity-mediated desires that turn others into instruments and objects, or whether they build affirmative communities in dialogue with the needs and desires of others. By identifying the historical reality behind the construction of television texts in the early 1950s, we demystify their "organic" character and reveal their implications as created artifacts. We uncover sedimented critiques from the past and potential forms of opposition for the present.

The historical specificity of early network television programs led their creators into dangerous ideological terrain. By examining them as part of our own history, we learn about both the world we have lost and the one we have yet to gain. Fredric Jameson claims that "history is what hurts, what sets inexorable limits to individual as well as collective praxis."[67] But the unfinished dialogue of history can also be what helps, what takes us back into the past in order to break its hold on the present. By addressing the hurt, and finding out how it came to be, we begin to grasp ways of understanding the past, and ending the pain.

NOTES

Reprinted from *Cultural Anthropology* 1:4 (November 1986), pp. 355–387, © 1986 American Anthropological Association.

Acknowledgments: I wish to thank Nick Browne, Gary Burns, Robert Deming, Tom Dumm, Michael Fischer, Jib Fowles, Mary Beth Haralovich, Susan Hartmann, Connie LaBelle, Elizabeth Long, Barbara Tomlinson, and Brian Winston for their comments and criticisms on previous drafts of this article.

1. Rick Mitz, *The Great TV Sitcom Book* (New York: Perigree, 1983), p. 458.

2. Stuart Ewen condemns these shows as hostile to immigrant life and imposing consumerism on it in his *Captians of Consciousness* (New York: McGraw-Hill, 1976), pp. 208–210; Marty Jezer takes a more favorable view in *The Dark Ages* (Boston: South End, 1982), pp. 191–194.

3. Erik Barnouw, *The Sponsor* (New York: Oxford, 1979).

4. Daniel Boorstin, *The Americans: The Democratic Experience* (New York: Vintage Press, 1973), pp. 392–397.

5. Of course, class, ethnicity, and race remained important, but their relationship to individual identity changed radically at this time. The bureaucratization of trade unions and xenophobic anti-Communism also contributed to declines in ethnic and class consciousness.

6. Robert Allen, *Speaking of Soap Operas* (Chapel Hill: University of North Carolina Press, 1985), p. 126; Richard deCordova, Unpublished paper presented at the Society for Cinema Studies Conference, New York, June 12, 1985.

7. See the discussion in this article of *Mama*, *The Goldbergs*, and *Amos 'n' Andy*.

8. Albert U. Romasco, *The Poverty of Abundance* (New York: Oxford, 1965).

9. Henry Berger, "Social Protest in St. Louis," Paper presented at the Committee for the Humanities Forum, St. Louis, Missouri, March 12, 1982.

10. George Lipsitz, *Class and Culture in Cold War America: A Rainbow at Midnight* (New York: Praeger, 1981).

11. Lipsitz, pp. 47–50.

12. Lipsitz, pp. 47–50.

13. *TV Facts* (New York: Facts on File, 1980), p. 141.

14. Neilsen ratings demonstrate television's view of the family as separate market segments to be addressed independently. For an analysis of the industry's view of children as a special market, see Patricia J. Bence, "Analysis and History of Typology and Forms of Children's Network Programming from 1950 to 1980," Paper presented at Society for Cinema Studies Conference, New York, June 12, 1985.

15. William Boddy, "The Studios Move Into Prime Time: Hollywood and the Television Industry in the 1950s," *Cinema Journal,* 24.4 (Summer 1985), pp. 23–37; Jeanne Allen, "The Social Matrix of Television: Invention in the United States," in *Regarding Television* ed. E. Ann Kaplan (Los Angeles: University Publications of America, 1983), pp. 109–119.

16. Lipsitz, pp. 46, 120–121.

17. Geoffrey Moore and Phillip Klein, "The Quality of Consumer Installment Credit," (Washington D.C.: National Bureau of Economic Research, 1967); Jezer, *The Dark Ages.*

18. Susan Hartmann, *The Home Front and Beyond* (Boston: Twayne, 1982), pp. 165–168.

19. John Mollenkopf, *The Contested City* (Princeton: Princeton University Press, 1983), p. 111.

20. Michael Stone, "Housing the Economic Crisis," in *America's Housing Crisis: What Is to be Done?,* ed. Chester Hartman, (London and New York: Routledge and Kegan Paul, 1983), p. 122.

21. Jezer, p. 127.

22. Ernest Dichter, *The Strategy of Desire* (Garden City: Doubleday, 1960), p. 210.

23. Dichter, p. 209.

24. Elizabeth Meehan and Bradford Ropes, "Mama's Birthday," Theater Art's Collection, University Research Library, University of California, Los Angeles, 1954.

25. Hartmann, p. 168.

26. Meehan and Ropes.

27. Meehan and Ropes.

28. Meehan and Ropes.

29. Meehan and Ropes.

30. Charles E. Swanson and Robert L. Jones, "Television Ownership and its Correlates," *Journal of Applied Psychology* 35 (1951), pp. 352–357.

31. Martha Wolfenstein, "The Emergence of Fun Morality," *Journal of Social Issues* 7:4 (1951), pp. 15–25.

32. *TV Guide* (May 7, 1954), p. 11.

33. *Ladies' Home Journal* 73 (September 1956), pp. 130–131; *TV Guide* (November 2, 1953,) p. 7.

34. *TV Guide* (November 2, 1953), p. 17.

35. Hartmann, pp. 164–165.

36. Joel Kovel, "Rationalization and the Family," *Telos* 37:5–21 (1978), p. 189.

37. Kovel, pp. 13–14.

38. Nancy Chodorow, *The Reproduction of Mothering: Psychoanalysis and the Sociology of Gender* (Berkeley: University of California Press, 1978), p. 189.

39. Chodorow, p. 181; Kovel, p. 19.

40. Horace Newcomb, *TV: The Critical View* (New York: Oxford 1978).

41. *TV Guide* (October 1, 1955), p. 14.

42. Stanley Aronowitz, *Working Class Hero* (New York: Pilgrim, 1983).

43. *TV Guide* (December 29, 1956), p. 17.

44. The *Mama* show relied on the Bay Ridge, Brooklyn chapter of the Sons of Norway for advice on authentic Norwegian folk customs and stories, according to Dick Van Patten and Ralph Nelson, in remarks made at the Museum of Broadcasting, New York City, on December 17, 1985.

45. Barnouw, *The Sponsor,* p. 106.

46. Erik Barnouw, *Tube of Plenty* (New York: Oxford, 1982), p. 126; Jezer, pp. 193–194; Stefan Kanfer, *A Journal of the Plaque Years* (New York: Atheneum Books, 1973), p. 194; *New Republic* (January 21, 1952), p. 8; *New Republic* (February 18, 1952), p. 22.

47. Nathan Huggins, *Harlem Rennaisance* (New York: Oxford, 1978).

48. Thomas Cripps, "The Amos 'n' Andy Controversy," in *American History/ American Television,* ed. John O'Connor (New York: Ungar, 1983), pp. 33–54; J. Fred Macdonald, *Blacks on White TV* (Chicago: Nelson Hall, 1983), pp. 27–28; *Newsweek* (July 9, 1951), p. 56.

49. The depiction of Kingfish's refusal to work had especially vicious connotations in an era where the crisis in black unemployment reached unprecedented depths.

50. Julius Lester, *All is Well* (New York: W. Morrow, 1976), p. 14.

51. For a discussion of this see Horace Newcomb, "On the Dialogic Aspects of Mass Communications," *Critical Studies in Mass Communications* 1:34–50, (1984), pp. 37–41.

52. Stuart Hall, "Culture, the Media and the 'Ideological Effect'," in *Mass Communication and Society*, ed. James Curran, Michael Gurevitch and Janet Woollacott (Beverly Hills: Sage, 1979), pp. 315–348.

53. Jürgen Habermas, *Legitimation Crisis* (Boston: Beacon Press, 1975).

54. For a discussion of the role of media borrowing from earlier forms see Daniel Czitrom, *Media and the American Mind* (Chapel Hill: University of North Carolina Press, 1983).

55. Hall, pp. 315–348.

56. Hall, pp. 315–348.

57. Gertrude Berg, *Molly and Me* (New York: McGraw Hill, 1961), p. 167.

58. This is not to single out *Mama* as an especially commercial program. In fact, its advertisers allowed the show to run with no middle commercial, using only the opening and closing commercial sequences. Yet other shows incorporated commercial messages into dramatic program-like segments, especially *The Goldbergs* and *Life with Luigi*.

59. Ralph Nelson, Press Release, Ralph Nelson Collection, Number 875, Box 44, Special Collections, University Research Library, University of California, Los Angeles, 1949.

60. Dichter, p. 209.

61. Habermas, pp. 71–75.

62. Habermas, p. 71.

63. Marc Daniels, Presentation at the Director's Guild of America, Los Angeles, California, July 11, 1984.

64. For an excellent discussion of 1970s television see the forthcoming book by Ella Taylor, *All in the Work-Family*.

65. Kovel, p. 19.

66. Protection of the family represents an old social theme for conservatives and a traditional device for creating dramatic tension. But never before have they been as thoroughly unified as dramatic and political themes and never before have they dominated conservative thought as they have in the last decade.

67. Fredric Jameson, *The Political Unconscious: Narrative as a Socially Symbolic Act* (Ithaca: Cornell University Press, 1981), p. 102.

The Honeymooners

Father Knows Best

Sit-coms and Suburbs: Positioning the 1950s Homemaker
Mary Beth Haralovich

The suburban middle-class family sit-com of the 1950s and 1960s centered on the family ensemble and its home life: breadwinner father, homemaker mother, and growing children placed within the domestic space of the suburban home. Structured within definitions of gender and the value of home life for family cohesion, these sit-coms drew upon particular historical conditions for their realist representation of family relations and domestic space. In the 1950s, a historically specific social subjectivity of the middle-class homemaker was engaged by suburban housing, the consumer product industry, market research, and the lifestyle represented in popular "growing family" sit-coms such as *Father Knows Best* (1954–1963) and *Leave It to Beaver* (1957–1963). With the reluctant and forced exit of women from positions in skilled labor after World War II and during a period of rapid growth and concentration of business, the middle-class homemaker provided these institutions with a rationale for establishing the value of domestic architecture and consumer products for quality of life and the stability of the family.

The middle-class homemaker was an important basis of this social economy—so much so that it was necessary to define her in contradictions which held her in a limited social place. In her value to the economy, the homemaker was at once central and marginal.[1] She was marginal in that she was positioned within the home, constituting the value of her labor outside of the means of production. Yet she was also central to the economy in that her function as homemaker was the subject of consumer product design and marketing, the basis of an industry. She was promised psychic and social satisfaction for being contained within the private space of the home; and in exchange for being targeted, measured, and analyzed for the marketing and design of consumer products, she was promised leisure and freedom from housework.

These social and economic appeals to the American homemaker were addressed to the white middle class whom Stuart and Elizabeth Ewen have described as "landed consumers," for whom "suburban homes were standardized parodies of independence, of leisure, and most important of all, of the property that made the first two possible."[2] The working class is marginalized in and minorities are absent from these discourses and from the social economy of consumption. An ideal white and middle-class home life was a primary means of reconstituting and resocializing the American family after World War II. By defining access to property and home ownership within the values of the conventionalized suburban family, women and minorities were guaranteed economic and social inequality. Just as suburban housing provided gender-specific domestic space and restrictive neighborhoods, consumer product design and market research directly addressed the class and gender of the targeted family member, the homemaker.

The relationship of television programming to the social formation is crucial to an understanding of television as a social practice. Graham Murdock and Peter Golding argue that media reproduce social relations under capital through "this persistent imagery of consumerism conceal[ing] and compensat[ing] for the persistence of radical inequalities in the distribution of wealth, work conditions and life chances." Stuart Hall has argued that the ideological effects of media fragment classes into individuals, masking economic determinacy and replacing class and economic social relations with imaginary social relations.[3] The suburban family sit-com is dependent upon this displacement of economic determinations onto imaginary social relations that naturalize middle-class life.

Despite its adoption of historical conditions from the 1950s, the suburban family sit-com did not greatly proliferate until the late 1950s and early 1960s. While *Father Knows Best*, in 1954, marks the beginning of popular discussion of the realism of this program format, it was not until 1957 that *Leave It to Beaver* joined it on the schedule. In the late 1950s and early 1960s, the format multiplied, while the women's movement was seeking to release homemakers from this social and economic gender definition.[4] This "nostalgic" lag between the historical specificity of the social formation and the popularity of the suburban family sit-com on the prime-time schedule underscores its ability to mask social contradictions and to naturalize woman's place in the home.

The following is an analysis of a historical conjuncture in which institutions important to social and economic policies defined women as homemakers: suburban housing, the consumer product industry, and market research. *Father Knows Best* and *Leave It to Beaver* mediated this address to the homemaker through their representations of middle-class family life. They appropriated historically specific gender traits and a realist *mise en scène* of the home to create a comfortable, warm, and stable family environment. *Father Knows Best*, in fact, was applauded for realigning family gender roles, for making "polite, carefully middle-class, family-type entertainment, possibly the most non-controversial show on the air waves."[5]

"Looking through a Rose-Tinted Picture Window into Your Own Living Room"

After four years on radio, *Father Knows Best* began the first of its six seasons on network television in 1954. This program about the family life of Jim and Margaret Anderson and their children, Betty (age 15), Bud (age 13), and Kathy (age 8), won the 1954 Sylvania Award for outstanding family entertainment. After one season the program was dropped by its sponsor for low ratings in audience polls. But more than twenty thousand letters from viewers protesting the program's cancellation attracted a new sponsor (the Scott Paper Company), and *Father Knows Best* was promptly reinstated in the prime-time schedule. It remained popular even after first-run production ended in 1960 when its star, Robert Young, decided to move on to other roles. Reruns of *Father Knows Best* were on prime time for three more years.[6]

Contemporary writing on *Father Knows Best* cited as its appeal the way it rearranged the dynamics of family interaction in situation comedies. Instead of the slapstick and gag-oriented family sit-com with a "henpecked simpleton" as family patriarch (this presumably refers to programs such as *The Life of Riley*), *Father Knows Best* concentrated on drawing humor from parents raising children to adulthood in suburban America. This prompted the *Saturday Evening Post* to praise the Andersons for being "a family that has surprising similarities to real people":

> The parents . . . manage to ride through almost any family situation without violent injury to their dignity, and the three Anderson children are presented as decently behaved children who will probably turn into useful citizens.[7]

These "real people" are the white American suburban middle-class family, a social and economic arrangement valued as the cornerstone of the American social economy in the 1950s. The verisimilitude associated with *Father Knows Best* is derived not only from the traits and interactions of the middle-class family, but also from the placement of that family within the promises that suburban living and material goods held out for it. Even while the role of Jim Anderson was touted as probably "the first intelligent father permitted on radio or TV since they invented the thing,"[8] the role of Margaret Anderson in relation to the father and the family—as homemaker—was equally important to post-World War II attainment of quality family life, social stability, and economic growth.

Leave It to Beaver was not discussed as much or in the same terms as *Father Knows Best*. Its first run in prime-time television was from 1957 to 1963, overlapping the last years of *Father Knows Best*. Ward and June Cleaver raise two sons (Wally, 12; Theodore, the Beaver, 8) in a single-family suburban home which, in later seasons, adopted a nearly identical floor plan to that of the Andersons. Striving for verisimilitude, the stories were based on the "real life" experiences of the scriptwriters in raising their own children. "In recalling the mystifications that every adult experienced when he [sic] was a child, 'Leave It to Beaver' evokes a humorous and pleasurably nostalgic glow."[9]

Like *Father Knows Best*, *Leave It to Beaver* was constructed around an appeal to the entire family. The Andersons and the Cleavers are already assimilated into the comfortable environment and middle-class lifestyle that housing and consumer products sought to guarantee for certain American families. While the Andersons and the Cleavers are rarely (if ever) seen in the process of purchasing consumer products, family interactions are closely tied to the suburban home. The Andersons' Springfield and the Cleavers' Mayfield are ambiguous in their metropolitan identity as suburbs in that the presence of a major city nearby is unclear, yet the communities exhibit the characteristic homogeneity, domestic architecture, and separation of gender associated with suburban design.

Margaret Anderson and June Cleaver, in markedly different ways, are two representations of the contradictory definition of the homemaker in that they are simultaneously contained and liberated by domestic space. In their placement as homemakers, they represent the promises of the economic and social processes that established a limited social subjectivity for homemakers in the 1950s. Yet there are substantial differences in the character traits of the two women, and these revolve around the degree to which each woman is contained within the domestic space of the home. As we shall see, June is more suppressed in the role of homemaker than Margaret is, with the result that June remains largely peripheral to the decision-making activities of family life.

These middle-class homemakers lead a comfortable existence in comparison with television's working-class homemakers. In *Father Knows Best* and *Leave It to Beaver*, middle-class assimilation is displayed through deep-focus photography exhibiting tasteful furnishings, tidy rooms, appliances, and gender-specific functional spaces: dens and workrooms for men, the "family space" of the kitchen for women. Margaret Anderson and June Cleaver have a lifestyle and domestic environment radically different from that of their working-class sister, Alice Kramden, in *The Honeymooners*. The suburban home and accompanying consumer products have presumably liberated Margaret and June from the domestic drudgery that marks Alice's daily existence.

The middle-class suburban environment is comfortable, unlike the cramped and unpleasant space of the Kramdens' New York City apartment. A major portion of the comedy of *The Honeymooners'* (1955–1956) working-class urban family is derived from Ralph and Alice Kramden's continual struggle with outmoded appliances, their lower-class taste, and the economic blocks to achieving an easy assimilation into the middle class through home ownership and the acquisition of consumer goods. Ralph screams out of the apartment window to a neighbor to be quiet; the water pipe in the wall breaks, spraying plaster and water everywhere. The Kramdens' refrigerator and stove predate the postwar era.

One reason for this comedy of *mise en scène* is that urban sit-coms such as *I Love Lucy* (1951–1957) and *The Honeymooners* tended to focus on physical comedy and gags generated by their central comic figures (Lucille Ball and Jackie Gleason) filmed or shot live on limited sets before studio audiences.[10] *Father Knows Best* and *Leave It to Beaver*, on the other hand, shifted the source of comedy to the ensemble of the nuclear family as it realigned the roles within the family. *Father Knows Best* was praised by the *Saturday Evening Post* for its "outright defiance" of "one of the more persistent clichés of television scriptwriting about the typical American family . . . the mother as the iron-fisted ruler of the nest, the father as a blustering chowderhead and the children as being one sassy crack removed from juvenile delinquency." Similarly, *Cosmopolitan* cited the program for overturning television programming's "message . . . that the American father is a weak-willed, predicament-inclined clown [who is] saved from his doltishness by a beautiful and intelligent wife and his beautiful and intelligent children."[11]

Instead of building family comedy around slapstick, gags and clowning, the Andersons are the modern and model American suburban family, one in which—judging from contemporary articles about *Father Knows Best*—viewers saw themselves. The *Saturday Evening Post* quoted letters from viewers who praised the program for being one the entire family could enjoy; they could "even learn something from it." In *Cosmopolitan,* Eugene Rodney, the producer of *Father Knows Best,* identified the program's audience as the middle-class and middle-income family. "It's people in that bracket who watch us. They don't have juvenile delinquent problems. They are interested in family relations, allowances, boy and girl problems."[12] In 1959 *Good Housekeeping* reported that a viewer had written to the program to thank *Father Knows Best* for solving a family problem:

> Last Monday my daughter and I had been squabbling all day. By evening we were both so mad that I went upstairs to our portable TV set, leaving her to watch alone in the living room. When you got through with us, we both felt like fools. We didn't even need to kiss and make up. You had done it for us. Thank you all very much.

Good Housekeeping commented fondly on the program's "lifelike mixture of humor, harassment, and sentiment that literally hits home with some 15 million mothers, fathers, sons, and daughters. Watching it is like looking through a rose-tinted picture window into your own living room." In this last season, *Father Knows Best* ranked as the sixth most popular show on television.[13]

The verisimilitude of *Father Knows Best* and *Leave It to Beaver* was substantially reinforced by being based at major movie studios (Columbia and Universal, respectively), with sets that were standing replications of suburban homes. The *Saturday Evening Post* described the living environment of *Father Knows Best:*

> The set for the Anderson home is a $40,000 combination of illusion and reality. Its two floors, patio, driveway and garage sprawl over Columbia Pictures Stage 10. One room with interchangeable, wallpapered walls, can be made to look like any of the four different bedrooms. The kitchen is real, however. . . . If the script calls for a meal or a snack, Rodney insists that actual food be used. . . . "Don't give me too much food," [Young said] "Jim leaves quickly in this scene and we can't have fathers dashing off without cleaning their plates."

The home is a space not for comedy riffs and physical gags but for family cohesion, a guarantee that children can be raised in the image of their parents. In *Redesigning the American Dream,* Dolores Hayden describes suburban housing

> as an architecture of gender, since houses provide settings for women and girls to be effective social status achievers, desirable sex objects, and skillful domestic servants, and for men and boys to be executive breadwinners, successful home handy men, and adept car mechanics.[14]

The narrative space of the suburban family home is not for comedy riffs and physical gags, but for family cohesion and the socialization of children.

"The Home Is an Image . . . of the Household and of the Household's Relation to Society"

As social historians Gwendolyn Wright and Dolores Hayden have shown, housing development and design are fundamental cornerstones of social order. Hayden argues that "the house is an image . . . of the household, and of the household's relation to society."[15] The single-family detached suburban home was architecture for the family whose healthy life would be guaranteed by a nonurban environment, neighborhood stability, and separation of family functions by gender. The suburban middle-income family was the primary locus of this homogeneous social formation.

When President Harry Truman said at the 1948 White House Conference on Family Life that "children and dogs are as necessary to the welfare of this country as is Wall Street and the railroads," he spoke to the role of home ownership in transforming the postwar American economy. Government policies supported suburban development in a variety of ways. The 41,000 miles of limited-access highways authorized by the Federal Aid Highway Act of 1956 contributed to the development of gender-specific space for the suburban family: commuter husbands and homemaker mothers. Housing starts became, and still continue to be, an important indicator of the well-being of the nation's economy. And equity in homeownership is considered to be a significant guarantee of economic security in the later years of life.[16]

But while the Housing Act of 1949 stated as its goal "a decent home and a suitable living environment for every American family," the Federal Housing Administration (FHA) was empowered with defining "neighborhood character." Hayden argues that the two national priorities of the postwar period — removing women from the paid labor force and building more housing — were conflated and tied to

> an architecture of home and neighborhood that celebrates a mid-nineteenth century ideal of separate spheres for women and men . . . characterized by segregation by age, race, and class that could not be so easily advertised.[17]

In order to establish neighborhood stability, homogeneity, harmony, and attractiveness, the FHA adopted several strategies. Zoning practices prevented multi-family dwellings and commercial uses of property. The FHA also chose not to support housing for minorities by adopting a policy called "red-lining," in which red lines were drawn on maps to identify the boundaries of changing or mixed neighborhoods. Since the value of housing in these neighborhoods was designated as low, loans to build or buy houses were considered bad risks. In addition, the FHA published a technical bulletin titled "Planning Profitable Neighborhoods," which gave advice to developers on how to concentrate on homogeneous markets for housing. The effect was to "green-line" suburban areas, promoting them by endorsing loans and development at the cost of creating urban ghettos for minorities.[18]

Wright discusses how the FHA went so far as to enter into restrictive or protective covenants to prevent racial mixing and "declining property values." She quotes the 1947 manual:

If a mixture of user groups is found to exist, it must be determined whether the mixture will render the neighborhood less desirable to present and prospective occupants. Protective covenants are essential to sound development of proposed residential areas, since they regulate the use of the land and provide a basis for the development of harmonious, attractive neighborhoods.

Despite the fact that the Supreme Court ruled in favor of the NAACP's case against restrictive covenants, the FHA accepted written and unwritten agreements in housing developments until 1968.[19]

The effect of these government policies was to create homogeneous and socially stable communities with racial, ethnic, and class barriers to entry. Wright describes "a definite sociological pattern to the household that moved out to the suburbs in the late 1940s and 1950s": the average age of adult suburbanites was 31 in 1950; there were few single, widowed, divorced, and elderly; there was a higher fertility rate than in the cities; and 9% of suburban women worked, as compared to 27% in the population as a whole. According to Hayden, five groups were excluded from single-family housing through the social policies of the late 1940s: single white women; the white elderly working and lower class; minority men of all classes; minority women of all classes; and minority elderly.[20]

The suburban dream house underscored this homogeneous definition of the suburban family. Domestic architecture was designed to display class attributes and reinforce gender-specific functions of domestic space. Hayden describes Robert Woods Kennedy, an influential housing designer of the period, arguing that the task of the housing architect was "to provide houses that helped his clients to indulge in status-conscious consumption . . . to display the housewife 'as a sexual being' . . . and to display the family's possessions 'as proper symbols of socio-economic class,' claiming that [this] form of expression [was] essential to modern family life." In addition to the value of the home for class and sexual identity, suburban housing was also therapeutic for the family. As Hayden observes, "whoever speaks of housing must also speak of home; the word means both the physical space and the nurturing that takes place there."[21]

A popular design for the first floor of the home was the "open floor plan," which provided a whole living environment for the entire family. With few walls separating living, dining, and kitchen areas, space was open for family togetherness. This "activity area" would also allow children to be within sight and hearing of the mother. Father could have his own space in a den or workroom and a detached garage for his car, while mother might be attracted to a modern model kitchen with separate laundry room. Bedrooms were located in the "quiet zone," perhaps on the second floor at the head of a stairway, away from the main activities of the household. While children might have the private space of individual bedrooms, parents shared the "master bedroom," which was larger and sometimes equipped with walk-in closets and dressing areas.[22]

This housing design, built on a part of an acre of private property with a yard for children, allowed the postwar middle-class family to give their children a lifestyle that was not so commonly available during the Depression and World War II. This domestic haven provided the setting for the socialization of girls into women and boys into men, and was paid for by the labor of the breadwinner father and maintained by the labor of the homemaker mother. The homemaker, placed in the home by suburban development and housing design, was promised release from household drudgery and an aesthetically pleasing interior environment as the basis of the consumer product industry economy.

"Leisure Can Transform Her Life Even If Good Design Can't"

Like housing design and suburban development, the consumer product industry built its economy on defining the social class and self-identity of women as homemakers. But this industrial definition of the homemaker underwent significant changes during the 1950s as suburban housing proliferated to include the working class. Two significant shifts marked discussions among designers about the role of product design in social life. The first occurred in 1955, when, instead of focusing on practical problems, the Fifth Annual Design Conference at Aspen drew a record attendance to discuss theoretical and cultural aspects of design. Among the topics discussed were the role of design in making leisure enjoyable and the possibility that mass communications could permit consumer testing of products before the investment of major capital. Design was no longer simply a matter of aesthetically pleasing shapes, but "part and parcel of the intricate pattern of twentieth-century life." The second shift in discussion occurred in early 1958, when *Industrial Design* (a major trade journal in the field) published several lengthy articles on market research, which it called "a new discipline—sometimes helpful, sometimes threatening—that is slated to affect the entire design process."[23]

Prior to the prominence of market research in the United States, designers discussed the contribution of product design to an aesthetically pleasing lifestyle, to the quality of life, and to making daily life easier. The homemaker was central to the growth and organization of the consumer product industry, but the editors of *Industrial Design* introduced the journal's fourth annual design review (December 1957) with an article positioning the homemaker as a problematic recipient of the benefits of design. Entitled "Materialism, Leisure and Design," this essay is worth quoting at some length. It first summarized the contribution of design to the leisure obtained from consumer products:

> We care very much about this world of things, partly because we are design-conscious and partly because we are American: this country is probably unique in that a review of the year's products is actually a measure of the material improvement in the everyday life of most citizens. . . . We think there is a good side [to American materialism], and that it does show up here—in quality, in availability and in the implication of increased leisure. Traditionally American design aims unapologetically at making things easier for people, at freeing them.

The article went on to respond to cynics who questioned whether homemakers *should* be freed from housework. *Industrial Design* argued for the potentially beneficial emancipation of the homemaker gained by product design:

> Automatic ranges and one-step washer-dryers leave the housewife with a precious ingredient: time. This has come to be regarded as both her bonus and her right, but not everyone regards it with unqualified enthusiasm. Critics belonging to the woman's-place-is-in-the-sink school ask cynically what she is free *for*. The bridge table? Afternoon TV? The lonely togetherness of telephone gossip? The analyst's couch? Maybe. But is this the designer's problem? Certainly it is absurd to suggest that he has a moral responsibility *not* to help create leisure time because if he does it is likely to be badly used. More choice in how she spends her time gives the emancipated woman an opportunity to face problems of a larger order than ever before, and this *can* transform her life, even if good design can't. In any case, the designer does have a responsibility to fill leisure hours, and *any* hours, with objects that are esthetically pleasing.[24]

These attempts to equate design aesthetics with leisure for the homemaker were occasionally challenged because they marginalized lifestyles other than the middle class. When Dr. Wilson G. Scanlon, a psychiatrist, addressed the 1957 meeting of the Southern New England Chapter of the Industrial Designers Institute, he argued that the act of "excessive purchasing of commodities [was] a form of irrational and immature behavior," that new purchases and increased leisure have not put anxieties to rest, and that "acceptance of some eccentricity rather than emphasis on class conformity should make for less insecurity [and for] a nation that is emotionally mature."[25]

Esther Foley, home services editor of MacFadden Publications, "shocked and intrigued" her audience at the "What Can the Consumer Tell Us?" panel at the 1955 conference of the American Society of Industrial Designers by discussing working-class homemakers. The flagship magazine of MacFadden Publications was *True Story*, with a circulation of two million nearly every year from 1926 through 1963. In addition to the confessional stories in the company's *True Romance*, *True Experience*, and other *True* titles, in the 1950s and 1960s some MacFadden publications were "family behavior magazines," appealing to working-class homemakers who were "not reached by the middle-class service magazine such as *McCalls* and *Ladies Home Journal*."[26]

Foley introduced a "slice of life" into the theoretical discussions of design by showing color slides of the homes of her working-class readers. She showed

> their purchased symbols—the latest shiny "miracle" appliances in badly arranged kitchens, the inevitable chrome dinette set, the sentimental and unrelated living room furnishings tied together by expensive carpets and cheap cotton throw rugs.[27]

While Scanlon complained of the psychological damage to the nation from class conformity through consumerism (an issue the women's movement would soon raise), Foley illustrated the disparity between the working class and an aesthetics of product design articulated for the middle class. These criticisms recognized the social and economic contradictions in the growing consumer economy.

In the mid-1950s, *Industrial Design* began to publish lengthy analyses of product planning divisions in consumer product corporations. The journal argued that changes in industrial organization would be crucial to the practice of design. There were three important issues: 1) how large corporations could summon the resources necessary for analyzing consumer needs and habits in order to succeed in the increasingly competitive market for consumer products; 2) how product designers must become aware of the role of design in business organizations; and 3) how industrial survival in the area of consumer goods would increasingly depend on defining new consumer needs.[28]

The close relationship between research and design is illustrated by GE's 1952 "advance industrial design group" test of a wall-mounted refrigerator. The first stages of design testing measured the "maximum reach-in for average housewife's height." The article was illustrated with a picture of a woman standing with arm outstretched into a cardboard mockup of the refrigerator. While at first glance this is an amusing notion, the homogeneity of suburban development and housing design suggests that this physical identification of "the average housewife" is consistent with her placement within limited social definitions.[29]

(*left*) The first stage of General Electric's refrigerator design testing: measuring the maximum reach-in for the height of the average housewife. (*right*) Consumers address the 1957 Design Symposium: a housewife explains her choice of flatiron to designers. Both reprinted from *Industrial Design Magazine 5* (February 1958), p. 42, and 4 (November 1957), p. 68. Copyright Design Publications, Inc., 330 West 42nd Street, New York, NY 10036.

This need for the consumer product industry to define the homemaker and, through her, its value to home life is well illustrated by a 1957 discussion among television set designers on whether to design television sets as furniture or as functional instruments like appliances. The designers talked about three aspects of this problem: 1) how to define the role and function of television in many aspects of daily life, not solely as part of living room viewing; 2) how to discover the needs of the consumer in television set design; and 3) the necessity of recognizing the role of television set design as part of an industry with a mass market. Whether modeled upon furniture or appliances, television set design should help the homemaker integrate the receiver into the aesthetics of interior decoration.[30]

The case for television as furniture was based on "better taste" on the part of consumers and the rapidly expanding furniture industry. Television set purchases exhibited a trend toward "good taste" and away from the "18th-century mahogany and borax-modern cabinets." In the previous year (1956), the furniture industry had had its best sales year in history. Given television's rapid installation rate in the 1950s (by 1960 it was in 87% of American households), designers agreed that people were spending more time at home and were more interested in the home's appearance. Designers needed to consider how the television set would play an important role in home redecoration and how they could assist homemakers in making aesthetic decisions concerning this new piece of furniture:

> There is not a homemaker who has not faced the problem of a proper room arrangement, lighting, color and decoration for television viewing — and even hi-fi listening. Yet let's be honest: the industry has not made an effort to solve this problem.[31]

The case for television as an instrument rested on its portability. Recent developments in the technology of television allowed for smaller, lighter sets that could be easily integrated into outdoor activities (on the deck behind the house) as well as into the kitchen decor (on the kitchen counter, color-coordinated with the appliances). For cues on how to proceed to fill this consumer need, television set designers suggested looking to the appliance industry, which had already proved effective in integrating products into complete and efficient packages for the kitchen.[32]

The consumer product design industry was aware of the significance of the homemaker in the economics of marketing and design. Before the introduction of systematic market research, her "needs" as a homemaker were partially determined by simply asking her what she wanted and then analyzing her responses. The 1957 Design Symposium at Silvermine invited five homemakers as conference participants, rather than merely as topics of discussion. They were not "typical housewives but five women with the ability to give serious thought and attention to shopping." These women helped the designers to analyze the way irons, washing machines, foreign cars, vacuum cleaners, and ranges functioned in their lives. But the feminine voice of the housewife was not the only voice heard at Silvermine. Four male "experts" discussed the need for consumers to communicate their "needs and wants" and described how the federal highway program, which fostered suburban expansion, would contribute to the development of a new mode of consumption: the shopping center. They also observed that deciding what product to buy produces tension that must be relieved.[33]

Hayden points out that housework is status-producing labor for the family, but at the same time it lowers the status of the homemaker by separating her from public life. The "psychological conflict" engendered by "guarantee[ing] the family's social status at the expense of her own . . . increases when women . . . come up against levels of consumption" that lie outside their potential for upward mobility.[34] Market research based its strength on turning these tensions around, placing them in the service of the consumer economy.

"Women Respond with Favorable Emotions to the Fresh, Creamy Surface of a Newly Opened Shortening Can"

By 1958, the "feminine voice" of the homemaker was even further enmeshed in expert opinion from the field of consumer science and psychology. With high competition in the consumer product industry, it was no longer adequate to determine the conscious needs of the homemaker through interviewing. Instead, market researchers sought to uncover the unconscious processes of consumption. *Industrial Design* described the market researcher as "a man with a slide rule in one hand and a copy of Sigmund Freud in the other," who quantified the unconscious motivations in purchasing.[35]

The class- and gender-related tensions inherent in consumer decisions could be identified through market research and alleviated through design. The status of the home and the identity of the homemaker, two important subjects of this research, were based on the development of suburban housing and the concomitant change in shopping patterns. With impersonal supermarkets replacing small retailers, market researchers argued that "sales talk had to be built into product and packaging."[36] Survey research, depth or motivational research, and experimental research sought to link design with class and gender characteristics, and ultimately to determine how product design could appeal to upward mobility and confirm the self-identity of homemakers. Survey research also helped to correlate the "social image" of products with their users in order to design products that would attract new groups as well as retain current buyers. The Index of Social Position, developed by August Hollingshead of Yale University, organized data on consumers into an estimation of their social status in the community. A multi-factor system rated residential position (neighborhood), power position (occupation), and taste level (education). The total score, he argued, would reveal a family's *actual* place in the community, replacing subjective judgments by interviewers.[37]

Other types of market research focused on the function of women as homemakers. Thus the economic responsibility for class status lay with the father while the mother was addressed through emotional connotations associated with homemaking. Depth research looked into the psychic motivations of consumers and revealed, for example, that "women reacted with favorable emotions to [the] fresh, creamy surface of a newly opened shortening can." Ernest Dichter redesigned the Snowdrift shortening label with this emotional response in mind. A swirl of shortening formed the letter *S* emerging from the can on a wooden spoon (to further associations with traditional cooking). The *s*-shape integrated the name of the product with the emotional appeal of the texture of the shortening. Proof of these researcher deductions and, presumably, the typicality of homemaker emotions was provided by IBM data-processing equipment, which could handle large samples and quantify the results.[38]

Experimental research included projective techniques that would elicit unconscious responses to market situations, on the theory that consumers would impute to others their own feelings and motivations. These techniques included word-association, cartoons in which word balloons were filled in, narrative projection in which a story was finished, role-playing, and group discussions. For example, women were shown the following two grocery lists and asked to describe the woman who used each list.

Shopping List 1	*Shopping List 2*
pound and a half of hamburger	pound and a half of hamburger
2 loaves of Wonder Bread	2 loaves of Wonder Bread
bunch of carrots	bunch of carrots
1 can Rumford's Baking Powder	1 can Rumford's Baking Powder
Nescafe instant coffee (drip)	1 lb. Maxwell House Coffee (ground)
2 cans Del Monte peaches	2 cans Del Monte peaches
5 lbs. potatoes	5 lbs. potatoes

Of the women polled, 48% described the first shopper as lazy, while only 4% attached that label to the second shopper. Women who considered using instant coffee a trait of the lazy housewife were less likely to buy it, "indicating that personality image was a motive in buying choice."[39]

In perception tests, machines measured the speed with which a package could be identified and how much of the design's "message" could be retained. Role-playing at shopping and group discussions at the Institute for Motivational Research's "Motivational Theater" were "akin to . . . 'psychodrama' " in that consumers would reveal product-, class-, and gender-related emotions that researchers would elicit and

(*top*) Ernest Dichter's redesign of the Snowdrift label: a swirl of shortening on a wooden spoon furthers associations with traditional cooking. (*bottom*) Perception studies measure the speed of package identification and reception of design message. Word associations reveal unconscious reactions to what subjects have seen below the perception threshold. Both reprinted from *Industrial Design Magazine* 5 (January 1958), pp. 37 and 42.

study. These techniques, it was noted in a contemporary article, "stimulate expression" by putting the subject "in another's position—or in one's own position under certain circumstances, like shopping or homemaking."[40]

Some designers complained that this application of science to design inhibited the creative process by substituting testable and quantifiable elements for aesthetics. In an address to the 1958 Aspen Conference, sociologist C. Wright Mills criticized designers for "bringing art, science and learning into a subordinate relation with the dominant institutions of the capitalist economy and the nationalist state." Mills's paper was considered to be "so pertinent to design problems today" that *Industrial Design* ran it in its entirety rather than publishing a synopsis of its major points, as it typically did with conference reports.[41]

Mills complained that design helped to blur the distinction between "human consciousness and material existence" by providing stereotypes of meaning. He argued that consumer products had become "the Fetish of human life" in the "virtual dominance of consumer culture." Mills attacked designers for promulgating "The Big Lie" of advertising and design, the notion that "we only give them what they want." He accused designers and advertisers of determining consumer wants and tastes, a procedure characteristic "of the current phase of capitalism in America . . . creat[ing] a panic for status, and hence a panic of self-evaluation, and . . . connect[ing] its relief with the consumption of specified commodities." While Mills did not specifically address the role of television, he did cite the importance of distribution in the postwar economy and "the need for the creation and maintenance of the national market and its monopolistic closure."[42]

Televisual Life in Springfield and Mayfield

One way that television distributed knowledge about a social economy that positioned women as homemakers was through the suburban family sit-com. These sit-coms promoted an image of the housewife and a mode of feminine subjectivity similar to those put forth by suburban development and the consumer product industry. In their representation of middle-class family life, series such as *Father Knows Best* and *Leave It to Beaver* mobilized the discourses of other social institutions. Realistic *mise en scène* and the character traits of family members naturalized middle-class home life, masking the social and economic barriers to entry into that privileged domain.

Deep-space composition and realist *mise en scène* display the open floor plan and place family narratives within the living space of the middle-class home.

The heterogeneity of class and gender that market research analyzed is not manifested in either *Father Knows Best* or *Leave It to Beaver*. The Andersons and the Cleavers would probably rank quite well in the Index of Social Position. Their neighborhoods have large and well-maintained homes; both families belong to country clubs. Jim Anderson is a well-respected insurance agent with his own agency (an occupation chosen because it would not tie him to an office). Ward Cleaver's work is ambiguous, but both men carry a briefcase and wear a suit and tie to work. They have the income that easily provides their families with roomy, comfortable, and pleasing surroundings and attractive clothing; their wives have no need to work outside the home. Both men are college-educated; the programs often discuss the children's future college education.

Father Knows Best and *Leave It to Beaver* rarely make direct reference to the social and economic means by which the families attained and maintain their middle-class status. Their difference from other classes is not a subject of these sit-coms. By effacing the separations of race, class, age, and gender that produced suburban neighborhoods, *Father Knows Best* and *Leave It to Beaver* naturalize the privilege of the middle class. Yet there is one episode of *Leave It to Beaver* from the early 1960s that lays bare its assumptions about what constitutes a good neighborhood. In doing so, the episode suggests how narrowly the heterogeneity of social life came to be defined.

Wally and Beaver visit Wally's smart-aleck friend, Eddie Haskell, who has moved out of his family's home into a rooming house in what Beaver describes as a "crummy neighborhood." Unlike the design of suburban developments, this neighborhood has older, rambling two-story (or more) houses set close together. The door to one house is left ajar, paper debris is blown about by the wind and left on yards and front porches. Two men are working on an obviously older model car in the street, hood and trunk open, tire resting against the car; two garbage cans are on the sidewalks; an older man in sweater and hat walks along carrying a bag of groceries. On a front lawn, a rake leans against a bushel basket with leaves piled up; a large canvas-covered lawn swing sits on a front lawn; one house has a sign in the yard: "For sale by owner—to be moved."

Wally and Beaver are uneasy in this neighborhood, one which is obviously in transition and in which work activities are available for public view. But everyone visible is white. This is a rare example of a suburban sit-com's demarcation of good and bad neighborhoods. What is more typical is the assumption that the homes of the Andersons and the Cleavers are representative of the middle class.

In different ways, the credit sequences that begin these programs suggest recurring aspects of suburban living. The opening of *Father Knows Best* begins with a long shot of the Anderson's two-story home, a fence separating the front lawn from the sidewalk, its landscape including trellises with vines and flowers. A cut to the interior entryway shows the family gathering together. In earlier seasons, Jim, wearing a suit and with hat in hand, prepares to leave for work. He looks at his watch; the grandfather clock to the left of the door shows the time as nearly 8:30 A.M. Margaret, wearing a blouse, sweater, and skirt, brings Jim his briefcase and kisses him goodbye. The three Anderson children giggle all in a row on the stairway leading up to the second-floor bedrooms. In later seasons, after the long shot of the house, the Anderson family gathers in the entryway to greet Jim as he returns from work. Margaret, wearing a dress too fancy for housework, kisses him at the doorway as the children cluster about them, uniting the family in the home.

The opening credits of *Leave It to Beaver* gradually evolved from an emphasis on the younger child to his placement within the neighborhood and then the family. The earliest episodes open with childlike etchings drawn in a wet concrete sidewalk. Middle seasons feature Beaver walking home along a street with single-family homes set back behind manicured, unfenced lawns. In later seasons, the Cleaver family is shown leaving their two-story home for a picnic trip: Ward carries the thermal cooler, June (in a dress, even for a picnic) carries the basket, and

Wally and Beaver climb into the Cleavers' late model car. While *Father Knows Best* coheres around the family ensemble, *Leave It to Beaver* decenters the family around the younger child, whose rearing provides problems that the older child has either already surmounted or has never had.

The narrative space of these programs is dominated by the domestic space of the home. *Father Knows Best* leaves the home environment much less often than does *Leave It to Beaver,* which often focuses on Beaver at school. This placing of the family within the home contributes in large measure to the ability of these programs to "seem real." During the first season of *Leave It to Beaver,* the Cleavers' home was an older design rather than a suburban dream house. The kitchen was large and homey, with glass and wood cabinets. The rooms were separated by walls and closed doors. By the 1960s, the Cleavers, like the Andersons, were living in the "open floor plan," a popular housing design of the 1950s. As you enter the home, to your far left is the den, the private space of the father. To the right of the den is the stairway leading to the "quiet zone" of the bedrooms. To your right is the living room, visible through a wide and open entryway the size of two doors. Another wide doorway integrates the living room with the formal dining room. A swinging door separates the dining room from the kitchen. The deep-focus photography typical of these sit-coms displays the expanse of living space in this "activity area."

While the Cleaver children share a bedroom, it is equipped with a private bathroom and a portable television set. Ward and June's bedroom is small, with twin beds. Since it is not a site of narrative activity, which typically takes place in the boys' room or on the main floor of the home, the parents' bedroom is rarely seen. These two small bedrooms belie the scale of the house when it is seen in long shot.

The Andersons' home makes more use of the potential of the bedrooms for narrative space. With four bedrooms, the Anderson home allows each of the children the luxury of his or her own room. Jim and Margaret's "master" bedroom, larger than those of their children, has twin beds separated by a nightstand and lamp, a walk-in closet, a dressing table, armchairs, and a small alcove. In this design, the "master" bedroom is conceived as a private space for parents, but the Anderson children have easy access to their parents' bedroom. The Andersons, however, have only one bathroom. Betty has commented that when she gets married she will have three bathrooms because "there won't always be two of us."

The Andersons and the Cleavers also share aspects of the decor of their homes, displaying possessions in a comfortably unostentatious way. Immediately to the left of the Andersons' front door is a large free-standing grandfather clock; to the right and directly across the room are built-in bookcases filled with hardcover books. In earlier seasons of *Leave It to Beaver,* the books (also hardbound) were on shelves in the living room. Later, these books were relocated to Ward's study, to line the many built-in bookshelves behind his desk.

The two families have similar tastes in wall decorations and furnishings. Among the landscapes in heavy wood frames on the Cleavers' walls are pictures of sailing vessels and reproductions of "great art," such as "Pinkie" by Sir Thomas Lawrence. While the Andersons do not completely share the Cleavers' penchant for candelabra on the walls and tables, their walls are tastefully decorated with smaller landscapes. Curiously, neither house engages in the prominent display of family photographs.

The large living room in each home has a fireplace. There is plenty of room to walk around the furniture, which is overstuffed and comfortable or of hardwood. The formal dining room in both homes includes a large wooden table and chairs that can seat six comfortably. It is here that the families have their evening meals. A sideboard or hutch displays dishes, soup tureens, and the like. The kitchen contains a smaller, more utilitarian set of table and chairs, where breakfast is eaten. Small appliances such as a toaster, mixer, and electric coffeepot sit out on counters. A wall-mounted roll of paper towels is close to the sink. The Andersons' outdoor patio has a built-in brick oven, singed from use.

While both homes establish gender-specific areas for women and men, *Father Knows Best* is less repressive in its association of this space with familial roles. Both Jim Anderson and Ward Cleaver have dens; Ward is often shown doing ambiguous paperwork in his, the rows of hardcover books behind his desk suggesting his association with knowledge and mental work. June's forays into Ward's space tend to be brief, usually in search of his advice on how to handle the boys. As Ward works on papers, June sits in a corner chair sewing a button on Beaver's shirt. Ward's den is often the site of father-to-son talks. Its doorway is wide and open, revealing the cabinet-model television that Beaver occasionally watches. While Jim also has a den, it is much less often the site of narrative action, and its door is usually closed.

Workrooms and garages are also arenas for male activity, providing storage space for paint or lawn care equipment or a place to work on the car. The suburban homemaker does not have an equivalent private space. Instead, the woman shares her kitchen with other family members, while the living and dining rooms are designated as family spheres. In typical episodes of *Leave It to Beaver,* June's encounters with family members generally take place in the kitchen, while Ward's tend to occur throughout the house. As her sons pass through her space, June is putting up paper towels, tossing a salad, unpacking groceries, or making meals. Margaret, having an older daughter, is often able to turn this family/female space over to her. She is also more often placed within other domestic locations: the patio, the attic, the living room.

June's son passes through her kitchen space where appliances help her maintain the comfortable environment of quality family life.

Both Margaret and June exemplify Robert Woods Kennedy's theory that housing design should display the housewife as a sexual being, but this is accomplished not so much through their positioning within domestic space as through costume. June's ubiquitous pearls, stockings and heels, and cinch-waisted dresses are amusing in their distinct contradiction of the realities of housework. While Margaret also wears dresses or skirts, she tends to be costumed more casually, and sometimes wears a smock when doing housework. Margaret is also occasionally seen in relatively sloppy clothes suitable for dirty work but marked as inappropriate to her status as a sexual being.

In one episode of *Father Knows Best*, Margaret is dressed in dungarees, sweatshirt, and loafers, her hair covered by a scarf as she scrubs paint from her youngest daughter, Kathy. When Betty sees her, she laughs, "If you aren't a glamorous picture!" As Jim arrives home early, Betty counsels Margaret, "You can't let Father see you like this!" Betty takes over scrubbing and dressing Kathy while Margaret hurries off to change before Jim sees her. But Margaret is caught, embarrassed at not being dressed as a suburban object of desire. Jim good-naturedly echoes Betty's comment: "If you aren't a glamorous picture!" He calms Margaret's minor distress at being seen by her husband in this departure from her usual toilette: "You know you always look great to me."

As this example shows, the agreement among Jim, Margaret, and Betty on the proper attire for the suburban homemaker indicates the success with which Betty has been socialized within the family. Yet even though both programs were created around "realistic" storylines of family life, the nurturing function of the home and the gender-specific roles of father and mother are handled very differently in *Father Knows Best* and *Leave It to Beaver*.

By 1960, Betty, whom Jim calls "Princess," had been counseled through adolescent dating and was shown to have "good sense" and maturity in her relations with boys. Well-groomed and well-dressed like her mother, Betty could easily substitute for Margaret in household tasks. In one episode, Jim and Margaret decide that their lives revolve too much around their children ("trapped," "like servants") and they try to spend a weekend away, leaving Betty in charge. While Betty handles the situation smoothly, Jim and Margaret are finally happier continuing their weekend at Cedar Lodge with all of the children along.

Bud, the son, participates in the excitement of discovery and self-definition outside of personal appearance. A normal boy in the process of becoming a man, he gets dirty at sports and tinkering with engines, replaces blown fuses, and cuts the grass. Unlike Betty, Bud has to be convinced that he can handle dating; Jim counsels him that this awkward stage is normal and one that Jim himself has gone through.

Kathy (whose pet name is "Kitten"), in contrast to her older sister, is a tomboy and is interested in sports. By 1959, *Good Housekeeping* purred that

> Kathy seems to have got the idea it might be more fun to appeal to a boy than to be one. At the rate she's going, it won't be long before [Jim and Margaret] are playing grandparents.[43]

Film and television writer Danny Peary was also pleased with Kathy's development, but for a very different reason: in the 1977 *Father Knows Best* "Reunion" show, Kathy was an unmarried gym teacher. Peary also felt that *Father Knows Best* was different from other suburban family sit-coms in its representation of women. "The three Anderson females . . . were intelligent, proud, and resourceful. Margaret was Jim's equal, loved and respected for her wisdom."[44] The traits that characterize Margaret in her equality are her patience, good humor, and easy confidence. Unlike Ward Cleaver, Jim is not immune to wifely banter.

In one episode, Jim overhears Betty and her friend Armand rehearsing a play, and assumes they are going to elope. Margaret has more faith in their daughter and good-naturedly tries to dissuade Jim from his anxiety: "Jim, when are you going to stop acting like a comic-strip father?" In the same episode, Jim and Margaret play Scrabble, an activity that the episode suggests they do together often. "Dad's getting beat at Scrabble again," observes Bud. Kathy notices, "He's stuck with the Z again." Margaret looks up Jim's Z word in the dictionary, doubting its existence. Margaret is able to continually best Jim at this word game and Jim is willing to play despite certain defeat.

In contrast to this easy-going family with character traits allowing for many types of familial interaction, *Leave It to Beaver* tells another story about gender relations in the home. June does not share Margaret's status in intelligence. In a discussion of their sons' academic performances, June remarks, "We can't all be *A* students; maybe the boys are like me." Ward responds, "No, they are *not* like you" and then catches himself. Nor does June share Margaret's witty and confident relationship with her husband. She typically defers to Ward's greater sense for raising their two sons. Wondering how to approach instances of boyish behavior, June positions herself firmly at a loss. She frequently asks, mystified, "Ward, did boys do this when you were their age?" Ward always reassures June that whatever their sons are doing (brothers fighting, for example) is a normal stage of development for boys, imparting to her his superior social and familial knowledge. Like her sons, June acknowledges the need for Ward's guidance. Unlike Margaret, June is structured on the periphery of the socialization of her children, in the passive space of the home.

Ward, often a misogynist, encourages the boys to adopt his own cynical attitude toward their mother and women in general. In an early episode, Ward is replacing the plug on the toaster. He explains to Beaver that "your mother" always pulls it out by the cord instead of properly grabbing it by the plug. Beaver is impressed by Ward's knowledge of " 'lectricity," to which Ward responds by positioning his knowledge as a condition of June's ineptness. "I know enough to stay about one jump ahead of your mother." Unlike *Father Knows Best*, *Leave It to Beaver* works to contain June's potential threat to patriarchal authority. When June asks why Beaver would appear to be unusually shy about meeting a girl, Ward wonders as well: "He doesn't know enough about life to be afraid of women."

In the episode in which Eddie Haskell moves out of the home, Ward sides with the Haskells by forbidding both his sons to visit Eddie's bachelor digs. As Ward telephones another father to ask him to do the same, June timidly asks (covering a bowl to be put in the refrigerator),

"Ward, aren't you getting terribly involved?" Ward answers that if this were their son he would appreciate the support of other parents. June murmurs assent as Ward and June continue the process of defining June's function within the family in terms of passivity and deference.

While *Father Knows Best* and *Leave It to Beaver* position the homemaker in family life quite differently, both women effortlessly maintain the domestic space of the family environment. In their representation of women's work in the home, these programs show the great ease and lack of drudgery with which Margaret and June keep their homes tidy and spotlessly clean. In any episode, these homemakers can be seen engaged in their daily housework. June prepares meals, waters plants, and dusts on a Saturday morning. She brings in groceries, wipes around the kitchen sink, and asks Wally to help her put away the vacuum cleaner (which she has not been shown using). Margaret prepares meals, does dishes, irons, and also waters plants. While June is often stationary in the kitchen or sewing in the living room, Margaret is usually moving from one room to another, in the process of ongoing domestic activity.

Margaret and June are not women of leisure, but it is nevertheless clear that their housework is not confining or time-consuming.

While one could argue that this lack of acknowledgment of the labor of homemaking troubles the verisimilitude of these sit-coms, the realist *mise en scène* that includes consumer products suggests the means by which the comfortable environment of quality family life can be maintained. Margaret and June easily mediate the benefits promised by the consumer product industry. They are definitely not women of leisure, but they are women for whom housework is neither especially confining nor completely time-consuming.

The visible result of their partially visible labor is the constantly immaculate appearance of their homes and variously well-groomed family members. (The older children are more orderly because they are further along in the process of socialization than are the younger ones.) The "real time" to do piles of laundry or the daily preparation of balanced meals is a structured absence of the programs. The free time that appliances provide for Margaret and June is attested to by their continual good humor and the quality of their interactions with the family. Unrushed and unpressured, Margaret and June are not so free from housework that they become idle and self-indulgent. They are well-positioned within the constraints of domestic activity and the promises of the consumer product industry.

We have seen how the homemaker was positioned in the postwar consumer economy by institutions that were dependent on defining her social subjectivity within the domestic sphere. In the interests of family stability, suburban development and domestic architecture were designed with a particular definition of family economy in mind: a working father who could, alone, provide for the social and economic security of his family; a homemaker wife and mother who maintains the family's environment; children who grow up in neighborhoods undisturbed by heterogeneity of class, race, ethnicity, and age.

The limited address to the homemaker by the consumer product industry and market research is easily understood when seen within this context of homogeneity in the social organization of the suburban family. Defined in terms of her homemaking function for the family and for the economy, her life could only be made easier by appliances. The display of her family's social status was ensured by experts who assuaged any uncertainties she may have had about interior decor by designing with these problems in mind. By linking her identity as a shopper and homemaker to class attributes, the base of the consumer economy was broadened, and her deepest emotions and insecurities were tapped and transferred to consumer product design.

The representation of suburban family life in *Father Knows Best* and *Leave It to Beaver* also circulated social knowledge that linked the class and gender identities of homemakers. Realist *mise en scène* drew upon housing architecture and consumer products in order to ground family narratives within the domestic space of the middle-class home. The contribution of the television homemaker to harmonious family life was underscored by the ease with which she negotiated her place in the domestic arena.

This brief social history has placed one television format — the suburban family sit-com — within the historical context from which it drew its conventions, its codes of realism, and its definitions of family life. Yet we must also ask about resistances to this social subjectivity by recognizing the heterogeneity of the social formation. For example, in the late 1950s and 1960s, when the suburban family sit-com proliferated on prime-time television, the women's movement was resisting these institutional imperatives, exposing the social and economic inequalities on which they were based.[45]

Oppositional positions point to the inability of institutions to conceal completely the social and economic determinations of subjectivity. But the durability of the suburban family sit-com indicates the degree of institutional as well as popular support for ideologies that naturalize class and gender identities. Continuing exploration of the relationship between the historical specificity of the social formation and the programming practices of television contributes to our understanding of the ways in which popular cultural forms participate in the discourses of social life and diverge from the patterns of everyday experience.

NOTES

I wish to thank Beverly O'Neil for suggesting and participating in the survey of design journals, and Robert Deming, Darryl Fox, and Lee Poague, who made helpful comments. An earlier version of this paper, entitled "Suburban Family Sit-Coms and Consumer Product Design: Addressing the Social Subjectivity of Homemakers in the 1950s," was presented to the 1986 International Television Studies Conference and appears in *Television and Its Audience: International Research Perspectives,* ed. Phillip Drummond and Richard Paterson (London: British Film Institute, 1988), pp. 38–60.

1. In *Women: The Longest Revolution* (London: Virago, 1984), p. 18, Juliet Mitchell argues that women are bound up in this contradiction: "[Women] are fundamental to the human condition, yet in their economic, social, and political roles, they are marginal. It is precisely this combination — fundamental and marginal at one and the same time — that has been fatal to them."

2. Stuart Ewen and Elizabeth Ewen, *Channels of Desire: Mass Images and the Shaping of American Consciousness* (New York: McGraw-Hill, 1982), p. 235.

3. Graham Murdock and Peter Golding, "Capitalism, Communication and Class Relations," and Stuart Hall, "Culture, Media and the 'Ideological Effect,' " in *Mass Communication and Society,* eds. James Curran,

Michael Gurevitch, and Janet Woollacott (Beverly Hills: Sage, 1979), pp. 12, 36, 336–339.

4. I began this study by considering prime-time network sit-coms with runs of three seasons or more from 1948 through 1960. Fourteen of these thirty-five sit-coms were structured around middle-class families living in suburban single-family dwellings. Eight of these fourteen defined the family unit as a breadwinner father, a homemaker mother, and children growing into adults: *The Ruggles* (1949–1952), *The Aldrich Family* (1949–1953), *The Stu Erwin Show* (1950–1955), *The Adventures of Ozzie and Harriet* (1952–1966), *Father Knows Best* (1954–1963), *Leave It to Beaver* (1957–1963), *The Donna Reed Show* (1958–1966), and *Dennis the Menace* (1959–1963).

The other six suburban family sit-coms shared some of these traits, but centered their narratives on situations or characters other than the family ensemble: *Beulah* (1950–1953) focused on a black maid to an apparently broadly caricatured white middle-class family; *December Bride* (1954–1961) concerned an attractive, dating widow living with her daughter's family; *The Bob Cummings Show* (1955–1959) concentrated on the adventures of a playboy photographer living with his widowed sister and nephew in a suburban home; *I Married Joan* (1952–1955) focused on the zany adventures of the wife of a domestic court judge; *My Favorite Husband* (1953–1957) had a couple working for social status in the suburbs; and *Bachelor Father* (1957–1962) featured an attorney who cared for his young niece in Beverly Hills.

This information was derived from the following sources: Tim Brooks and Earle Marsh, *The Complete Directory of Prime Time Network Television Shows, 1946–Present* (New York: Ballantine Books, 1981); Les Brown, *The New York Times Encyclopedia of Television* (New York: Times Books, 1977); Henry Castleman and Walter J. Podrazik, *The TV Schedule Book* (New York: McGraw-Hill, 1984).

5. Kenneth Rhodes, "Father of *Two* Families," *Cosmopolitan* (April 1956), p. 125.

6. Rhodes, p. 125; Bob Eddy, "Private Life of a Perfect Papa," *Saturday Evening Post* (April 27, 1957), p. 29; Brooks and Marsh, pp. 245–246.

7. Rhodes, p. 125; Eddy, p. 29.

8. Newspaper critic John Crosby, quoted in Eddy, p. 29.

9. "TV's Eager Beaver," *Look* (May 27, 1958), p. 68.

10. Brooks and Marsh, pp. 340–341, 352–353.

11. Eddy, p. 29; Rhodes, p. 126.

12. Eddy, p. 29; Rhodes, p. 127.

13. "Jane Wyatt's Triple Threat," *Good Housekeeping* (October 1959), p. 48.

14. Eddy, p. 176; Dolores Hayden, *Redesigning the American Dream: The Future of Housing, Work and Family Life* (New York: Norton, 1984), p. 17.

15. Hayden, p. 40; see also Gwendolyn Wright, *Building the Dream: A Social History of Housing in America* (Cambridge: MIT Press, 1981).

16. Hayden, pp. 35, 38, 55; Wright, pp. 246, 248.

17. Hayden, pp. 41–42; Wright, p. 247.

18. Wright, pp. 247–248.

19. Wright, p. 248.

20. Hayden, pp. 55–56; Wright, p. 256.

21. Hayden, pp. 63, 109.

22. Hayden, pp. 17–18; Wright, pp. 254–255.

23. "The fifth international design conference at Aspen found 500 conferees at the crossroads, pondering the direction of the arts, and, every now and then, of the American consumer," *Industrial Design* 2:4 (August 1955), p. 42; Avrom Fleishman, "M/R, a Survey of Problems, Techniques, Schools of Thought in Market Research: Part 1 of a Series," *Industrial Design* 5:1 (January 1958), pp. 33–34.

24. "Materialism, Leisure and Design," *Industrial Design* 4:12 (December 1957), pp. 33–34.

25. Dr. Wilson G. Scanlon, "Industrial Design and Emotional Immaturity," *Industrial Design* 4:1 (January 1957), pp. 68–69.

26. "Eleventh Annual ASID Conference: Three Days of Concentrated Design Discussion in Washington, D.C.," *Industrial Design* 2:6 (December 1955), p. 128; Theodore Peterson, *Magazines in the Twentieth Century* (Urbana: University of Illinois Press, 1964), pp. 255, 298, 301–302.

27. "Eleventh Annual ASID Conference," p. 123.

28. Richard Tyler George, "The Process of Product Planning," *Industrial Design* 3:5 (October 1956), pp. 97–100. See also Deborah Allen, Avrom Fleishman, and Jane Fiske Mitarachi, "Report on Product Planning," *Industrial Design* 4:6 (June 1957), pp. 37–81; "Lawrence Wilson," *Industrial Design* 2:5 (October 1955), pp. 82–83; "Sundberg-Ferar," *Industrial Design* 2:5 (October 1955), pp. 86–87; "10 Work Elements of Product Planning," *Industrial Design* 4:6 (June 1957), p. 47.

29. Avrom Fleishman, "M/R: Part 2," *Industrial Design* 5:2 (February 1958), p. 42.

30. "IDI Discusses TV, Styling and Creativity," *Industrial Design* 4:5 (May 1957), pp. 67–68.

31. A. C. Nielsen Company, "The Nielsen Ratings in Perspective" (1980), p. 20; "IDI Discusses TV," pp. 67–68.

32. "IDI Discusses TV," pp. 67–68. On television technology and set design, see "Design Review," *Industrial Design* 6:9 (August 1959), p. 89; "TV Sets Get Smaller and Smaller," *Industrial Design* 4:1 (January 1957), pp. 39–43; "Redesign: Philco Crops the Neck of the Picturetube to Be First with Separate-Screen Television," *Industrial Design* 5:6 (June 1958), p. 52; "Design Review," *Industrial Design* 6:9 (August 1959), p. 88; Tenite advertisement, *Industrial Design* 6:7 (July 1959), p. 23; Tenite advertisement, *Industrial Design* 8:11 (November 1961), p. 25.

33. "The Consumer at IDI," *Industrial Design* 4:11 (November 1957), pp. 68–72.

34. Hayden, p. 50.

35. Fleishman, "M/R, a Survey of Problems," pp. 27, 29. While Fleishman recognized Paul Lazarsfeld's contribution to market research, this article did not mention Lazarsfeld's work in the television industry or his development of The Analyzer, an early instrument for audience measurement, for CBS. See Laurence Bergreen, *Look Now, Pay Later* (New York: New American Library, 1981), pp. 170–171.
36. Fleishman, "M/R, a Survey of Problems," p. 27.
37. Fleishman, "M/R, a Survey of Problems," p. 35.
38. Fleishman, "M/R, a Survey of Problems," p. 37.
39. Fleishman, "M/R, a Survey of Problems," p. 40.
40. Fleishman, "M/R, a Survey of Problems," pp. 41–42.
41. Fleishman, "M/R: Part 2," pp. 34–35; C. Wright Mills, "The Man in the Middle," *Industrial Design* 5:11 (November 1958), p. 70; Don Wallace, "Report from Aspen," *Industrial Design* 5:8 (August 1958), p. 85.
42. Mills, pp. 72–74.
43. "Jane Wyatt's Triple Threat," p. 48.
44. Danny Peary, "Remembering 'Father Knows Best,' " in *TV Book*, ed. Judy Fireman (New York: Workman, 1977), pp. 173–175.
45. Long-running suburban family sit-coms that ran on network prime time during the early years of the women's movement were *Father Knows Best* (1954–1963), *Leave It to Beaver* (1957–1963), *The Donna Reed Show* (1958–1966), *The Dick Van Dyke Show* (1961–1966), *Hazel* (1961–1966), *Dennis the Menace* (1959–1963), and *The Adventures of Ozzie and Harriet* (1952–1966). This information was obtained from Brooks and Marsh, pp. 15–16, 193, 199–200, 211, 245–246, 322, 423–424.

Julia

"Is This What You Mean by Color TV?" Race, Gender, and Contested Meanings in NBC's *Julia*

Aniko Bodroghkozy

America in 1968: Police clash with the militant Black Panthers while one of the group's leaders, Huey Newton, is sentenced for murder; civil rights leader Martin Luther King is assassinated in Tennessee, sparking violent uprisings and riots in the nation's black ghettos; the massive Poor People's Campaign, a mobilization of indigent blacks and whites, sets up a tent city on the Mall in Washington, D.C.; at Cornell University, armed black students sporting bandoliers take over the administration building and demand a black studies program.[1] In the midst of all these events—events that many Americans saw as a revolutionary or at least an insurrectionary situation among the black population— NBC introduced the first situation comedy to feature an African-American in the starring role since *Amos 'n' Andy* and *Beulah* went off the air in the early 1950s.[2] *Julia*, created by writer-producer Hal Kanter, a Hollywood liberal Democrat who campaigned actively for Eugene McCarthy, starred Diahann Carroll as a middle-class, widowed nurse trying to bring up her six-year-old-son, Corey. After the death of her husband in a helicopter crash in Vietnam, Julia and Corey move to an integrated apartment complex, and she finds work in an aerospace industry clinic.

NBC executives did not expect the show to succeed.[3] They scheduled it opposite the hugely successful *Red Skelton Show*, where it was expected to die a noble, dignified death, having demonstrated the network's desire to break the prime-time color bar. Unexpectedly, the show garnered high ratings and lasted a respectable three years.

Despite its success, or perhaps because of it, *Julia* was a very controversial program. Beginning in popular magazine articles written before the first episode even aired and continuing more recently in historical surveys of the portrayals of blacks on American television, critics have castigated *Julia* for being extraordinarily out of touch with and silent on the realities of African-American life in the late 1960s. While large numbers of blacks lived in exploding ghettos, Julia and Corey

143

Baker lived a luxury lifestyle impossible on a nurse's salary. While hostility and racial tensions brewed, and the Kerner Commission Report on Civil Disorders described an America fast becoming two nations separate and unequal, tolerance and colorblindness prevailed on *Julia*.

The show came in for heavy criticism most recently in J. Fred MacDonald's *Blacks and White TV: Afro-Americans in Television Since 1948*. MacDonald describes *Julia* as a "comfortable image of black success . . . in stark juxtaposition to the images seen on local and national newscasts."[4] The show, according to MacDonald, refused to be topical; when dealing with racial issues at all, it did so only in one-liners. He also describes black and white discomfort with the show, claiming that the series was a sell-out intended to assuage white consciences and a "saccharine projection of the 'good life' to be achieved by those blacks who did not riot, who acted properly, and worked within the system."[5]

MacDonald's text-based criticism of *Julia* would appear to be quite justified. However, there was a whole range of politically charged meanings attributed to the program during its network run that critics like MacDonald haven't discussed. What critics of the program have ignored are the diverse and often conflicted ways in which both the producers and viewers of *Julia* struggled to make sense of the show in the context of the racial unrest and rebellions erupting throughout American society. Historically situated in a period of civil dislocations when massive numbers of black Americans were attempting, both peacefully and not so peacefully, to redefine their place within the socio-political landscape, *Julia* functioned as a symptomatic text — symptomatic of the racial tensions and reconfigurations of its time.

The extent to which *Julia* functioned as a site of social tension is particularly evident in the viewer response mail and script revisions in the files of producer Hal Kanter, and it is also apparent in critical articles written for the popular press at the time.[6] These documents allow us to begin to reconstruct the contentious dialogue that took place among audiences, magazine critics, and the show's producer and writers. They also provide clues to how such conflicts materialized in the program narrative itself. A key feature of this dialogue was a discursive struggle over what it meant to be black and what it meant to be white at the close of the 1960s. Black viewers, white viewers, and critics all made sense of the program in notably different ways. Although a struggle over racial representation was the overt issue, their responses to the program also occasionally exhibited a nascent, if conflicted, attempt to speak about gender and the representation of women.

Producing Difference

The script files in the Hal Kanter papers show quite clearly how Kanter and his production team struggled to construct images of African-Americans in the context of the civil rights movement. Particularly revealing is the file for a 1968 episode entitled "Take My Hand, I'm a Stranger in the Third Grade," which contains the initial six-page outline (the first working out of the episode's storyline) and a thirty-six-page first draft script (the first fleshing out of the story in dialogue form) written by Ben Gershman and Gene Boland, the latter one of the series' four black writers.[7]

The story revolved around Corey's friend Bedelia Sanford, a black schoolmate who tried to win his affection by stealing toys for him. In the original storyline, Julia confronted Bedelia's mother, who lived in a slum with numerous children. She flared up at Julia's expressions of sympathy for her situation, calling Julia "one of those uppitty [*sic*] high-class Colored ladies who thinks she's somebody because she went to college and has a profession. Well, says Mrs. S., she's got a profession too—she's on welfare." Hal Kanter underlined that final line and wrote in the margin next to it:"*NO, SIRS!*"

In the first draft script, Mrs. Sanford had suddenly metamorphosed into an upper-class black woman whose preoccupation with money-making pulled her away from attending to her daughter. When Julia accused her of trying to buy Bedelia's love, Mrs. Sanford accused Julia of "always tearing down our own." She called Julia a mediocre Negro who had attained all the status she would ever have. Julia retorted, "[B]ut that Gauguin print and that Botticelli and your *white maid* all rolled together isn't going to change the fact that you are a failure as a mother."

The adjustment of the Sanfords' economic status upward indicates that Kanter and his writers were uncertain and anxious about their depiction of black Americans. The characters were either demeaning ghetto stereotypes or they were upper-class "white Negroes," a term used by critics to describe Julia. The stereotypical images of African-American life that most whites had previously taken for granted had, by the late sixties, become, at least to *Julia*'s creators, problematic constructs. As predominantly white creators of black characters, Kanter and his writing team wanted to avoid racist representations but appeared stumped in their attempt to come up with something that wasn't merely a binary opposition. The repertoire of black images was inadequate and there was no new repertoire on which to draw.

While racial depiction and definition functioned as a highly politicized dilemma for the producers of *Julia*, the question of gender representation was another matter. One might expect that a program dealing with a working woman's attempts to raise her child alone would open a space for questioning sexual inequality. If scenes from the series' first episode and pilot are any indication, this appears not to have been the case. While racist depictions of blacks were being questioned, sexist portrayals of women were not. The show and its creators seemed as blithely unconscious in their portrayal of women as they were self-conscious in their portrayal of blacks.

The first episode of the series, "The Interview," written by Hal Kanter and aired September 24, 1968, includes the following scene between Julia and her future boss, Dr. Chegley.[8] Julia had just entered Chegley's office to be interviewed for a nurse's position. Chegley had his back to Julia as she entered. He looked at an X-ray and, without looking at her, asked her to identify it. She replied that it was a chest X-ray. He then turned to face her and the following dialogue ensued:

CHEGLEY: You have a healthy looking chest. . . . I believe you're here to beg me for a job.
JULIA: I'm here at your invitation, Doctor, to be interviewed for a position as a nurse. I don't beg for anything.
CHEGLEY: I'll keep that in mind. Walk around.
JULIA: Beg your pardon?
CHEGLEY: You just said you don't beg for anything.
JULIA: That's just a figure of speech.
CHEGLEY: I'm interested in your figure without the speech. Move. Let me see if you can walk.
JULIA: I can. [*Walking*] I come from a long line of pedestrians.
CHEGLEY: Turn around. [*As she does*] You have a very well-formed fantail. [*As she reacts*] That's Navy terminology. I spent thirty years in uniform. [*Then*] Do you wear a girdle?
JULIA: No, sir.
CHEGLEY: I do. I have a bad back. Now you can sit down.

The pilot, "Mama's Man," also written by Kanter, contains a similar scene.[9] Julia was being interviewed by a manager at Aerospace Industries, Mr. Colton, who became very flustered when he saw Julia. He told her that all her qualifications were in order, but that she was not what he expected. Julia asked whether she should have been younger or older, or, "Should I have written at the top of that application—in big, bold, black letters, 'I'm a Negro?!' " Colton told her that had nothing to do with it. The problem was that she was too pretty. "When we employ nurses far less attractive than you, we find that we lose many man-hours. Malingerers, would-be Romeos, that sort of thing. In your case, you might provoke a complete work stoppage."

In contemporary terms these two scenes display examples of the most egregious sexism and sexual harassment. However, when the episodes aired, the women's liberation movement, which dates its public birth to the Miss America pageant protest on September 7, 1968, was not yet a part of public consciousness. *Julia*'s creators thus did not yet have to contend with the oppositional voices of the women's movement. On the other hand, the producers were quite concerned with the highly visible civil rights and black power movements, and were well aware of the fact that representations of racial discrimination and harassment were now socially and politically unacceptable. The scenes from these two episodes of *Julia* reveal a self-conscious understanding of that unacceptability; however, anxiety about that situation resulted in a displacement. Discrimination and harassment were shifted from racism onto sexism. Both job interview scenes needed to relieve the anxiety created over Julia's difference. The writers could not allow her racial difference to function as an appropriate reason for the denial of a job or for demeaning banter, but there were no such political taboos in relation to her sexual difference.

Conflicted Reception

The conflicted production process can indicate some of the ways in which *Julia* worked through social and political anxieties in American culture in the late 1960s. However, the interpretive strategies brought to bear upon the text both by critics and by viewers are even more significant because they can show us how these tensions and conflicts were dealt with by different social groups within American society at the time.

Recent work in cultural studies has demonstrated that meanings are not entirely determined by the text or by its producers. As Stuart Hall's "encoding-decoding" model has shown, readers of a text are active agents and need not accept the meanings constructed by a text's producers. Readers can oppose or negotiate with the meanings that the text promotes as the correct or preferred interpretation.[10] By examining how audiences interpreted *Julia*, we can see how the crisis in race relations grew as people attempted to come to grips with the meanings of racial difference in the face of militant challenges by a black oppositional movement.

By juxtaposing the interpretive strategies and discourses mobilized by critics writing in the popular press and by viewers writing to Kanter or to the network, we can examine how privileged cultural elites interpreted the show as well as how television viewers constructed meanings often at odds with those of the critics. The viewer mail (some 151 letters and postcards) filed in the Hal Kanter papers provides a particularly rich case study of how *Julia*'s audiences attempted to make sense of the program and how they grappled with racial difference and social change through their engagement with the show. At times, the statements in the letters echo those in the popular press; more frequently, both the reading strategies and the debates are different. Many of the letters have carbon copy responses from Kanter attached, setting up a fascinating, often contentious dialogue. But what is most compelling about the letters is the way they reveal the remarkably conflicted, diverse, and contradictory responses among audience members.

These letters, the majority of which came from married women, should not be seen as representative of the larger audience's responses to the program.[11] Letter writers tend to be a particularly motivated group of television viewers. There is no way to determine whether the sentiments that crop up over and over again in the letters were widespread among viewers who did not write to the producers. Thus my analysis of these letters is not an attempt to quantify the *Julia* audience or to use the documents as a representative sample. While neither the letter writers nor the critics in the popular press were representative of the audience as a whole, their readings were symptomatic of struggles over racial definition. Perhaps, then, the best way to work with these documents is to see them as traces, clues, parts of a larger whole to which we have no access. Indeed, like all histories of audience reception, this one presents partial knowledge, pieces of the past that we must interpret in a qualified manner.[12]

One trend that became evident almost immediately among the favorable letters written by white viewers was a marked self-consciousness about racial self-identification: "I am white, but I enjoy watching 'Julia.' "[13] "Our whole family from great grandmother down to my five year old, loved it. We just happen to be caucasian." "As a 'white middle class Jewish' teacher, may I say that it is finally a pleasure to turn on the T.V. and see contemporary issues treated with honesty, humor, and sensitivity."[14]

One way in which to account for the self-consciousness of many letter writers identifying themselves as whites was that the novelty of a black-centered program raised questions about traditional and previously unexamined definitions of racial identity and difference. One mother of two boys in Ohio struggled with this very issue in her letter:

> Being a white person I hope this program helps all of us to under-
> stand each other. Maybe if my children watch this program they will
> also see the good side of Negro people [rather] than all the bad side
> they see on the news programs such as riots, sit-ins, etc. I know this
> program will help my two sons so when they grow up they won't be
> so prejudice[sic].

While the woman made some problematic distinctions between good
black people and bad black people, there was an attempt to grapple
with racial difference. Definitions of what it meant to be white had suddenly become an uncertain terrain. The crisis in race relations signified
by "riots, sit-ins, etc." made the black population visible, and the
depiction of African-Americans had ceased to be a stable field. As
representations of black people had become an arena of contested
meanings, so too had self-representations of whites become uncertain.
One manifestation of that uncertainty was self-consciousness. In the aftermath of the civil rights movement and in the midst of black power
sentiment, the question of what it now meant to be white in America
was an issue that needed working through.

Another way to think about race was, perhaps paradoxically, to
deny difference. A letter from a rather idealistic fifteen-year-old girl in
Annandale, Virginia, affirmed, "Your new series has told me that at
least SOME people have an idea of a peaceful and loving existence. So
what if their skin pigmentation is different and their philosophies are
a bit different than ours *they are still people*." Another woman from
Manhattan Beach, California, who described her race as Caucasian
and her ancestry as Mexican, wrote, "I love the show. Keep up the
good work. This way the world will realize that the Negro is just like
everyone else, with feelings and habits as the Whites have." A mother
of twins in Highland Park, New Jersey, observed, "And it's immensely
valuable to the many non-Negroes who just don't know any Negroes,
or don't know that all people mostly behave like people."

Perhaps these viewers engaged in a denial of the "otherness" of black
people in an attempt to reduce white anxiety about racial difference.
By affirming that blacks were "just people" and just like everyone else,
these viewers defined "everyone else" as white. White was the norm
from which the Other deviated. In their sincere attempts to negotiate
changing representations of race, these viewers denied that blacks
historically had not fit the constructed norm of the white middle-class
social formation. In this move, the viewers were, of course, assisted by
the program itself. The show's theme music was a generic sit-com jingle
lacking any nod to the rich traditions of African-American musical
forms. Julia's apartment, while nicely appointed, and with a framed

photo of her dead hero husband prominently displayed, was also completely generic. Unlike a comparable but more recent black family sit-
com, *The Cosby Show*, with its lavish townhouse decorated with
African-American artworks, Julia's home contained no culturally specific touches. Diahann Carroll's speech was also completely uninflect-
ed, on the one hand differentiating her from her prime-time predecessors such as *Amos 'n' Andy* and *Beulah*, but on the other hand
evacuating as much ethnic and cultural difference as possible. For viewers picking up on the interpretive clues provided by the show, black
people were "just people" to the extent that they conformed to an unexamined white norm of representation.

While this denial of difference may have been typical, it was by no
means the dominant interpretive strategy employed by viewers who
wrote letters. In fact, many viewers were clearly struggling with the
problem of representation, both of blacks and of whites. The criticism
leveled by many viewers—that the show was unrealistic and was not
"telling it like it is"—reveals a struggle over how reality should be
defined.

The refrain "tell it like it is" became a recurring theme in debates
about *Julia*, both in the popular press and among the viewer letters. In
a rather scathing review, *Time* magazine criticized the show for not
portraying how black people really lived: "She [Julia] would not recognize a ghetto if she stumbled into it, and she is, in every respect save
color, a figure in a white milieu."[15] Robert Lewis Shayon, the TV-radio
critic for *Saturday Review*, was also particularly concerned with *Julia*'s
deficiencies in representing this notion of a black reality. In the first of
three articles on the series, he, like the *Time* reviewer, castigated the
program for turning a blind eye to the realities of black life in the ghettos. For Shayon, the reality of the black experience was what was
documented in the Kerner Commission report: "Negro youth, 'hustling
in the jungle' of their 'crime-ridden, violence-prone, and poverty-
stricken world'—that's the real problem, according to the commission
report."[16] The world of *Julia*, on the other hand, was a fantasy because
it did not focus on the problems of black youth (which for Shayon
meant young black males) and because it did not take place in a ghetto
environment. The unconsciously racist notion that the black experience was essentially a ghetto experience remained unexamined in
these popular press accounts.

This attempt to define a singular, totalized "Negro reality" became
a point of dispute in Shayon's follow-up columns on May 25 and July
20, 1968. Shayon received a letter in response to his first column from
M.S. Rukeyser, Jr., NBC's vice president for press and publicity. He
also received a letter from Dan Jenkins, an executive at the public rela-

tions firm handling television programming for General Foods, one of *Julia*'s main sponsors. Shayon juxtaposed the responses of these men to an interview given by Hal Kanter, which affirmed that the show would tell the truth, show it like it is. Shayon noted that Jenkins appeared to hold a contradictory view:

> Jenkins, the publicity agent, wrote: "It is not, and never has been the function of a commercial series to 'show it as it is, baby.' On those rare occasions when the medium has taken a stab at limning the unhappy reality of what goes on in much of the world (e.g., *East Side, West Side*), the public has quickly tuned out.[17]

Shayon went on to quote from Rukeyser's letter: "We have no real quarrel with your [Shayon's] subjective judgment on the degree of lavishness of Julia's apartment, wardrobe, and way of life. There has been controversy within our own group about this."[18] Shayon also quoted from another interview with Kanter, who seemed to step back from his earlier stance. By "showing 'it like it is,' [Kanter] was talking not of ghetto life, but of 'humorous aspects of discrimination . . . properly handled . . . without rancor, without inflammation, and withal telling their attempts to enjoy the American dream.' "[19] In his article of July 20, 1968, Shayon added Diahann Carroll's response, quoting from an Associated Press story about the controversy generated by Shayon's initial article: "We're dealing with an entertainment medium. . . . *Julia* is a drama-comedy; it isn't politically oriented. Because I am black that doesn't mean I have to deal with problems of all black people."[20]

By bringing together the sentiments of the show's creator and its network, sponsor, and star, the Shayon pieces revealed just how conflicted the production process for *Julia* was. There was no consensus on what "telling it like it is" meant. Rukeyser's letter openly admitted to controversy over how Julia and her world should be depicted. Shayon's series of articles opened up for examination the problem of representation. If black identity had become a shifting field in the wake of the crisis in race relations, then "telling it like it is" would be impossible. Shayon thought he knew how *Julia* should tell it, but his articles indicated that in 1968 the program's creators were far less certain.

Unlike the critics, viewers generally did not want to relocate Julia and Corey to a ghetto. Instead, viewers who criticized the show for not "telling it like it is" were more concerned with the presentation of black characters than they were with the upscale setting. A male viewer in Chicago wrote:

> On another point which bears remarks is the unwillingness to allow the program to be "black." I do not object to white people being in

the cast. What I do object to is selecting the black cast from people (black people) who are so white oriented that everybody has a white mentality, that is, their expressions are all that of white people. Choose some people whose expressions and manners are unquestionably black. The baby-sitter was, for example, so white cultured that you would have thought she was caucasian except for the color of her skin.

Hal Kanter's reply to this letter indicated how contested this issue was: "We all make mistakes, don't we, Mr. Banks? Please try to forgive me for mine in the spirit of universality and brotherhood we are attempting to foster."

Mr. Banks's letter revealed an uncertainty over how to portray black people. Kanter's testy reply indicated that despite his rhetoric of brotherhood (and sameness), this was a problem that plagued the show's creators—a problem already evident in the script development for "Take My Hand." How would one represent "unquestionably black" expressions and manner? The representation of "black" was defined by Mr. Banks negatively by what it was not: it was not white. The dilemma of what "black" signified outside a cultural system in which "white" was the norm was still left open to question.[21]

Other viewers, also uncomfortable with the unrealistic quality of the program, pointed out more problems in the representation of blacks. A woman in Berkeley, California, observed:

> Your show is in a position to dispell [sic] so *many* misconceptions about Black people & their relationships to whites. I am just one of many who are so *very* disappointed in the outcome of such a promising show.
> *Please*, help to destroy the misconceptions—not reinforce them! Stop making Miss Carroll super-Negro and stop having blacks call themselves "colored" and make your characters less self-conscious and tell that "babysitter" to quit overacting.

This concern with representing blacks as "Super Negro" was also voiced in the popular press. In a *TV Guide* article in December 1968, Diahann Carroll was quoted saying:

> With black people right now, we are all terribly bigger than life and more wonderful than life and smarter and better—because we're still proving. . . . For a hundred years we have been prevented from seeing accurate images of ourselves and we're all overconcerned and overreacting. The needs of the white writer go to the superhuman being. At the moment, we're presenting the white Negro. And he has very little Negro-ness.[22]

These references to the "Super Negro" or the "white Negro" indicated an unmasking of an ideologically bankrupt representational system unable to come to terms with a representation of blacks that was independent of white as the defining term. The self-consciousness to which Diahann Carroll and the letter writer alluded was similar to the self-consciousness of other viewers who felt a need to identify themselves by race. Racial identity and its representation may have become an uncertain and contested field as "black" and "white" became unhinged from their previous definitions, but they were still imbricated within a white representational system.

This problem of racial definition was raised by other viewers who objected to blacks being differentiated and defined at the expense of white characters. Many viewers, particularly white housewives, took exception to the juxtaposing of Julia to her white neighbor, Mrs. Waggedorn. One mother of a four-year-old in Philadelphia said she would not watch the program anymore "as I believe you are protraying [sic] the white mother to be some kind of stupid idiot. —The colored boy & mother are sharp as tacks which is fine but why must the other family be portrayed as being dumb, dumb, dumb." Another "white suburban mother of four" in Fort Worthington, Pennsylvania, complained that Mrs. Waggedorn was a "dumb bunny" while Julia was a "candidate for 'Mother of the Year.' " A third letter from a "quite typical New England housewife and mother of three" in Hyde Park, Massachusetts, stated:

> If Diahann Carroll were to play the roll [sic] of the neighborly housewife, and vice verser [sic], the black people of this country would be screaming "Prejudice." Why must Julia be pictured so glamorously dressed, living in such a luxurious apartment, dining off of the finest china while her white neighbor is made to appear sloppy, has rollers in her hair. . . .
>
> If your show is to improve the image of the negro woman, great! But—please don't accomplish this at the expense of the white housewife.

The reading strategy these viewers brought to the text was one of polarization. They saw a form of reverse discrimination. Explicit in their letters was an anxiety over the representation of race, black versus white. Implicit, however, was a nascent critique of the representation of gender. All three of these letter writers self-consciously defined themselves by occupation: white housewives and mothers. In the depiction of Mrs. Waggedorn, they saw a stereotypical representation of themselves and were quite aware that they were being demeaned as women.

The positions articulated by these women to a certain extent mirror concerns raised in a number of women's magazines. Articles written about the series, or more specifically the series' star, Diahann Carroll, focused not on questions of race but rather on questions of motherhood. An article in *Ladies' Home Journal* written by the widow of slain civil rights activist Medgar Evers, while not ignoring the question of race representation, emphasized a theme of female bonding between Mrs. Evers and Diahann Carroll, two black women forced to raise children on their own.[23] A *Good Housekeeping* article completely evacuated the issue of race, dealing only with dilemmas Diahann Carroll faced attempting to raise her daughter while pursuing a career.[24]

Thus, while questions of race representation were highly politicized both in the popular press and among viewers, questions about the representation of gender and motherhood were rendered entirely apolitical in both articles in the women's magazines. Instead, the issues were personalized: they were Diahann Carroll's problems or Mrs. Medgar Evers's problems, but they were not discussed as social problems. Similarly, the white housewives who objected to the portrayal of Mrs. Waggedorn had no political discourse through which to articulate their anger at an offensive female stereotype. Both the women's magazine writers and the housewives seemed aware that there was something problematic about the gender-based positions of mothers and housewives within the social order. However, they lacked the means to shift their analysis of the problem from the personal to the social. One could argue that the women's movement, still in its infancy in the late 1960s, provided such an analysis, at least for middle-class white women who formed the main constituency for the emergent women's liberation movement. Just as the black oppositional movement revealed that the position of African-Americans within the social landscape was politically, economically, and socially circumscribed and required political solutions, so the emergence of the women's movement revealed a similar set of concerns about the position of women. However, such an analysis, widely available in relation to race, was not yet accessible to a general female audience.[25]

The viewer response letters examined so far attempted, either by denying difference or by trying to grapple with it, to engage with the program in order to think through ways in which to rework race relations. While many of the letters exhibited unexamined racist discourses, the racism seemed unintended and unconscious, a manifestation of the shifting ground. *Julia*, as a text that worked hard to evacuate politically charged representations and potentially disturbing discourses of racial oppression, would appear to be an unlikely candidate for overtly racist attacks. However, a surprisingly large number of the letters in the Hal Kanter papers reveal an enormous amount of unmediated anxiety felt by some viewers about changes being wrought in the wake of the civil rights and black oppositional movements.

Concerns that reappeared in these letters tended to focus on a discomfort with seeing increasing numbers of African-Americans on television, fears that traditional racial hierarchies were being eradicated, and anxieties about interracial sexuality. While *Julia* never dealt with issues of miscegenation or intermarriage, many of these viewers read them into the program anyway. Some of these viewers may have done so because, unlike the black mammy figures traditionally predominant in the mass media, Julia conformed to white ideals of beauty. That her white male bosses were shown recognizing her sexuality may have provided the cues some viewers needed to construct scenarios such as the one provided by an anonymous viewer from Los Angeles:

> What are you trying to do by making "Julia." No racial problems — she is playing opposite a white, she is suppose [*sic*] to live in an all white apt house. It's racial because you will have it so Nolan [Dr. Chegley, Julia's boss] will fall in love with her and have to make her over — repulsive — You had better write a part for a big black boy so he can mess with a white girl or they will get mad.

Anxiety over social change and transformations in race relations erupted here in a full-blown fear of interracial sexuality. For this viewer, integration created a moral panic whereby the sudden visibility of blacks in "white society" could only mean that "big black boys" wanted to mess with white girls.

Other viewers, less obsessed with questions of miscegenation, exhibited fears about integration by expressing anger at television as an institution. They blamed television for creating social strife and causing blacks to forget their proper place. One anonymous viewer from Houston, Texas, who signed her or his comments "the silent majority," wrote:

> Living in Texas all my life I have always lived around the negroes and they used to be really fine people until the T.V. set came out & ruined the whole world! Not only have you poor white trash taken advantage of them & ruined their chances now you have ruined the college set. You are good at getting people when they are most vulnerable and changing their entire thinking!

These letters indicate how besieged some people were feeling in the midst of the turmoil of the late 1960s. In Julia, some viewers may have seen the "new Negro" as one who threatened their racially hierarchized universe. All the anxiety-reducing mechanisms employed by the program's creators to defuse notions of difference merely exacerbated anxiety for these viewers. They did not need to see explicit interracial sexuality dealt with on the television screen to see miscegenation as the logical (and inevitable) outcome of the erasure of racial difference. Such letters show the ideological extremes viewers could go to in their meaning-making endeavors. *Julia* as a text certainly did not encourage these interpretations. But since meanings are neither entirely determined nor controlled by the text and since viewers are active agents in the process of constructing their own meanings, we can see how disturbing the process can be. Cultural studies theorists analyzing oppositional reading strategies have generally focused on how such viewers position themselves against dominant ideology. By implication such reading positions are often seen as positive evidence of cultural struggle against the constraining policies, perspectives, and practices of the ruling social order or "power bloc."[26] However, as these letters show, an oppositional reading strategy need not be a liberatory or progressive strategy.

Another issue that seemed to bother the hostile viewers was the mere presence of blacks on television. Blacks were slowly becoming more visible as supporting players in such popular programs as *I Spy, The Mod Squad, Hogan's Heroes,* and *Daktari.* Blacks were also occasionally being featured in commercial advertisements by 1967. But in the summer of 1968, the networks, at the urging of the Kerner Commission, outdid themselves offering an unprecedented number of news documentaries on the state of black America, including CBS's acclaimed *Of Black America,* a seven-part series hosted by Bill Cosby.[27] For some viewers this was clearly too much: "We have had so much color shoved down our throats on special programs this summer its [*sic*] enough to make a person sick," wrote one viewer from Toronto. An anonymous viewer from Eufaula, Oklahoma, wrote, "After the riots and [the] network filled 'Black American' shows all summer, white people aren't feeling to [*sic*] kindly toward colored people shows. You are ahead of the time on this one." Yet another anonymous viewer from Red Bluff, California, asserted, "I will not buy the product sponsoring this show or any show with a nigger in it. I believe I can speak for millions of real americans [*sic*]. I will write the sponsors of these shows. I am tired of niggers in my living room." A third anonymous viewer from Bethpage, Long Island, asked, "Is this what you mean by color T.V. ugh. *Click*!!" Moreover, many of these people made no distinction between documentary representations of civil strife and the fictional world of *Julia.* Since both in some way concerned black people, *Julia* was really no different from the news specials about ghetto riots.

In the end, the reason it is useful to consider these disturbing and offensive letters is because of what they can tell us about the polysemic nature of reception. *Julia* was heavily criticized for constructing a

"white Negro," for playing it safe in order not to scare off white viewers, for sugar-coating its racial messages. While all of that may be true,
the show's "whiteness," middle-classness, and inoffensiveness did not
defuse its threat to entrenched racist positions. This threat was also
made evident by the fact that many of the hostile letters carried no return address. Unlike other viewers who wrote letters, both favorable
and unfavorable, these letter writers were not interested in opening up
a dialogue with the show's producers. The anonymity both shielded
their besieged positions and revealed that such positions were no longer
easily defensible.

While the majority of letters in the Hal Kanter papers appear to be
from white viewers, there are a significant number of letters from viewers who identified themselves as black.[28] Some of these letters share minor similarities with some of the responses from white viewers. For the
most part, however, the reading strategies differ markedly. Jacqueline
Bobo, drawing on the work of David Morley and Stuart Hall, has discussed the importance of "cultural competencies," or cultural codes, in
order to make sense of how black women made their own meanings
of The Color Purple.[29] As David Morley has stated:

> What is needed here is an approach which links differential interpre-
> tations back into the socio-economic structures of society, showing
> how members of different groups and classes sharing different "cul-
> tural codes" will interpret a given message differently, not just at the
> personal idiosyncratic level, but in a way "systematically related" to
> their socio-economic position.[30]

Bobo shifts the emphasis from social and economic structures to those
of race in order to determine what codes black women employed when
interpreting the film. This model can also help us understand the
unique ways in which black viewers of Julia made sense of the
program.

One crucial distinction between black and white viewers was that
many of the black viewers displayed a participatory quality in their engagement with the program. They tended to erase boundaries between
themselves and the text. Many letter writers asked if they could write
episodes or play parts on the show. An eleven-year-old boy from the
Bronx wrote:

> I am a Negro and I am almost in the same position as Corey. . . .
> Your show really tells how an average black or Negro person lives.
>   I like your show so much that if you ever have a part to fill I
> would be glad to fill it for you.[31]

A teenage girl from Buffalo wanted to create a new character for the
show: Julia's teenage sister. She proceeded to describe what the sister's

characteristics would be and how she would like to play the part. A female teacher from Los Angeles wrote:

> The thought occurred to me that *Julia* may be in need of a close friend on your television show — and/or Corey Baker may need a *good* first grade teacher (me). . . . I am not a militant but a *very proud Negro*.[32]

The viewers who wanted to write episodes generally made their offer at the end of the letter after having detailed what they considered wrong with the show. Other viewers wanted to get together with Kanter personally to discuss the matter. One young woman from Detroit, studying mass media at college, suggested a meeting with Kanter: "Perhaps I can give you a better idea of what the Black people really want to see and what the white person really *needs* to see."[33]

While white viewers offered criticisms of the program, only the black viewers took it upon themselves to offer their assistance in improving the show. Their participatory relationship to the text indicated a far more active attempt at making the show meaningful. For the black viewers the struggle over representation was between the actual program as created by white producers and a potential, but more authentic, program to be created by the black viewers. By acting in and writing for the show, they became producers of meaning, rather than mere recipients of meaning constructed by whites. Asserting the values of their cultural codes, they attempted to bring their own knowledge to the text. The positive engagement evidenced by these viewers arose from an articulation of self-affirming representation.

Ebony, a mass-circulation magazine targeted at a primarily middle-class black readership, also tried to find racially-affirming representations in the program. Unlike other popular press accounts, *Ebony* took pains to emphasize the show's positive aspects while acknowledging its shortcomings. Pointing to *Julia*'s four black scriptwriters, the article indicated that the show would provide new opportunities for African-Americans in the television industry.[34] *Ebony* appeared to support the program specifically because the magazine saw that blacks were assisting (even if in a limited way) in its production.

One of the main areas of concern for many black viewers was whether the representation of blacks was realistic or whether the program portrayed a white world for white viewers. The denial of difference that numerous white viewers applauded was challenged by many, although not all, black viewers. A black woman from Los Angeles wrote:

> Your show is geared to the white audience with no knowledge of the realness of normal Negro people.

> Your work is good for an all white program—but something is
> much missing from your character—Julia is unreal.
>   To repeat again—Julia is no Negro woman I know & I'm Negro
> with many friends in situations such as hers.

Kanter replied somewhat sarcastically: "I'm glad you think our work
is 'good for an all white program.' I'll pass your praise along to our
black writer and black actors."

While some of the white viewers, who had self-consciously identified
themselves by race, appeared to think *Julia* was addressed primarily to a
black audience, this black viewer had the opposite impression. The black
audience was evacuated by a text that denied the "realness" of black identity. The mass-media student quoted above made a similar observation:

> The show does not portray the life of the typical probing Black wom-
> an, it is rather a story of a white widow with a Black face. Even
> though she does possess the physical appearance of a Black woman
> (minus expensive clothing, plush apartment, etc.) she lacks that cer-
> tain touch of reality.

The problem of realism was again a manifestation of a crisis in
representation, a crisis in how to define black identity and who would
be authorized to do so. In his reply to the student, Kanter acknowledged the problem, stating, "I have considered its [your letter's]
content and have come to the conclusion you may be right."

Those white viewers who agreed that the show was unrealistic and
that Julia was a "white Negro" were more likely to do reality checks
with other white characters with whom they could identify, such as
Mrs. Waggedorn. Black viewers who found the show unrealistic and
who found Julia to be a "white Negro" had difficulty identifying with
any of the characters. The woman with many friends in Julia's situation
searched the text in vain looking for confirmation of her identity as a
black woman. Unlike the black women Jacqueline Bobo studied who
found positive, progressive, and affirming meanings about black
womanhood in *The Color Purple*, this particular woman found nothing in *Julia*. The text did not speak to her experiences. It did not construct a reading position from which she could use her cultural codes
and find useful meanings. On the contrary, her experience as a black
woman, along with those of her friends, blocked any possibility of
finding a place for herself within the text. The strategy of breaking
down textual boundaries and inserting oneself into the program by
offering to write episodes or play a role may have functioned to avert
this problem. It may have given some black viewers a mechanism by
which to place themselves within the program and assert their own
identities as African-Americans.

The other major arena of concern for black viewers, as well as for some white critics, was the depiction of the black family. This issue is a difficult one for feminist theory. The reading strategies employed by black viewers of *Julia* present a problematic situation since, from a (white) feminist perspective, it would be difficult to see their readings as empowering for women. Only one of the viewers who commented on the portrayal of the black family took an anti-patriarchal position. The other black viewers (all of whom were women) criticized the show for not having a strong male head of the family.

The one woman who did not take the creators of *Julia* to task for omitting a strong patriarch was herself reacting to *Saturday Review* critic Shayon's remarks that *Julia* was perpetuating the "castration theme in the history of the American Negro male."[35] Offering her services as a writer of short stories and plays, the viewer went on to provide the following observations:

> No one ever let the Negro woman have her say even the middle class one. No one really knows how hard it is for the Negro woman when her man walks out on her leaving her with four or five babies.

Another woman from Chicago offered an analysis more representative of black viewers:

> I don't think any more of you for excluding the black man from this series than I think of the "original" slave owners who first broke up the black family!
>
> You white men have never given the black man anything but a hard time.
>
> If you really want to do some good you'll marry "Julia" to a strong black man before the coming TV season is over and take her from that white doctor's office and put her in the home as a housewife where she belongs!
>
> Otherwise a lot of black women—like me, who love, respect, and honor their black husbands will exclude "Julia" from our TV viewing just as you have excluded our black male from your show!

A married woman from Brooklyn who signed herself "An Ex-Black Viewer" wrote:

> After viewing the season premiere of "Julia," I, as a black woman find myself outraged. Is this program what you call a portrayal of a typical Negro family (which is, incidentally, fatherless?) If so, you are only using another means to brainwash the black people who, unfortunately, may view your program weekly.

The problems associated with the show's portrayal of black family life were also discussed in black academic circles. In an article on blacks in American television that appeared in *The Black Scholar* in 1974, Marilyn Diane Fife strongly attacked *Julia* for ignoring black men. By making the central character a widowed black woman, the program neatly sidestepped the critical issue of black men and their position within African-American culture, as well as their position within American society. Fife observed:

> Traditionally the black female has accommodated more to the white power structure. The real social problems of blacks have always turned around the black man's inability to have dignity, and the power and respect of his family. "Julia" disregards all this by turning the only black male roles into potential suitors, not actual male figures involved in the overall series.[36]

Fife thus suggested that the focus on a female black lead rendered the series safer, less likely to grapple with issues that might upset white viewers.

White feminists may be particularly uneasy with such analyses since they seem to affirm the very conditions of patriarchal family structures that they have challenged. However, for black women, this critique of patriarchy has ignored questions of racism that are seen as crucial to an understanding of the situation of black women. The historically different positions occupied by black and (middle-class) white women within the social order should alert us to the problems of grafting feminist perspectives developed within a white middle-class milieu onto the experiences of black women. However, this necessity of acknowledging difference seems to render problematic the mobilization of much feminist theory to apply to anything but the experiences of white women. Given this dilemma, I (along with other feminists) would suggest that feminist theory needs to respond to the specific historical situations of different women living in patriarchal systems.[37]

Indeed, a more historically grounded examination of the unique experiences of black women within family structures can help explain the responses of these women to *Julia*. As Angela Davis and Jacqueline Jones have pointed out in their histories of black women, the life of a housewife within a patriarchal familial structure was quite uncommon for black women. For these women, work generally meant exploitative labor for whites that took black women away from their own families and communities.[38] Unlike middle-class white women, who may have seen work outside the home as potentially liberating, the history of work for black women had no such emancipatory connotations. The viewer who wanted Julia taken out of the white doctor's office was thus making sense of Julia's labor from within this larger history of black women's work. That Julia resorted to leaving Corey locked up alone in their apartment while she went off to her job interview may have had deeper meanings for black women who historically had been forced to leave their children to fend for themselves while they cared for the children of either white owners or white employers.

Another way in which to examine the perspectives of these black women is to situate them in relation to dominant ideas about the black family that were in circulation at the time. It is likely that these discourses would have been familiar to educated, professional, middle-class members of the African-American community. Many of the black letter writers identified themselves by profession — teachers, nurses, students — and tended to write grammatically and stylistically sophisticated letters. This leads me to assume that they were most likely middle-class viewers. The dominant perspective on the black family, with which these viewers were likely to be familiar, was an intensely misogynistic view of a destructive "black matriarchy."

This thesis was first put forth by the influential African-American sociologist E. Franklin Frazier, who began writing about the black family in the 1930s. He attributed a matriarchal character to black familial structure and found its source in the dislocation and stresses of slavery and discrimination. While this familial structure remained strong within the black community after emancipation, Frazier contended that matriarchal formations predominated in mostly lower-class, impoverished urban and rural families. Rather than give much credit to the strength and resiliency of black women, Frazier saw their power within the family as a sign of dysfunction. Those families who managed to achieve middle-class or upper-middle-class status assumed patriarchal characteristics mirroring white families, thus assimilating more successfully into the American norm. Frazier felt that blacks had been unable to retain their African cultural heritage when ripped away from their homeland by slave traders. He therefore felt blacks needed to adopt the familial arrangements dominant in their new homeland in order to survive as a people. Thus the two-parent nuclear family with a strong male head, a structure Frazier saw in upwardly mobile black families, was desirable.[39]

Frazier, like many of the white viewers of *Julia* who attempted to deny difference, did not see any problems with this white norm. Patriarchy seemed to work in constructing successful families if we view the white middle-class model as normative. But Frazier, like most theorists of the black family, was concerned primarily with the black male and was thus rather blind to the position of the female in familial structures, whether black or white.

Frazier's perspective can help us understand why the familial structure in *Julia* was considered so problematic for many black viewers as well as for numerous critics who may also have been familiar with this thesis. On the one hand, the Baker family seemed the epitome of an upwardly mobile black family. Julia, as a nurse, was a professional who had joined the middle class. She and Corey, living in an integrated apartment building with white neighbors, appeared to be completely assimilated into white society. On the other hand, this assimilated, middle-class black family had no male head. Like lower-class and ghettoized black families, a woman took sole responsibility for running the family. The black family depicted in *Julia* thus threatened the dichotomized model Frazier had described. The Bakers collapsed the distinctions between the upwardly mobile middle-class family predicated on patriarchy and the impoverished and dysfunctional lower-class family predicated on matriarchy.

The Moynihan Report was even more influential in distributing ideas about the black family in the 1960s.[40] Produced by the Department of Labor in 1965 (around the time of the Watts uprising), the report described black families caught within a "tangle of pathology." One characteristic of this so-called pathology was the supposed preponderance of female-headed black households in comparison to white households. Echoing the misogynist stance of Frazier, Moynihan felt this situation had grave consequences for African-Americans as a people:

> In essence, the Negro community has been forced into a matriarchal structure which, because it is so out of line with the rest of the American society, seriously retards the progress of the group as a whole, and imposes a crushing burden on the Negro male and, in consequence, on a great many Negro women as well.[41]

The report was denounced by many in the black community who felt that it put as much, if not more, of the blame on the black family structure as it did on white racism and discrimination in order to explain the dire situation of many blacks in American society.[42] While some scholars attempted to trace matriarchal or matrilinear familial structures back to black cultural ancestry in West Africa, few in the 1960s were championing female-dominated families within scholarly or popular discourses.

Within this cultural climate, where so much attention was being focused on the apparently pathological and destructive quality of female-headed black households, *Julia* was a likely target for criticism from black viewers. As an unattached, independent woman, Julia could be seen as a threatening figure, yet another strong matriarch perpetuating in the realm of popular culture a familial model menacing African-American social life. It is unfortunate that the emergent women's movement, which would most likely embrace a figure such as Julia precisely because she was independent and career-oriented, would find it impossible to speak to the unique oppressions of black women. The perniciousness of the black matriarchy myth remained unexposed.[43]

The readings provided by viewer letters and popular press critics should indicate that there was no one preferred, dominant, or definitive set of meanings attached to *Julia*. Different viewers brought their socially, culturally, racially, and historically determined interpretive strategies to bear upon the program. And because of the historically specific moment of *Julia*'s appearance, a moment of racial strife when previously unquestioned categories of racial identity and definition no longer held firm, the program itself was as conflicted as the interpretations of it. Even Kanter at times acquiesced to the dissenting views of his audience.

By looking at *Julia* as a symptomatic text — symptomatic of the crisis in race relations and its concomitant representations — we can see how a document of popular culture can serve as a piece of historical evidence, embodying within itself tensions working their way through American society at a particular moment. The social and political turmoil of the 1960s manifested itself within a multitude of institutions and sectors of American civil society. Even television, saddled with the moniker "the vast wasteland" for its vapid and blithely apolitical programming in the 1960s, could not escape the turmoil. *Julia* straddled the vacuous "wasteland" and the more socially relevant programming inaugurated at CBS with *All in the Family* in 1970.[44] Despite flirting with relevance, Julia tended to slide toward innocuous cuteness. However, when we shift our attention away from the program and onto its audiences, we find contentious and sometimes highly politicized responses. By concentrating on reception, we can thus begin to chart the dynamics of historical and social change. In the process, American television in the 1960s starts to look less and less like a vast wasteland.

NOTES

I would like to extend my thanks to Lynn Spigel, John Fiske, Charlotte Brunsdon, David Morley, Julie D'Acci, the graduate students of the Telecommunications section of the Communications Arts Department, University of Wisconsin-Madison, and David Aaron for their suggestions and comments on various drafts of this paper.

1. David Caute, *The Year of the Barricades: A Journey Through 1968* (New York: Harper & Row, 1988).

2. *Amos 'n' Andy* remained in syndication until 1966. NBC attempted a short-lived variety show with Nat King Cole in 1957.

3. Les Brown, *Television: The Business Behind the Box* (New York: Harcourt Brace Jovanovich, 1971), pp. 78–79.

4. J. Fred MacDonald, *Blacks and White TV: Afro-Americans in Television since 1948* (Chicago: Nelson-Hall Publishers, 1983), p. 116.

5. MacDonald, p. 117. *Julia* was also criticized by the U.S. Commission on Civil Rights in its influential publication *Window Dressing on the Set: Women and Minorities in Television* (Washington, D.C.: U.S. Commission on Civil Rights, August 1977).

6. The Hal Kanter papers are located at the Wisconsin Center Historical Archives, State Historical Society, Madison, Wisconsin. The Kanter papers contain primarily final draft scripts for all the *Julia* episodes; Kanter's personal correspondence, production materials for the series, and ratings information; and a large selection of viewer letters. Most of the letters to which I will be referring later in this paper are filed in folders labeled "fan letters, favorable" and "fan letters, unfavorable." Some viewer letters are also scattered among Kanter's correspondence folders.

7. This script is located in the Hal Kanter papers, Box 18.

8. This script is filed in the Hal Kanter papers, Box 19.

9. This script is filed in the Hal Kanter papers, Box 18.

10. Stuart Hall, "Encoding/Decoding," *Culture, Media, Language*, ed. Hall et al. (London: Hutchinson, 1980), pp. 128–138.

11. Sixty-one of the letters came from married women and twenty-three from single women or those whose marital status was unidentifiable. Thirty-three letters came from men. The rest were either unidentifiable by gender or from children and young people. The preponderance of women viewers is mirrored in ratings materials located in a ratings folder in Hal Kanter papers, Box 18. A breakdown of the *Julia* audience for a two-week period ending Sept. 28, 1969, showed that women between the ages of 18 and 49 formed the largest bulk of the audience, followed by female teens. Men between the ages of 18 and 49 formed the smallest share of the audience.

12. Carlo Ginzburg, "Morelli, Freud and Sherlock Holmes: Clues and Scientific Method," *History Workshop* 9 (Spring 1980), pp. 5–36. Ginzburg argues that for historians a conjectural approach (the analysis of clues) "holds the potential for understanding society. In a social structure of ever-increasing complexity like that of advanced capitalism, befogged by ideological murk, any claim to systematic knowledge appears as a flight of foolish fancy. To acknowledge this is not to abandon the idea of totality. On the contrary; the existence of deep connection which explains superficial phenomena can be confirmed when it is acknowledged that direct knowledge of such a connection is impossible. Reality is opaque; but there are certain points — clues, signs — which allow us to decipher it" (p. 27).

13. All of the following viewer letters, unless marked otherwise, are in the Hal Kanter papers, Box 18.

14. The writers of these letters are, respectively, a male viewer from DuBois, Pennsylvania, a female viewer from Colton, California, and a female viewer from New York City.

15. "Wonderful World of Color," *Time* (December 13, 1968), p. 70.

16. Robert Lewis Shayon, " 'Julia': Breakthrough or Letdown," *Saturday Review* (April 20, 1968), p. 49.

17. Robert Lewis Shayon, " 'Julia' Symposium: An Opportunity Lost," *Saturday Review* (May 25, 1968), p. 36.

18. Shayon, " 'Julia' Symposium," p. 36.

19. Shayon, " 'Julia' Symposium," p. 36.

20. Robert Lewis Shayon, " 'Julia': A Political Relevance?" *Saturday Review* (July 20, 1968), p. 37.

21. For an examination of white as norm see Richard Dyer's "White," *Screen* 29:4 (Autumn 1988), pp. 44–64. Dyer observes, "In the realm of categories, black is always marked as a colour . . . and is always particularising; whereas white is not anything really, not an identity, not a particularising quality, because it is everything—white is no colour because it is all colours" (p.45).

22. Richard Warren Lewis, "The Importance of Being Julia," *TV Guide* (December 14, 1968), p. 26.

23. Mrs. Medgar Evers, "A Tale of Two Julias," *Ladies' Home Journal* (May 1970), pp. 60–65.

24. "Diahann Carroll's Juggling Act," *Good Housekeeping* (May 1969), pp. 38–51.

25. Betty Friedan's groundbreaking text of second-wave feminism, *The Feminine Mystique* (New York: Dell, 1963), analyzed the discontented housewife stories that began to crop up in women's magazines in the early 1960s. Despite her enormously influential work, Friedan's analysis did not appear to affect the type of stories published in magazines such as *Ladies' Home Journal*. The blindness of this particular magazine to the emergent women's liberation movement was made plain in March, 1970, when over a hundred feminists occupied the magazine's offices demanding sweeping editorial and policy changes. See Alice Echols, *Daring to Be Bad: Radical Feminism in America 1967–1975* (Minneapolis: University of Minnesota Press, 1989), pp. 195–197.

26. See, for instance, John Fiske, *Television Culture* (London & New York; Methuen, 1987) and *Understanding Popular Culture* (Boston: Unwin Hyman, 1989).

27. MacDonald, pp. 138–139.

28. Thirteen women, one man, and three children or young people identified themselves as black. There was also a group of thirteen letters from an inner-city grade school writing class. From the tone of the letters, I suspect the class was predominantly made up of black children.

29. Jacqueline Bobo, "*The Color Purple*: Black Women as Cultural Read-

ers," *Female Spectators: Looking at Film and Television,* ed. E. Deidre Pribram (London & New York: Verso, 1988), pp. 90–109.

30. David Morley, *The Nationwide Audience* (Chapel Hill & London: University of North Carolina Press, 1985), p. 14.

31. This letter is located in the Hal Kanter papers, Box 1, among Kanter's general correspondence. A significant number of letters from self-identifying black viewers can be found in this general correspondence rather than in the fan letter files.

32. Hal Kanter papers, Box 1.

33. Hal Kanter papers, Box 1.

34. *Ebony* (November 1968), pp. 56–58.

35. *Saturday Review* (April 20, 1968), p. 49.

36. Marilyn Diane Fife, "Black Images in American TV: The First Two Decades," *The Black Scholar* (November 1974), pp. 13–14.

37. For an overview of this debate see Linda Gordon, "On Difference," *Genders* (forthcoming).

38. See Angela Y. Davis, *Women, Race & Class* (New York: Vintage Books, 1981), and Jacqueline Jones, *Labor of Love, Labor of Sorrow: Black Women, Work and the Family, From Slavery to the Present* (New York: Vintage Books, 1985).

39. See E. Franklin Frazier, *The Family: Its Function and Destiny* (New York: Harper & Row, 1959), and his classic statement on black families, *The Negro Family in the United States* (Chicago: University of Chicago Press, 1939). For a good introduction to the various debates about the black family in the 1960s and early 1970s see *Black Matriarchy: Myth or Reality?,* ed. John H. Bracey, Jr., August Meier, and Elliott Rudwick (Belmont, Calif.: Wadsworth, 1971).

40. Daniel P. Moynihan, *The Negro Family: The Case for National Action* (Washington, D.C.: U.S. Department of Labor, Office of Planning and Research, March 1965).

41. Moynihan in Bracey, Meier, and Rudwick, p. 140.

42. See, for instance, noted black sociologist Andrew Billingsley's book *Black Families in White America* (Englewood Cliffs, N.J.: Prentice-Hall, Inc., 1968), pp. 199–202.

43. Black feminists have more recently begun to explode this myth. For a critique of Frazier, Moynihan, and other discourses on the black family, see Bonnie Thornton Dill, "The Dialectics of Black Womanhood," in *Feminism and Methodology,* ed. Sandra Harding (Bloomington and Indianapolis: Indiana University Press, 1984), pp. 97–108.

44. Todd Gitlin discusses the "turn toward relevance" in network programming in the wake of the social movements of the 1960s in his book, *Inside Prime Time* (New York: Pantheon Books, 1983), pp. 203–220.

Defining Women:
The Case of *Cagney and Lacey*
Julie D'Acci

On Monday nights between 1983 and 1988, CBS attracted millions of American women to its "ladies' night line-up."[1] The last program in this line-up, a thorn in the network's side for its controversial women characters and its mediocre ratings, was also renowned for delivering a deluxe "quality audience" to CBS and its advertisers week after week.[2] According to CBS research department vice president David Poltrack, *Cagney and Lacey* attracted women viewers who, by and large, watched less television than the average audience member, were college educated, over thirty-five, and earned over $40,000 a year.[3]

Upscale female audiences were the coveted plum of the television industry in its 1980s quest for the "working-women's market," and female characters—acting out the industry's fantasies of the "new working women"—were fashioned to lure their "real-life" counterparts to prime time as never before. However, the territory of 1980s working women and the adjacent territory of feminism posed difficulties for network television. Clashes over exactly what these new women characters could or could not be, in fact, left scars in the prime-time offerings of the period that demonstrate just how well guarded particular definitions of women are by those who hold them and just how dangerous new ones are perceived to be. Many of the new working-women shows introduced during the early 1980s—*9 to 5*, *Remington Steele*, *Gloria*, *It Takes Two*, and *Cagney and Lacey*—underwent overhauls and modified their depictions of women in order to bring their characters back in line with conventional television notions of femininity. Because of its six-year run, its departure from traditional norms of the "TV woman," and its embattled history, *Cagney and Lacey* provides a rich case study of the struggles over competing definitions of what it means to be a woman.

In 1981, the time of *Cagney and Lacey*'s first production as a made-for-TV movie, the cultural definitions of "woman," both in American society at large and in the representational practices of television, were multiple and open to debate. Traditional cultural meanings of femininity in a number of spheres (economy, labor, family, and sexuality, to name a few) were challenged by the women's movements. Television, in its general quest for "relevance" and its specific attempt to reach the new working-women's market, was producing representations of women that drew, in varying ways and degrees, on the new feminist consciousness—particularly that of the American liberal women's movement. Some of these representations, especially those of *Cagney and Lacey* in its initial stages, were in sharp contrast to television's conventional ways of depicting women. But these innovations would be tempered and transformed as a backlash against feminism gained force (notably evident in the defeat of the Equal Rights Amendment), and as television's tendency to filter out potentially controversial subject matter began to take hold.

A detailed study of *Cagney and Lacey* generally, then, offers to reveal the *actual terms* of cultural struggle over the meanings of femininity as this was played out on prime-time television during the period from 1981 to 1988. Since the original *Cagney and Lacey* script was written in 1974 and offered (without takers) to every major motion picture studio in Hollywood, it also offers insight into that earlier period. Furthermore, the issues contested during the late 1970s and through the 1980s continue to provoke the television industry and its audiences today.

Cagney and Lacey was the first dramatic program in television history to star two women. It appeared on CBS between 1982 and 1988 and dealt with two white middle-class and upper middle-class female detectives in the New York City Police Department. Created by Barbara Avedon and Barbara Corday, its executive producer was Barney Rosenzweig and its production company was Orion Television. The characters—Cagney (played by Meg Foster and Sharon Gless, respectively) and Lacey (played by Tyne Daly)—were represented as active heroines who solved their own cases (both mentally and physically), were rarely shown as "women in distress" and were virtually never rescued by their male colleagues.[4] In addition to their roles as active protagonists in the narrative, they were also active subjects, rarely objects, of sexual desire. Christine Cagney, a single woman, had an ongoing sexual life in which she often pursued men who interested her. Similarly, Mary Beth Lacey, a married woman, was a sexual initiator with her husband, Harvey. Lacey was also the primary breadwinner of the family, while Harvey, an often unemployed construction worker, cooked and took care of the house and their two children. Cagney and Lacey were depicted as close friends who took a lot of pleasure in one another's company and spent a lot of screen time talking to each other.

When the program first appeared, the actresses and characters were in their mid-thirties, and there was a distinct minimization of glamour

in their clothing, hairstyles, and makeup. The characters were originally from working-class backgrounds and were both "working women."
Much of the initial script material was modeled on the concerns of the
early liberal women's movement in America, especially equal pay and
sexual harassment at work. The first scripts dealt with male discrimination on the job and contained such material as a riff between Cagney
and Lacey about the various ways in which Lt. Samuels, their com-
manding officer, was a "pig."

During its creation, and for the whole of its production, *Cagney and
Lacey* became the site of intense public debates over various definitions
of femininity. Many of the key players involved in the series' production and reception continuously battled over what women on television
should and should not be. Among these players were those we would
expect to be part of any negotiation of television content—the network, the individual production company and production team, the
television audience, the press, and various interest and pressure
groups.

These players, of course, were invested in definitions of women that
suited their particular interests, whether those were political, economic, social, personal, or some combination thereof. The television industry, for instance, was looking for relevance and topicality while simultaneously hoping to preserve many of its conventional ways of
depicting female characters. These conventions included the depiction
of women as young, white, middle class, stereotypically "beautiful,"
and demure. They also included the presentation of female characters
who were wives, mothers, heterosexual sex objects, subsidiaries to
men, "vulnerable," and "sympathetic."[5] Within such conventions
women were destined to be cast in situation comedies rather than in
prime-time dramas. *Cagney and Lacey*'s production company, Orion
Television (formerly Filmways), was at least somewhat committed to
generating more innovative representations of women. Richard Rosen-
bloom, Orion Television's president, was, in fact, known in Hollywood at the time for producing the highest percentage of properties
written by women.[6] The individual production team was, for its part,
directly influenced by the liberal women's movement, and quite explicitly fashioned *Cagney and Lacey* according to early feminist terms.
A significant segment of the women's audience for *Cagney and Lacey*,
and for other programs aimed at working women, was actively seeking
progressive, interesting, and, in an often-cited viewer term, "real"
representations of women in television fiction. As can be imagined, the
mainstream press was extremely varied in its interests. One sector, very
much influenced by feminism, agitated for a wider range of women
characters, and specifically for roles shaped by the concerns of the

women's movements. Other segments called for a return to "tried and true" femininity. Similarly, a number of interest and pressure groups had stakes in greatly divergent depictions of women. The National Gay Task Force, for example, vehemently protested the network's effort to ward off connotations of lesbianism in *Cagney and Lacey* by replacing one Cagney actress (Meg Foster) with another "more feminine" one (Sharon Gless). The National Right to Life Committee fiercely opposed Cagney and Lacey's support of a woman character who choses to have an abortion. Planned Parenthood and the National Abortion Rights League applauded the series' embrace of reproductive rights. And spokespeople for the liberal women's movement generally and consistently championed the series for depicting "independent" working women and women's friendship.[7]

Getting New Representations of Women to the Screen

Cagney and Lacey's earliest period, from its conception in 1974 to its production as a made-for-TV movie in 1981, is rife with conflicts over different definitions of women. Generally speaking, representations of women in motion pictures and television programs were highly contradictory throughout the 1970s. Films such as *Alice Doesn't Live Here Anymore*, *Julia*, *The Turning Point*, and *An Unmarried Woman* expressed tensions between the emerging interests of the women's movements and more traditional notions of femininity. On prime-time television, social, economic, and political conditions combined to spawn a collection of amazingly paradoxical depictions. Beginning in 1970, the television industry's search for the upscale urban audience produced "socially conscious" or "socially relevant" programs that drew in large measure on the civil rights, black power, anti-war, and women's movements of the period.[8] Simply keeping its programming up to date might have led the industry to draw on the social ferment of the late 1960s and early 1970s for subject matter, but the push to attract specifically upscale urban audiences intensified the mining of thematic material that television executives thought would appeal to young, educated city-dwellers. Programs featuring working women, black women, older women, divorced women, single mothers, and working-class women suddenly filled the screen. *The Mary Tyler Moore Show*, *Rhoda*, *Alice*, *Good Times*, *The Jeffersons*, *Maude*, *One Day at a Time*, and *All in the Family* are prominent examples of the new fare. However, as scholars such as Lauren Rabinovitz and Serafina Bathrick have pointed out, these programs often produced contradictory representations of women.[9]

Beginning in the mid-1970s and continuing until the end of the decade, different industry and social conditions combined once again to generate even more paradoxical female characters. This time, pressure on the industry to reduce incidents of televised violence led quite directly to the display of women's bodies as sexual attractions. "If you can't have Starsky pull a gun and fire it fifty times a day on promos," said Brandon Tartikoff (at the time vice president of NBC's programming), "sex becomes your next best handle."[10] Prior to this period, images of women on television were not charged with the sexual spectacle of motion picture imagery; instead, female television characters were domesticated. From the mid-1970s to the early 1980s, however, female sex objects populated the television landscape in what is often called the "jiggle" era, or in the industry's non-euphemistic tag, the "T&A" (for "tits and ass") period. It is, of course, no accident that these representations coincided with a time of mounting backlash over the concerns and demands of the women's movements. One of the major paradoxes of this period, however, is that women starred in more dramatic programs than at any other time in television history. Series such as *Police Woman*, *Get Christie Love*, *Charlie's Angels*, *Wonder Woman*, *Flying High*, and *American Girls* are major legacies of the time.

Cagney and Lacey's first script was conceived in 1974 squarely within the conceptual terms of the liberal women's movement: it featured role reversals, that is, women in a traditionally male profession, and women in a standard male public-sphere genre. Historically and industrially speaking, its creators considered it an idea whose time had come.[11] According to Barbara Avedon, Barbara Corday, and Barney Rosenzweig, *Cagney and Lacey* was specifically conceived as a response to an early and influential book from the women's movement, Molly Haskell's *From Reverence to Rape: The Treatment of Women in the Movies*. Avedon and Corday were engaged in the literature and politics of the early women's movement, and both were in women's groups. Rosenzweig was "setting out to have his consciousness raised."[12] They read Haskell's book and were intrigued by the fact that there had never been a Hollywood movie about two women "buddies" comparable to *M*A*S*H* or *Butch Cassidy and the Sundance Kid*.[13] According to Rosenzweig:

> The Hollywood establishment had totally refused women those friendships, the closest thing being perhaps Joan Crawford and Eve Arden in *Mildred Pierce*, the tough lady boss and her wise-cracking sidekick. So I went to my friend Ed Feldman, who was then head of Filmways (now Orion), and I said, "I want to do a picture where we turn around a conventional genre piece like *Freebie and The Bean* with its traditional male situations and make it into the first real hit feminist film."[14]

One of the main motivations behind *Cagney and Lacey* from its inception was the creators' notion that two women could, in fact, be represented as friends who worked and talked together, rather than as conventionally portrayed competitors. Both Avedon and Corday recall the ways in which the relationship between Cagney and Lacey was modeled (if somewhat unconsciously) on their own eight-year relationship as writing partners and friends.

Ed Feldman at Filmways was interested in the idea Rosenzweig had pitched to him, and he gave the seed money to hire Avedon and Corday as writers.[15] Barbara Avedon recalls that although Filmways was "excited" about the idea, they had difficulty understanding the view of women involved. They persisted in situating the characters in the film industry's terms of women as spectacles and sex objects. According to Avedon, "They [Filmways] told us things like, when [Cagney or Lacey] rips her shirt back and shows her badge to the guys, they can all stare [at her breasts]." "That," continued Avedon, "was the level of consciousness, even though they [Filmways] were doing a women-buddy movie."[16]

Avedon and Corday prepared for writing the script by spending ten days with New York policewomen. Avedon recalled, "The women cops we met were first and foremost cops. Unlike Angie Dickinson in *Police Woman* who'd powder her nose before she went out to make a bust, these women took themselves seriously as police officers."[17] Both Corday and Avedon were convinced that the only way for *Cagney and Lacey* to work was if they cast "strong, mature" women, with "senses of humor." They envisioned Sally Kellerman as Cagney and Paula Prentiss as Lacey.[18] Corday, Avedon, and Rosenzweig all felt that because they were dealing with potentially controversial "feminist" material, their film would have to be first and foremost "entertaining."[19] The original script, "Freeze," was a spoof in which *Cagney and Lacey* uncover the existence of The Godmother, the female intelligence behind a brothel where men are the prostitutes and women the patrons.[20] Again, the major narrative device was the early women's movement's notion of role reversals.

After getting the script financed by Filmways, Rosenzweig needed a major motion picture studio to pick it up and do the actual production. He took the original property to every studio in Hollywood and got predictably "Hollywood" responses, such as "these women aren't soft enough, aren't feminine enough."[21] At MGM, Sherry Lansing (who was later to become the first woman head of a major motion picture studio, Twentieth Century Fox) persuaded her boss, Dan Melnik, to make the movie. MGM said it would but only if well-known "sex symbols" Raquel Welch and Ann-Margret starred. (Welch and Ann-

Margret had not yet demonstrated their true versatility as actresses at this point in Hollywood history.) The other stipulation was a 1.6-million-dollar budget which, in a kind of Catch-22 fashion, prohibited the hiring of such high-priced actresses.[22] The property, therefore, lay dormant for the next five years.

In 1980, Rosenzweig decided to have another go at it. This time, he took it to the television networks as a pilot for a weekly series. Corday and Avedon reconceived the script to update it and make it less of a spoof and more of a "realistic" crime drama.[23] Although CBS would not pick up *Cagney and Lacey* as a series, it decided it would take it as a less costly, less risky, made-for-TV movie, and it also suggested that Rosenzweig cast "two sexy young actresses."[24] According to Rosenzweig, he told CBS:

> You don't understand, these policewomen must be mature women. One has a family and kids, the other is a committed career officer. What separates this project from *Charlie's Angels* is that Cagney and Lacey are women; they're not girls and they're certainly not objects.[25]

During this impasse, CBS, which had an outstanding "pay-or-play" commitment to Loretta Swit of *M*A*S*H*, asked Rosenzweig to cast her as Cagney.[26] Avedon and Corday, who had recently worked with Sharon Gless on the TV series *Turnabout*, wanted her for the part.[27] Avedon said she had actually considered Gless the model for Cagney while writing the new script.[28] Because Gless could not be released from her contract to Universal, Rosenzweig cast Swit as Cagney, even though her contract with *M*A*S*H* would preclude her availability should an opportunity to turn *Cagney and Lacey* into a series arise. He cast Tyne Daly as Lacey. The movie was scheduled for broadcast on October 8, 1981, and was publicized in various ways by the women's movement, the television industry, and the mainstream press.

The pre-production publicity represented Cagney and Lacey as important for the causes of the women's movement. Gloria Steinem at *Ms* magazine had been sent a script by the creators and was so enthusiastic that she appeared with Loretta Swit on the *Phil Donahue Show* to plug the movie. According to one media critic, they were so "reverential" it "sounded as though they were promoting the first woman president."[29] Steinem also featured Loretta Swit and Tyne Daly, in police uniforms as Cagney and Lacey, on the cover of the October issue of *Ms*.[30] The issue contained a feature article on *Cagney and Lacey* written by Marjorie Rosen, a well-known feminist film critic and author of *Popcorn Venus: Women, Movies and the American Dream*. The article told the troubled history of the property, emphasized its importance for feminism, underscored specific feminist characteristics it saw Cagney and

Lacey as bringing into "distinctive focus," and ended with a pitch for a weekly series. The feminist characteristics especially applauded by *Ms* included women as the subjects of narrative action and adventure, as active in traditionally male-dominated genres and jobs, and as friends. Also emphasized were the notions of women as autonomous, individualistic, and independent.[31]

CBS's promotion department, with its own motivations and vested interests, publicized the movie according to a standard television industry advertising practice called "exploitation advertising." This is a practice, with precedents in the Hollywood film industry, in which a sensational (usually sexual or violent) aspect of a program is highlighted for the purposes of attracting audiences. In the *Cagney and Lacey* movie advertisement in *TV Guide*, a large close-up of Loretta Swit with long blonde hair dominates the left side of the composition, while her clasped, outstretched hands contain a pointed revolver, which dominates the right. A significantly smaller medium shot of the lesser-known (at the time) Tyne Daly in police coat, shirt, and tie is under the Swit close-up. On the far left of the page, under and smaller than the Daly image, is a shot of Swit lying on her back (presumably naked) with a sheet draped over her. One bare shoulder and arm, and one bare leg bent at the knee, are exposed. A man, depicted only from his waist up (also naked) is leaning over and on top of her, his arm across her body. The copy reads, "It's their first week as undercover cops! Cagney likes the excitement. Lacey cares about the people she protects. They're going to make it as detectives—or die trying."[32]

Various conceptions of women are set into play here, and it seems evident that the television industry, in dealing with a movie about women in non-traditional roles, is careful to invoke not only connotations regarding the "new woman" but also more traditional notions of femininity. Swit is shown as a cop with an aimed revolver but also as a conventionally beautiful woman with eye makeup, lipstick, and long blonde hair. She is also shown as a conventional object rather than subject of sexual desire. Lacey is shown in traditionally male clothing but is described in the conventionally feminine way of "caring about the people she protects." And although they are both trying to "make it" as detectives, they are also stereotypical "women in distress" who may "die trying." The emphasis on stereotyped feminine behaviors and predicaments in an ad for a movie about women in new roles fulfills the formula for exploitation advertising by suggesting sexual and dangerous content to the audience, while also reassuring the audience about women's traditional role and position in relation to social power.

The movie aired at 8:00 P.M. on Thursday, October 8, 1981, and captured an astonishing 42 share of the television audience (CBS had been getting a 28 or 29 share in this time period).[33] Within 36 hours, CBS was on the telephone to Barney Rosenzweig asking him to get a weekly program together.[34] Gloria Steinem and *Ms* magazine staff members had already lobbied members of the CBS board, urging them to make a series out of the movie.[35]

Controversial Representations of Women

The second phase of *Cagney and Lacey*'s history, the television series starring Tyne Daly and Meg Foster (as Swit's replacement for Cagney), was aired from March 25, 1982, to August 1982 (including summer reruns). This period coincides with that during which the network was most ardently courting an audience of working women. The massive entry of women into the labor force in the 1970s and 1980s produced what advertisers in the mid-1970s began to call the "new working women's market," a demographic group made up of American women in control of and spending their own disposable income. Other culture industries including magazines, movies, radio, and cable TV channels had pursued such women well before prime-time network television did, but in the late 1970s the three major networks began casting about for programs to attract them. The prime-time soaps (beginning with *Dallas* in 1978) and a series of made-for-TV movie melodramas were the first forms successful at capturing this new target audience. By the early 1980s, the television industry, having cloned and spun off a crop of prime-time soaps, was looking for other vehicles with which to do the same. The huge ratings success of the *Cagney and Lacey* made-for-TV movie seemed to indicate that women-oriented programming that drew on feminist discourses and subject matter was a good bet. Such a hunch, in the midst of the Reagan years' backlash against the women's movements, only intensified the contestatory nature of the negotiations surrounding the production and reception of female television characters at the time.

The first *Cagney and Lacey* series script was written by Barbara Avedon, Barbara Corday, and Barney Rosenzweig. Gloria Steinem and *Ms* magazine, keeping alive the link between the women's movement and the program, organized a reception for the stars and creators in early March.[36] The series was publicized by Filmways in press releases as "two top-notch female cops who fight crime while proving themselves to male colleagues."[37] The angle of women working in nontraditional jobs, in roles that called for rough physical action, and as fighting sexism was emphasized both in the industry's publicity for the series and the scripts.

The very night and hour *Cagney and Lacey* premiered, the series *9 to 5*, based on the hit movie of the same name (and dealing with secretaries agitating for better working conditions), premiered on the competing ABC network.[38] The fact that *Cagney and Lacey* and *9 to 5* were scheduled opposite one another would prove costly for both series in terms of ratings. Gloria Steinem, speaking at a Hollywood Radio and Television Society luncheon a month before the premieres, had protested this scheduling, saying it might "split the audience and hurt each other's [the two series'] chances."[39]

Of the thirty-five press reviews I read on the series' premiere, most were lukewarm or favorable. Most mentioned the feminist elements in the script: the exposure of "chauvinism" among the male detectives, Mary Beth and Harvey's role reversals, and the "juggling" of women's personal lives and careers.[40] Several articles said such things as "the show's message of female discrimination is too obvious and heavy-handed," and "the not-too-subtle message here is that women have to be twice as good to look equal with a man—a topic which could be the Achilles' heel of the series if pounded home too strongly."[41] Many also pointed out the difference between Cagney and Lacey and other female television characters. Such phrases as "no racy 'Charlie's Angels'-style glamour here," "mature women, not girls or sex objects," "not clothes horses à la Angie Dickinson," and "realistic crimebusting from the female perspective minus the giggle and jiggle," were common.[42] Other articles commented with impunity on the women's bodies, appraising them with regard to conventional television notions of glamour. "Ms. Daly," one of the articles reads, "has a plain face, a schlumpy figure, a thick Eastern accent. She's not sexy on the outside. . . . Meg Foster is the better looking but far more of a tomboy than a sex symbol."[43] Another reads, "While Foster and Daly are attractive, they look and act ordinary enough to be believable. . . . They are even occasionally permitted to look rumpled, discouraged, crabby."[44] And again:

> Past shows have had one token woman—with the exception of
> "Charlie's Angels," which featured a team of Wonder Women dressed
> and coifed from Rodeo Drive rather than DC Comics. Cagney and
> Lacey, on the other hand, are cops. They look like real people. They
> are cute rather than beautiful.[45]

For the next full year, such running commentary on the bodies of the two characters was standard in many articles on the series. The practice demonstrates several things. First, the critics perceived a difference between Cagney and Lacey and other television representations of women on the level of the body. This difference, of course, is produced through the televisual technique of *mise en scène* and relates to the characters' hairstyle, makeup, clothing, gestures, and mannerisms.[46] However, the critical commentary evidences a tendency to halt the play of difference with regard to representations of women. By focusing on the bodies of the women represented, the critics reproduced a traditional way of assessing the value of women and thus worked (at least in part and in many instances despite themselves) to *contain* the difference set into play by *Cagney and Lacey*. Women in this commentary become identified with, and to some degree limited to, their bodies. The phenomenon demonstrates how difficult it is for women to escape being "pinned to" their biological difference, or to exceed the conventional equation of women with sex or sex object. It also demonstrates the presumed access to women's bodies and the license to discuss and evaluate them that television, film, and photographic representations have helped to routinize.

Despite the favorable press, and without much consideration for the fact that it was scheduled in competition with *9 to 5*, the network wanted to cancel *Cagney and Lacey* after two episodes.[47] In fact, CBS did not allocate advertising money to promote the series' third episode in *TV Guide* (*9 to 5* had a half-page ad).[48] There is no doubt that the first episodes of *Cagney and Lacey* were a ratings disappointment to the network and were responsible for losing the large lead-in audience attracted by *Magnum P.I.*, the program that immediately preceded it.[49]

The show would have been canceled abruptly had not Rosenzweig persuaded Harvey Shephard, vice president in charge of programming for CBS, to give *Cagney and Lacey* a *Trapper John* rerun spot on Sunday, April 25, at 10:00 PM. Rosenzweig argued that *Cagney and Lacey* was an adult program that required a time slot later than 9:00 PM.[50] Shephard reluctantly agreed, but once again voiced CBS's ambivalence by telling Rosenzweig to "save his money" when Rosenzweig told him that Filmways planned to spend $25,000 on new publicity.[51] However, Filmways did take the financial risk, sending Foster and Daly on a cross-country tour. In a one-week campaign, organized by the Brocato and Kelman public relations company, Daly and Foster traveled to major urban areas and gave approximately fifty radio, television, and print interviews, including a Washington, D.C., television talk show interview with Tyne Daly and Betty Friedan "on the topic of women's rights."[52]

The Sunday, April 25, episode of *Cagney and Lacey* pulled in an impressive 34 share and ranked 7 in the overall ratings. Despite the success, Harvey Shephard told Rosenzweig that many members of the CBS board (responsible for the final renewal decisions) would consider the 34 share "a fluke."[53] He said he would fight for the series' renewal only if Rosenzweig made a significant change in the program. The change was to replace Meg Foster.[54]

At this point in the history of *Cagney and Lacey*, a number of factors influencing CBS's ambivalence about the program began to emerge. These factors are directly related to notions of femininity generated by the series and seem to be the most salient in CBS's hesitation. In a *Daily Variety* article on May 25, 1982, and a *Hollywood Reporter* article on May 28, Harvey Shephard spoke publicly about Foster's replacement. Shephard was quoted in both articles as saying that "several mistakes were made with the show in that the stories were too gritty, the characterizations of both Cagney and Lacey were too tough and there was not enough contrast between these two partners."[55] Several weeks after the statements appeared, an article in *TV Guide* revealed yet other factors behind CBS's ambivalence and its decision to replace Foster. According to critic Frank Swertlow, *Cagney and Lacey* was to be "softened" because CBS believed the main characters were "too tough, too hard and not feminine." The article quoted an unnamed CBS programmer who said the show was being revised to make the characters "less aggressive." "They were too harshly women's lib," he continued. "These women on 'Cagney and Lacey' seemed more intent on fighting the system than doing police work. We perceived them as dykes."[56]

It would appear that the association of *Cagney and Lacey* with the "masculine woman" and with lesbianism gave CBS a way in which to think about and cast its objections to the unconventional and apparently threatening representations of women on the series. This would explain why CBS rushed to cancel the program and remove Foster. It would also explain why the network gave such importance to the comments it may have picked up in the audience research rather than, for instance, to the positive comments in the press reviews cited earlier.

New and expanded representations of women could not, apparently, include even a hint of lesbianism. This, of course, must be situated within the history of lesbianism's representation on prime time, but space permits only a few comments. During the 1970s quest for "relevance" and socially "hip" subject matter, several programs featured episodes about lesbians, including *All in the Family*. Likewise, into the 1980s, prime-time programs such as *Kate and Allie*, *Hotel*, *Hill Street Blues*, *St. Elsewhere*, and *The Golden Girls* included lesbianism as a single-episode storyline, and the daytime serial *All My Children* had an ongoing lesbian character for several weeks in 1983. By the late 1980s,

Heartbeat featured an ongoing lesbian character whose inclusion was instrumental in the show's cancellation by ABC after protests from religious groups. The main point to be made here is that each of these "liberal" representations of lesbianism, in one way or other and to varying degrees (*Heartbeat* and *All My Children* trying to downplay this facet), underscore the "social problem" aspect of lesbianism and play off the notion that lesbianism is an "aberration."[57] That viewers would interpret the relationship between Cagney and Lacey as having lesbian overtones, or that two strong women characters would be perceived as "dykey" without the accompanying suggestion that "dykeyness" was considered a deviation from the norm, was something the television industry simply could not permit. Indeed, this stretched the limits of difference regarding the representation of women well beyond the boundaries of television's permissible zone.

CBS's official explanation of Meg Foster's removal from the show was that audience research had discovered objections to the characters. According to Arnold Becker, chief of research for CBS, audience research drawn from a sample of 160 persons had picked up such comments on *Cagney and Lacey* as "inordinately abrasive, loud and lacking warmth" and "they should be given a measure of traditional female appeal, especially Chris."[58] However, Becker also gave his own (not based on audience research) opinion about the characters: "Even in the first show," he said, "when they [Cagney and Lacey] dressed like hookers, they weren't sexy looking—they were sort of like burlesque." And, "There's a certain amount of resistance to women being in male-oriented jobs. I think it's fair to say, in light of what has happened to ERA, that most people favor equal pay for equal work, but not women as truck drivers or ditch diggers or that sort of male work." He added that the allusion "to homosexuality" in *TV Guide* was "quite unfair." "Those tested," he said, "thought of Cagney and Lacey as masculine, not that they were lovers."[59]

The differential treatment given to the characters and the actresses during this incident demonstrates some of the specific dimensions of the network's anxiety. The *TV Guide* article says the *married* character played by Tyne Daly was being kept because CBS considered her "less threatening." Conversely, CBS thought that the original Chris Cagney's non-glamorous, feminist, sexually active image and her working-class and single status manifested too many "non-feminine" traits. She also had no acceptable class, family, or marriage context that could contain, domesticate, or "make safe" those threatening differences.

The press and viewer response to the changes in the series and the firing of Meg Foster generated significant public discussion and debate

over the meanings of "femininity" (and "masculinity"). These definitions touched on many dimensions of *mise en scène:* the characters'
clothing, hairstyles, facial mannerisms, and the use of props such as
cigarettes. The debates consistently referred to femininity and women's
bodies in the social world beyond the domain of the television
characters.

Howard Rosenberg of the *Los Angeles Times* began a satiric column
on many of the issues raised by the incident, with the questions "What
is feminine? What is masculine? What is CBS doing?" He then asked,
"Are the old Cagney and Lacey too strident? Even too masculine?" He
continued, "For the definitive answer, I contacted Detective Helen Kidder and Detective Peggy York, partners in the Los Angeles Police
Department." He quoted Kidder as saying:

> I watched the show once and I was so turned off. They looked rough
> and tough, and they weren't terribly feminine, just in the way they
> dressed and acted. They were so, you know, New York. . . . Peggy
> and I wear good suits, nylons and pretty shoes, silk blouses, the hair,
> everything. Not that that keeps you from being a dyke.

Rosenberg concluded with his own analysis of the characters:

> Although Cagney is the character to be softened, Lacey seemed to be
> far the toughest of the two. . . . Many of the symbols were conflict-
> ing, however. Cagney frequently spoke admiringly of men, which
> was good, but wore slacks more than Lacey did, which was suspi-
> cious. Yet, Cagney had pink bed sheets and longer and curlier hair
> than Lacey. . . . In Lacey's favor, there was a scene in which she
> sank amorously into bed with Hawvey [*sic*] and another in which she
> cooked breakfast for the family. Good signs. Yet she also dangled a
> cigarette from her mouth like Bogie. Cagney always drove, and Lacey
> didn't, which could mean something. But Lacey talked without mov-
> ing her mouth. Lacey convinced me, however, when she took off her
> skirt in one sequence, she was wearing a slip, not boxer shorts.[60]

Rosenberg's column was one among many that appeared after the
removal of Meg Foster, and numerous women reporters vented their
outrage. Sharon Rosenthal of the *New York Daily News* wrote, "Not
feminine enough? By whose standards? I wondered. Wasn't the whole
point of the show to portray women on television in a new, more en-
lightened manner?"[61] And Barbara Holsopple of the *Pittsburgh Press,*
in writing about what the network wanted for *Cagney and Lacey,* said,
"Not tough cops, mind you. Nice feminine, good ones. Those yo-yos
at the network were second-guessing us again."[62]

As Howard Rosenberg's interview with the Los Angeles policewomen indicates, it is plausible and even predictable that a portion of viewers would find Cagney and Lacey problematic, and some for the specific reasons mentioned by CBS. The viewer reaction in the letters I have seen, however, was critical of CBS.[63] A sample of *Cagney and Lacey* audience letters in Rosenzweig's files contains such remarks as, "The program *Cagney and Lacey* is being ruined. I have thoroughly enjoyed it: the actresses had good chemistry and I enjoyed seeing a tough female." Another viewer commented:

> I read in last week's *TV Guide* something about replacing Meg Foster for such reasons as she is too threatening? I don't understand where TV executives come up with such craziness. I get the feeling there's a card game at the Hillcrest Country Club called "Let's go with the path of least resistance when it comes to women on TV." There seems to be a NEED for all women TV stars to be a carbon copy of Cheryl Ladd. Where's the female Al Pacino? Where's the female Bobby de Niro?

Still another viewer stated, "Foster and Daly did a marvelous job of portraying strong, confident women living through some trying and testing circumstances. Too strong? Too aggressive? Come on! They are cops in the city. They aren't supposed to be fragile, delicate wimps." And a final one from England: "The excuse that Cagney and Lacey are too butch is pathetic. A policewoman in America let alone Britain not butch enough wouldn't last in the public streets."[64]

Two months after the removal of Meg Foster, CBS may have, in the words of one reviewer, "shuddered a little" when a previously unaired Meg Foster/Tyne Daly episode, which was broadcast on June 21, scored a 38 share and ranked number 2 in the overall ratings.[65] However, the network continued to manifest its caution and discomfort regarding potentially controversial representations of women when it pulled the other new Foster/Daly episode scheduled for June 28 from the lineup a few hours before air time. The network said it had received phone calls and letters protesting the episode, which was about a Phyllis Schlafly-type anti-ERA spokesperson whom Cagney and Lacey were assigned to protect.[66] Even though the attempt to move the Equal Rights Amendment into the constitution had already failed, CBS decided to avoid controversy, pull the episode and air it later in August. The network, furthermore, had asked Rosenzweig not to invite Gloria Steinem to appear on the episode as he had originally intended.[67] In the two *TV Guide* advertisements for these June episodes, a considerable "feminization" of the images of Daly and Foster is evident—especially when compared to the previous *TV Guide* advertisements for the series.

Bringing Women Back in Line

CBS's ultimate decision on Cagney and Lacey was that the series should be revised to "combine competency with an element of sensuality."[68] Its solution was twofold: to replace Meg Foster with someone more "feminine" (Sharon Gless) and to change Chris Cagney's socio-economic background.[69] The Gay Media Task Force, in light of the allegations that the original characters were "too masculine," protested the replacement, saying that Gless's acting was "very kittenish and feminine."[70]

Instead of being from the working class, Cagney would now have been raised by a wealthy Westchester mother and grandmother. Her father, a retired New York policeman who had already been featured in the series, would be the divorced husband of that mother, and the marriage a cross-class mistake. A new CBS press kit was issued to publicize the series in a different way. "Cagney and Lacey," it read, "are two cops who have earned the respect of their male counterparts and at no expense to their femininity."[71]

Furthermore, after the Meg Foster episodes, Cagney underwent a radical fashion change to accompany her class transformation. A network memo stated that "the new budget will include an additional $15,000 for wardrobe costs, the revised concept for character calls for Cagney to wear less middle-class, classier clothes so that her upward mobility is evidenced."[72] This revision must also be seen in relation to the history of television's skewed representations of class and to the advertising industry's decision, at this time, to target the upscale professional segment of the working women's market.[73]

The new Chris Cagney was more of a rugged individualist than a feminist and was actually conservative on many social issues. Lacey espoused most of the feminism and liberal politics. A CBS promo for the 1982–1983 season made these new differences between the characters explicit and also foregrounded Cagney's heterosexuality. The promo ran like this:

MARY BETH: Ya know Chris, there've been some great women in the 20th century.
CHRIS: Yeah! And some great men (dreamily).
MARY BETH: Susan B. Anthony!
CHRIS: Jim Palmer!
MARY BETH: Madame Curie. . .
CHRIS: Joe Montana. . . ooo can he make a pass!
MARY BETH: (lightly annoyed with Chris) Amelia Airhart! [sic]
CHRIS: The New York Yankees!
MARY BETH: Chris, can't you think about anything else than men?[74]

Struggling over Femininity: The Press and the Viewers

The new and revised *Cagney and Lacey* with Sharon Gless and Tyne Daly began in the fall of 1982 and generated a good deal of attention and enthusiasm in the press. This revised program makes the most sense when seen in the context of the overall changes in the new television programs directed toward working women and drawing on feminism, and in the context of a backlash against the women's movements. During this same period, the program *9 to 5*, with Jane Fonda as executive co-producer, endured revisions that led to an episode in which the once-politicized secretaries spent much of the program dressed in negligées. *Remington Steele*, about a woman running her own detective agency, underwent changes in which the lead female character became considerably less aggressive and much more traditionally feminine in her relationship with the male character.[75]

The mainstream press, in commenting on the first season of the Gless/Daly *Cagney and Lacey*, focused on the "changes" from the previous run. Many wrote of the general "softening" and "feminization" of the program. For example, one critic noticed that "the entire show this season appears less gritty than last year's style," while another remarked, "some of the rougher, tougher edges are gone."[76]

A large number of articles appeared in response to Gless's replacement of Foster and the feminization of the program. They read like a semiotic register of the word "feminine," and function (not always intentionally) to problematize its various meanings. Many singled out specific elements such as clothing, hairstyles, makeup, voice qualities, body movements, personality traits, and behaviors as evidence for the presence or absence of "femininity," while some also wrote of the unconventional, potentially problematic character of Gless's and Cagney's "femininity." Carol Wyman of the *New Haven Register* said of Gless/Cagney, "She's one of those people who is very pretty, and at the same time a jock, the kind of person who ruins her good stockings to chase a crook, talks loud when she gets drunk and gets impatient with a woman witness who cries too much."[77]

Some articles that commented on the "feminization" also wrote of the changes in the relationship between the characters and the innuendos of lesbianism:

> Miss Daly's tomboy quality was balanced by the introduction of a partner with more feminine characteristics than her original co-star. . . . This second-season rematch [is] perhaps more compatible with the network's definition of a conventional female relationship. . . [but] who cares if a cop is gay or not as long as he or she shoots straight.[78]

Judging from audience letters, viewers were at first reluctant to accept Gless, but within two months a large and avid following began to develop. An exemplary letter from a woman who had been angered by Meg Foster's removal reads:

> I thought Meg Foster and Tyne Daly were a great combination, but apparently some "genius" of the male persuasion, obviously, decided that Meg Foster wasn't "feminine" enough. My Gawd, should cops wear aprons and be pregnant? Gimme a break! However, *Lady* Luck was with you when you found Sharon Gless. I must admit that you did something right by putting her in the Cagney role. . . . She's extremely feminine with just the right amount of "butch" to strike a very appealing balance.[79]

An irony in the history of the series, and a strong testament to the operation of multiple and contradictory viewer interpretations, is that Sharon Gless (according to published articles and viewer letters) had a large lesbian following at the time of the series' first run and now in reruns.[80] And this audience interpreted the Cagney character according to a variety of unpredictable and unconventional viewing strategies. When seen in relation to the viewer response letters surrounding the removal of Meg Foster and the press comments on the appeal of the friendship between Cagney and Lacey, this development demonstrates the ways in which the television industry's investments in particular notions of "femininity" and at least certain viewer investments can be at odds. The potential homoerotic overtones in the representation of the two women that formed the basis for the network's discomfort were, in fact, the bases of certain viewers' pleasure. There was, of course, a continuum of response ranging from viewers who responded pleasurably to the fictional representation of a close friendship between Cagney and Lacey to those whose viewing strategies purposely highlighted the homoerotic overtones in the relationship.

After the initial run of articles on the "feminization" of the characters and the series, a wide array of feminist-oriented pieces highlighting the importance of *Cagney and Lacey* to women appeared in mainstream newspapers. The series was hailed as "pioneering the serious role of women on TV" and "helping to break new TV ground."[81] Many of these articles emphasized the notion that Cagney and Lacey, unlike previous television characters, portrayed "real women." Despite this critical acclaim the first season of the Gless/Daly *Cagney and Lacey* did not do well in the overall ratings and did only marginally well with a women-only target audience. Its competition during much of the season was female-oriented prime-time movies. Consequently, CBS put *Cagney and Lacey* on its cancellation list. In an effort to save the series,

Barney Rosenzweig coordinated a large letter-writing campaign in which CBS and major newspapers throughout the country were deluged with thousands of viewer letters protesting the impending cancellation.[82] The Los Angeles chapter of the National Organization for Women and National NOW publicized the campaign and urged their members to write. According to state delegate Jerilyn Stapleton, the Los Angeles chapter had only two goals for the period: to get Ronald Reagan out of office and to keep *Cagney and Lacey* on the prime-time schedule.[83]

Virtually all the letters mentioned the uniqueness of *Cagney and Lacey*'s representation of women and the relationship between the two characters. The writers repeatedly suggested that Cagney and Lacey were good "role models" for women and girls; that they were unique because they were "real" and "different from all previous TV portrayals of women"; and that they were extremely important to the culture, to the individual writers, and to the writers' friends and families. Almost all related *Cagney and Lacey*'s depictions of women to their own everyday lives, the writers often placing themselves in a particular social situation and at a specific point on the "feminism spectrum." Phrases such as, "I'm a thirty-three year old nursing administrator," a "single working mother," a "married woman and mother who works inside the home," "a feminist" or "not a women's libber—just a concerned woman" appeared often. Many of the letters reverberated with discourses stemming from the liberal women's movement and demonstrated the workings of an "interpretive community" or a "community of heightened consciousness" described in the work of such feminist scholars as Elizabeth Ellsworth and Jacqueline Bobo.[84] They also displayed many specific ways in which the women letter writers were reconfiguring and redefining their notions of what it means to be a woman.

Repeatedly, writers said such things as "It's good to see smart, functioning, strong women"; "It's a pleasure to see women in such active roles"; "It's one of the few programs that neither glamorizes nor degrades women"; and "At last women are being portrayed as three-dimensional human beings." There were numerous long letters describing the particular significance of the series to the writer. One viewer wrote:

> My office alone contains six technical editors, RABID fans of "Cagney and Lacey." We're all highly paid, well-educated women in our forties with very different life-styles. Since we are "specialists" and work very closely with each other, each of us regards the others as "extended family," and we nurture and support each other in the best ways possible. We enjoy "Cagney and Lacey" because it contains so many moments that ring familiar in a woman's daily life. We see our-

selves in it so often, even though OUR jobs are unbelievably unexciting. It's gotten so that Tuesday mornings are spent hashing over Monday night's episode. We're really addicted.

Another said:

It's such an exciting show from a woman's point of view. Watching those two women makes one realize how much more attractive we are as women when we dare to be all our possible dimensions rather than the stereotypical images we have been taught to be and continually see on the screen. You have affected some of us profoundly.

The relationship between the two actresses and characters and its effect on the viewers were written about with equal enthusiasm. The actresses, Tyne Daly and Sharon Gless, were described as a "superb combination," a "winning team," who "together have great charisma" and "natural and genuine chemistry." "The vivid interaction of Chris and Mary Beth," wrote one viewer, "has actually made honest female relationships into major dramatic entertainment." Another claimed, "In the final analysis, it was the friendship between the two lead characters wherein lay the show's strongest appeal for me."

Despite the volume of viewer mail, and despite the fact that it primarily came from the desired target audience (upscale working women between the ages of 18 and 54), the series was canceled in the spring of 1983. However, several factors combined to cause CBS to reverse its decision and bring it back on the air. First, people continued to send letters. Second, after cancellation, *Cagney and Lacey* received four Emmy nominations, and Tyne Daly won an Emmy for best dramatic actress. Third, *Cagney and Lacey* scored number one in the ratings for the first week of summer reruns and remained in the top ten throughout the period. Nonetheless, CBS hedged its bets by reinstating the series with a very limited seven-episode trial run.

The Struggle Continues: The Production Team, the Network, and Interest Groups

The period of *Cagney and Lacey*'s history that begins with the reinstated Gless/Daly series in the spring of 1984 reveals several industry trends occurring at the time. With regard to television's portrayal of feminism, the period was characterized by "mainstreaming." Hence, the radical edge of feminist issues was tempered and channeled into character traits and behaviors. In addition, the meaning of feminism itself was becoming increasingly ambiguous so that programs offered "something for everyone" to fulfill many different viewers' political po-

sitions and interpretations. Terry Louise Fisher, a producer/writer for
Cagney and Lacey, described this as a move from political issues to "entertainment value."[85] During this period, some of the key players on
Cagney and Lacey's production team, particularly Barney Rosenzweig,
began to think more in industry terms and less in women's movement
terms when it came to portraying the characters. This resulted in dis-
putes among the production team members over the representations of
Cagney's and Lacey's hairstyles, makeup, and clothing. Determined to
get the series renewed beyond the limited seven episodes, Rosenzweig
called for a general upgrading of the style and "looks" of the two
characters.[86] He wanted a renovation of the Cagney "look" to include
more "stylish," "glamorous" outfits, and a new hairstyle that would
"move" and "bounce."

For several months, Rosenzweig had wanted to change Lacey's
wardrobe and hairstyle. Tyne Daly, who had designed the Mary Beth
Lacey "look" by shopping with wardrobe designer Judy Sabel in the
sale and basement sections of New York department stores, continually refused to change the character's plain, eccentric style.[87] Battles over
Lacey's hair were also frequent occurrences on the set. Rosenzweig
would ask Daly's hairdresser to get to her between takes and tease and
spray her hair.[88] During one such incident, Daly shouted to the crew
and staff, "Can anyone tell me why my producer wants me to look like
Pat Nixon?"[89]

During this period, there were also negotiations and struggles over
the representation of female characters at the level of script development. An episode involving Cagney's pregnancy scare (the last of the
seven trial episodes in May 1984) is a powerful example. The negotiations revolved around how to represent a single woman, an unmarried
woman's pregnancy, the topic of working women and childbearing,
and the issues of contraception and abortion. A synopsis from my personal observation and notes gathered during producer-writer meetings
in February and March of 1984 reveals some of the actual processes
involved.

Conceived by Terry Louise Fisher, the story originally dealt with
Cagney's discovery that she was pregnant. Fisher had struggled with
how to resolve the pregnancy. Knowing that the network would never
allow abortion as a possibility for Cagney, Fisher self-censored the consideration and was less than satisfied in resorting to the hackneyed mis-
carriage route. After working on the script, however, she felt it opened
up interesting possibilities. Tony Barr, an executive at CBS, rejected
the script, saying that the network did not "want to shine the spotlight
on pregnancy" and the problems of a pregnant unmarried woman. Barney Rosenzweig, Barbara Corday (creative consultant for the series),

Terry Louise Fisher (writer-producer), P.K. Knelman (co-producer), and Peter Lefcourt (writer-producer) discussed various options at a meeting. CBS had suggested that they turn the episode into a "biological clock" story in which Cagney is faced with the decision of whether or not she will ever have children. Fisher felt that the biological clock angle was not dramatically sound because it would offer no "resolution" or "closure." She asked Rosenzweig if he would fight for the original story with the network. But Corday wondered if they wanted to fight for it at this point, thinking it would be better to hold off and do it next season (if CBS were to renew the series) in, for instance, the fifth show so they could build up to Cagney being seriously involved with one person. Since the subplot of the script involved the officers at the precinct preparing for the sergeant's exam, and since attaining the rank of sergeant was one of Cagney's immediate ambitions, Lefcourt suggested that the issue revolve around a "my job or having a baby kind of choice." Fisher said she refused to do that to working women: "It sounds too much like waiting for Prince Charming" to come. Lefcourt agreed, "You're right, the Cinderella story."

Finally, Rosenzweig suggested they leave the first act exactly as it was—Cagney *thinks* she's pregnant. In actuality, however, she is not. Since the network had seemed so adamant about not focusing at all on pregnancy, Rosenzweig immediately called Tony Barr with his compromise option. Barr agreed that Cagney could *think* she was pregnant, but only on the condition that Lacey accuse her of being totally irresponsible. A long discussion on how they would cast Cagney's irresponsibility then followed. Someone wondered, "Should we say it was a night of passion?" Another suggested, "Cagney could say something like, 'I know it was my fault, I was acting like a teenager;' or 'Well, it happens, I mean the diaphragm is not foolproof.' " Rosenzweig objected that "as the father of four daughters, I don't want to put down the diaphragm." The other four agreed that it was the only "safe method for women's bodies," and they did not want to represent Cagney as "being on the pill."

In the final episode entitled "Biological Clock," Cagney thinks she is pregnant but is not, and Lacey is only mildly accusatory. There is no mention of specific birth control technologies or how the "mistake" might have happened. There is no mention of what Cagney would do if she were pregnant, although Lacey strongly pushes marriage. Cagney seems to be developing a relationship with the alleged baby, and abortion is never mentioned.

During this period, the producers and writers also talked about where, in general, to go with the Cagney character.[90] The discussions revolved around making Cagney a more "sympathetic" character.

They decided they would do this by making her more "committed" as a character, and this would be done by having her become seriously involved with one man. According to Terry Louise Fisher and Barbara Avedon the word "sympathetic" is industry jargon directed almost exclusively toward female characters and used to describe female roles that evoke "feminine" behavior and situations.[91] But the decision to make Cagney sympathetic by having her in a committed relationship with her boyfriend, Dory, was unpopular with viewers. One of the reporters on *60 Minutes* during the "letters-from-viewers" segment read a viewer letter that called for the removal of Dory from the *Cagney and Lacey* series.

During the 1984–1985 season, the Cagney character was once again associated with some conventionally feminist actions. In the episode in which she brings an end to her relationship with Dory, she overtly rejects (in a long conversation with Lacey) the institution of marriage. In other episodes, she files sexual harassment charges against a captain in the police department, urges Lacey to get a second opinion on a mastectomy, and consequently introduces the option of a lumpectomy. The season concludes with Cagney being the only one in her precinct to make the rank of sergeant, thereby emphasizing the importance of her career and her goal to become the first woman chief of detectives. With critical and industry acclaim, a more secure place in the ratings (at least with the target female audience) and the requisite changes in class and glamour, the network, it appears, became less skittish about the less conventional representations of women.

A number of episodes between 1984 and 1988, particularly those dealing with wife-beating, abortion, breast cancer, sexual harassment, date rape, and alcoholism, treated issues of enormous social importance to women and raised questions about the use of "exploitation topics" in programs for and about women.[92] These episodes both "cashed in on" and became part of intense public debates involving the institutional and social control over women's bodies and what women generally should and should not be. They also brought several social interest groups and institutions into the overall discursive struggle over defining what it meant to be a woman.

An episode about abortion, for example, broadcast November 11, 1985, became a central part of the ongoing public battles over the issue. Anti-abortion groups, led by the National Right to Life Committee (a group heavily invested in traditional definitions of women and their bodies), appealed to CBS to pull the episode, which centered on the bombing of an abortion clinic and the support by Cagney and Lacey (after considerable debate) of a woman's choice to have an abortion. The NRLC called the program a "piece of pure political propaganda."[93] After CBS said that they found the program to be "a fair and well-balanced view" and refused to pull it from the schedule, the NRLC asked CBS affiliates to black it out. If the affiliate did not want to black it out, NRLC asked it to offer to show a half-hour film of NRLC's choice (such as the anti-abortion film *Matter of Choice*) or to make available to NRLC a half-hour to "put some of our folks on to rebut this." If none of this worked, NLRC's next plan was to "call for a nationwide blackout of CBS during the balance of the month of November which is their rating month."[94]

Tyne Daly and Barney Rosenzweig flew to Washington, D.C., for a luncheon co-sponsored by the National Abortion Rights Action League and Orion Television to "counter [the] opposition" to the episode.[95] Daly said, "We feel we've done something very balanced. . . . I don't think I know a woman who hasn't struggled or knows someone who hasn't struggled with this issue."[96] Planned Parenthood also organized a press conference in New York on the episode, and NRLC President John Wilke and Barney Rosenzweig debated the issue on the *MacNeil/Lehrer News Hour*. To Wilke's charges that "this program is the most unbalanced, most unfair program we've seen in a number of years. . . . We did not hear a single right-to-life answer properly given," Rosenzweig replied:

> A year ago we had an episode in which Christine Cagney believed she was pregnant, and never once considered abortion as an alternative. I didn't hear from the National Organization for Women or the Voters for Choice then about banning the show or boycotting us. I just got some rather nice letters from the pro-life people.[97]

One CBS affiliate "pulled the show," while WOWT-TV in Omaha, Nebraska, agreed to offer equal time to NRLC.[98] After the broadcast, the political struggle continued: an anti-abortion spokesperson suggested that "any further violence at abortion clinics would be on CBS's conscience."[99] In an article in the *Washington Post*, Judy Mann praised the actions of CBS and the episode, and she said of television that "no other medium is as capable of dramatizing and educating the public about some of life's most difficult experiences."[100]

Closing Thoughts

Many more things, of course, can be said about women, television, and *Cagney and Lacey*. But the case I have outlined does raise some general points. First, as is obvious by now, television is a social institution and discursive practice which must be studied in all its complexity. On the one hand, it is, as Teresa de Lauretis (following Foucault) might say, a "technology of gender"—an apparatus that contributes to the social and cultural construction of femininity and masculinity that defines the possibilities of what it means to be a woman or a man.[101] On the other hand, as with any mass medium, it attracts diverse audiences who can interpret its texts in many different ways. As we have seen in *Cagney and Lacey*, different players in the overall television enterprise generate, and compete for, their own definitions of femininity according to their own investments and imaginations.

One of the most vexing issues for popular culture scholars at the present time involves the relationship of polysemy (or the multiplicity of meaning) to the limitations on meaning in texts produced by mainstream culture industries. From my point of view, television should be seen as a negotiation among the industry, the texts, and audience members.[102] But it is similarly apparent to me that we must acknowledge and analyze more thoroughly the many ways the television industry works to pin down meaning in particular and often predictable ways. This involves, among other things, attending to the ways in which the industry continues to depict women on the basis of its own institutional and advertising-based exigencies. Just as the 1970s quest for young, urban audiences led to a spate of "socially relevant" television programs and to the increased representation of black women, working-class women, and single mothers, the quest for the working women's market in the late 1970s and 1980s led to women-oriented programs and feminist subject matter in prime time. But as we have seen, when these representations deviated too much from the acceptable conventions of the industry, they were quickly brought back in line. Given the outpouring of letters about *Cagney and Lacey* from women viewers who were desperate for new representations, and the fact that *Cagney and Lacey* attracted so many working women to the prime-time screen, we might have expected the networks to be more adventurous in future programs, more eager to please female audiences. Although they have featured some female leads in dramatic programs since the mid-1980s (*Kay O'Brien*, *The Days and Nights of Molly Dodd*, *China Beach*, *Heartbeat*, *Nightingales*, and *The Trials of Rosie O'Neill*), many of which met with cancellation or controversy, the networks continued to channel women, and especially "transgressive" women (such as Roseanne and Murphy Brown) into situation comedies.

The case of *Cagney and Lacey* ultimately illuminates, I think, two major facets of a complex phenomenon: the specific ways television texts tend to "shut down" and limit the meanings of "woman," and the ways in which large numbers of viewers, voracious for innovative representations, continued throughout the history of the series and its changes to read the text for meanings that echoed and shored up their conceptions of themselves as "non-traditional" women. The fact, moreover, that many lesbian viewers continued to find homoerotic overtones in the program and continued to generate pleasure from active "misreadings" confirms that textual limits do not shut down audience interpretations. But, from my point of view, the production of oppositional or alternative readings is not, finally, enough. I am confident that those of us who spend time in front of television sets will always interpret programming in creative ways, always produce meanings that escape the confines of the text. I hope, however, we will also continue to analyze television texts and industry practices for the ways they contribute to constraining the representations of gender, sexuality, race, class, and ethnicity. And finally, I hope we continue to agitate for a greater representation of *difference* in all the mass media.

This seems particularly necessary in the current cultural retrenchment from feminism now manifest on our television screens. ABC, for example, canceled *Heartbeat* after religious watchdog groups protested its lesbian characters; and NBC, besieged by the same groups in early 1991, assured advertisers and the public that it had no intention of continuing a storyline on *L.A. Law* involving a possible love relationship between two women characters. Later in 1991, however, CBS (fearing it was losing viewers to less conservative cable channels) announced it would continue stories about its bisexual female character; and for the same reason, the Network Television Association (a trade group representing ABC, CBS, and NBC) urged marketers not to be "intimidated" by boycott organizations.[103] Faced with these developments, I see it as strategic to generate ways of intervening in the popular struggle over meanings. Although agitating for changes in television does not necessarily change the world, the alternative course of resignation leaves the outlook even more bleak. At the very least, it is important not to concede television and its representations to the discourses and energies of the New Right.

NOTES

1. For articles on the "ladies' night line-up" see Ella Taylor, "Ladies' Night: CBS's Monday Night Mystique," *Village Voice* (December 3, 1985), pp. 55–56; and Pat Dowell, "Ladies' Night," *American Film* (January–February 1985), pp. 44–49.
2. A quality audience is an audience made up of the exact demographic characteristics desired by the network for the particular time slot the program occupies. Upscale, working women between the ages of 23

and 54 were the desired demographics for Monday night prime time on CBS. For a discussion of quality audiences and "quality" programs see Jane Feuer, Paul Kerr, and Tise Vahimagi, eds., *MTM: "Quality Television"* (London: BFI, 1984).

3. Quoted in Karen Stabiner, "The Pregnant Detective," *New York Times Magazine* (September 22, 1985), p. 103. *Cagney and Lacey,* as audience letters and rating information demonstrate, also drew in many working women from a lower range on the economic spectrum.

4. At the conclusion of the *Cagney and Lacey* made-for-TV movie, Swit's Cagney appears as a "woman in distress" and is rescued by the squad (most of whom, with the exception of Lacey, are men). The representation of the protagonists as classic "women in distress," however, is absent from the Foster/Daly series. The Gless/Daly series does have a few sequences that feature "women in distress" figures. Lacey, for instance, is rescued from a high beam by Harvey, and Lacey is taken hostage. Mimi White, "Ideological Analysis and Television," *Channels of Discourse*, ed. Robert Allen (Chapel Hill: University of North Carolina Press, 1987), pp. 154–158 cites two instances in which Cagney is shown as "trapped" or "caged" by the framing and the *mise en scène*. White finds this problematic for the series' representation of women. By and large, however, the characters are not, I would maintain, regularly produced as the classic "women in distress" or in need of help from male colleagues.

5. These are the two terms used most often by the television networks to describe what they want in women characters. From Terry Louise Fisher and Barbara Avedon, personal interviews, February 1984, Los Angeles.

6. Michael Leahy and Wallis Annenberg, "Discrimination in Hollywood: How Bad Is It?" *TV Guide* (October 13–19, 1984), p. 14. According to Leahy and Annenberg, Orion TV hired women to write 37% of its projects.

7. The liberal women's movement had such an enormous effect on *Cagney and Lacey*'s production and reception that I want to clarify my conception of it here. In America, the movement is generally associated with *Ms* magazine, with Gloria Steinem and with the National Organization for Women. Its primary emphasis, especially in the 1970s and early 1980s, was on equality in the labor force, with a focus on white middle-class women, and its programs for social change were oriented toward reform rather than radical structural reorganization of American social and cultural life. Nonetheless, the movement was vigilant in keeping public attention on the material conditions of women's everyday lives, on women's solidarity, and on the importance of mass media to social change.

8. Jane Feuer, in "MTM Enterprises: An Overview," Feuer et al., pp. 1–28. Todd Gitlin, *Inside Prime Time* (New York: Pantheon, 1983), p. 266.

9. Serafina Bathrick, "*The Mary Tyler Moore Show*: Women at Home and at Work," in Feuer et al., pp. 99–131. Lauren Rabinovitz, "Sitcoms and Single Moms: Representations of Feminism on American TV," *Cinema Journal* 29:1 (Fall 1989), pp. 3–19.

10. Cited in Todd Gitlin, p. 72.

11. Barbara Corday, personal interview, February 1984, Los Angeles; Barney Rosenzweig, personal interview, October 1983, Los Angeles.

12. Barney Rosenzweig, personal interview.

13. Barbara Corday, personal interview; Barney Rosenzweig, personal interview.

14. Marjorie Rosen, "Cagney and Lacey," *Ms* 4 (October 1981), pp. 47–50, 109.

15. Rosen, p. 49; Barbara Corday, "Dialogue on Film," *American Film* 9 (July–August 1985), p. 12.

16. Barbara Avedon, personal interview.

17. Avedon quoted in Rosen, p. 49.

18. Barbara Corday, personal interview; Barbara Avedon, personal interview.

19. Barney Rosenzweig, personal interview; Rosen, p. 49.

20. Rosen, p. 49.

21. Rosen, p. 49.

22. Rosen, p. 49.

23. Rosen, p. 50.

24. Barney Rosenzweig, personal interview.

25. Rosen, p. 50.

26. Barney Rosenzweig, personal interview, October 1983.

27. Barbara Avedon, personal interview; Barbara Corday, personal interview.

28. Barbara Avedon, personal interview.

29. Sharon Rosenthal, "Cancellation of 'Cagney and Lacey' to Mean Loss of 'Rare' TV Series," *New York Daily News* (June 3, 1983), pp. 31, 35.

30. Barney Rosenzweig, personal interview; *Ms* 4 (October 1981), cover.

31. Some of these characteristics demonstrate the ways in which advertising definitions of women and the liberal women's movement definitions (particularly at this point in the history of the American women's movement) may be brought together without much trouble. Later in the 1980s, the liberal women's movement was more attentive to issues involving women of color, poor and working-class women, and lesbians, and it also recognized structural reasons for women's oppression which require more than personal solutions. In the early 1980s, however, the emphasis of the movement was most squarely on equality in the labor force, primarily for white, middle-class women.

32. *TV Guide* (October 3–10, 1981), p. A-137.

33. Richard Turner, "The Curious Case of the Lady Cops and the Shots That Blew Them Away," *TV Guide* 41 (October 8–14, 1983), p. 52.

34. Turner, p. 52.

35. *Soho News* (March 9, 1982), page unknown, from clipping file of Barney Rosenzweig, Los Angeles.

36. *Soho News* (March 9, 1982), page unknown, from clipping file of Barney Rosenzweig, Los Angeles.

37. Filmways News Release, "Meg Foster to Join Tyne Daly as CBS 'Cagney and Lacey' Duo," (1982), Barney Rosenzweig files.

38. Six months later, in the fall of 1982, three other working-women-oriented and women's movement-influenced programs, *Gloria*, *Remington Steele*, and *It Takes Two*, also joined the schedule.

39. Tom Bierbaum, "Steinem Takes Right Turn on TV Violence," *Daily Variety* (February 2, 1982), p. 25.

40. See, for example, Bowden's Information Service, "Tyne Daly Returns to Detective Role," *The Leader Post* (March 12, 1982), page unknown, from clipping file of Barney Rosenzweig.

41. Barbara Holsopple, "Two New Series on Women: All Work, No Play," *Pittsburgh Press* (March 25, 1982), page unknown, from clipping file of Barney Rosenzweig, Los Angeles.

42. Beverly Stephen, "Policewomen: TV Show on the Case," *Los Angeles Times* (April 11, 1982), page unknown, from clipping file of Barney Rosenzweig, Los Angeles; Bonnie Malleck, "Real Women at Last: Pinch-Hitter 'Cagney and Lacey' Is a Mid-Season Bonus," *Kitchner-Waterloo Record* (April 1982), page unknown, from clipping file of Barney Rosenzweig.

43. Ed Bark, "Ratings May Kill Quality Cop Show," *Dallas Texas Morning News* (April 1, 1982), page unknown, from clipping file of Barney Rosenzweig, Los Angeles.

44. Malleck, page unknown.

45. Bill Musselwhite, "No There's No Farm Raising Tiny Animals for Airlines," *Calgary Herald* (April 3, 1982), page unknown, from clipping file of Barney Rosenzweig, Los Angeles.

46. The technique of *mise en scène* includes, among other things, characters' body size, makeup, hairstyle, clothing or costume; character movement, gestures, mannerisms, and use of props. See David Bordwell and Kristin Thompson, *Film Art* (New York: Alfred A. Knopf, 1985), pp. 119–150.

47. Turner, p. 53; Barney Rosenzweig, personal interview.

48. *TV Guide* (April 3–10, 1982), pp. A-116–117.

49. *Magnum PI* was getting an average share of 38. When *Cagney and Lacey* aired it pulled in a 25 share the first week and 24 the second week. According to Rosenzweig, "At 9 o'clock all over America, 12 million people were getting up out of their seats *en masse* and walking away, or leaving the network." Cited in Turner, p. 53.

50. Turner, p. 53.

51. Turner, p. 53.

52. Brocato and Kelman, Inc., Public Relations, "Itinerary for Tyne Daly and Meg Foster" (April 27, 1982), Barney Rosenzweig files.

53. Turner, p. 54.
54. Turner, p. 54; Barney Rosenzweig, personal interview. After Meg Foster was released from her contract she had initial difficulty getting other work. According to a United Feature syndicate article (Dick Kleiner, "TV Scout Sketch #1: Cagney and Lacey Situation, The Story Behind Meg's Ouster," week of August 23, 1982), prior to that she "was an in-demand actress. But there was no official announcement of why she was fired, so people jumped to some pretty wild conclusions. . . . They want no part of a troublemaker." The article continues, "Later an official story came out and from then on Meg's offers picked up again." Rosenzweig says he tried to save Foster's job by suggesting to CBS that they dye her hair blonde (as a way of achieving character contrast with the brunette Daly). He admits, however, to giving in to the network rather quickly and making Foster the "scapegoat" in order to save the series. Barney Rosenzweig, personal interview, 1983, Los Angeles. As of this writing, Foster appears as a district attorney on *The Trials of Rosie O'Neil*, starring Sharon Gless and produced by Barney Rosenzweig.
55. Richard Hack, "TeleVisions," *The Hollywood Reporter* (May 28, 1982), p. 6; Dave Kaufman, "CBS Ent Prez Grant Asks Crix for Fair Chance," *Daily Variety* (May 25, 1982), p. 19.
56. Frank Swertlow, "CBS Alters 'Cagney' Calling it 'Too Women's Lib,' " *TV Guide* (June 12–18, 1982), p. A-1.
57. My point here is that even though the programs were presenting "positive" representations of lesbians, they highlighted the fact that lesbianism is considered socially "deviant" as the organizing principle of the story—the point of the humor or drama.
58. Howard Rosenberg, " 'Cagney and (Uh) Lacey,' a Question of a Pink Slip," *Los Angeles Times* (June 23, 1982), Calendar Section, p. 7.
59. Rosenberg, p. 7. It is possible, of course, that the research survey also inadvertently elicited particular responses from the viewers tested.
60. Rosenberg, pp. 1, 7.
61. Rosenthal, pp. 31, 35.
62. Barbara Holsopple, " 'Cagney and Lacey' Hanging by (Blond) Thread," *Pittsburgh Press* (November 19, 1982), p. B-38.
63. *TV Guide* printed a series of angry responses in its subsequent issue. *TV Guide* (June 10–16, 1982), p. A-4.
64. Viewer letters, 1982, Rosenzweig files.
65. Frank Torrez, "TV Ratings," *Los Angeles Herald Examiner* (July 2, 1983).
66. Sal Manna, "Sorry This Show Wasn't Seen," *Los Angeles Herald Examiner*, 1982, pp. B-1 and B-7, exact date unknown, from clipping file of Barney Rosenzweig, Los Angeles.
67. Manna, pp. B-1 and B-7. Steinem, due to an overcrowded schedule, had actually already declined.
68. Arnold Becker quoted in Rosenberg, p. 7.

69. John J. O'Connor, in speaking of the "new" Cagney, described Gless as "blond, single, [and] gorgeous in the imposing manner of Linda Evans on *Dynasty*." See his " 'Cagney and Lacey'—Indisputably a Class Act," *The New York Times* New Service to *The Patriot Ledger* (July 5, 1984), p. 42.

70. Tim Brooks and Earle Marsh, *The Complete Directory to Prime Time Network TV Shows: 1946–The Present* (New York: Ballantine Books, 1985), p. 136.

71. Rick Du Brow, "Cagney and Lacey Hang Tough," *Los Angeles Herald Examiner* (January 25, 1983), pp. C-1, C-4.

72. *Cagney and Lacey* offices, "Analysis of Costs for CBS for 'Cagney and Lacey,' " 1982, Rosenzweig files.

73. Since the mid-1950s advertisers made it clear that they did not want their products associated with lower-class characters and settings. See Eric Barnouw, *The Image Empire* (New York: Oxford University Press, 1970), pp. 5–8.

74. CBS Entertainment, Advertising and Promotion, "Program Promotion," 1982, Rosenzweig files.

75. Elaine Warren, "Where Are the Real Women on TV?" *Los Angeles Herald Examiner* (October 31, 1983), Section E, pp. 1, 10.

76. "Review," *Daily Variety* (October 28, 1982), p. 9.

77. Carol Wyman, " 'Cagney and Lacey' Has Grown," *New Haven Register* (February 24, 1983), page unknown, from clipping file of Barney Rosenzweig, Los Angeles.

78. Terrence O'Flaherty, "Women in the Line of Fire," *San Francisco Chronicle* (October 11, 1983), p. B-9.

79. Viewer letters from Barney Rosenzweig files, Los Angeles.

80. Barbara Grizzuti Harrison, "I Didn't Think I Was Pretty: An Interview with Sharon Gless," *Parade Magazine* (February 23, 1986), pp. 4–5.

81. Caption for cover photo of Tyne Daly and Sharon Gless, *Los Angeles Herald Examiner* (January 25, 1983).

82. I am quoting from a sample of 500 letters from this period which I arbitrarily pulled and duplicated from Barney Rosenzweig's files. The letters are written to Bud Grant (president of CBS entertainment), Barney Rosenzweig, Tyne Daly, Sharon Gless, and Orion Television. Since each letter was written to save the series from the network's ax, the sample is thoroughly biased in favor of the series and its representations. No critical letters or letters of complaint are present.

83. Jerilyn Stapelton, personal interview, February 1984, Los Angeles.

84. Elizabeth Ellsworth, "Illicit Pleasures: Feminist Spectators and *Personal Best*," in *Becoming Feminine*, ed. Leslie G. Roman, Linda K. Christian-Smith, and Elizabeth Ellsworth (Philadelphia: The Farmer Press, 1988), pp. 102–119. Jacqueline Bobo, "*The Color Purple*: Black Women as Cultural Readers," in *Female Spectators*, ed. E. Deidre Pribram (London and New York: Verso, 1988), pp. 90–108. This work draws on that of Stanley Fish, David Morley, and Charlotte Brunsdon.

85. Terry Louise Fisher, personal interview, February 1984, Los Angeles.

86. Barney Rosenzweig, personal interview, January 1984, Los Angeles.

87. Judy Sabel, personal interview, February 1984, Los Angeles.

88. Personal observation on the set of *Cagney and Lacey* and conversation with Eddie Barron, hairdresser for Tyne Daly, February 1984, Los Angeles.

89. Personal observation on the set of *Cagney and Lacey*, February 1984.

90. Personal notes, writer-producer meetings, January–March, 1984, Los Angeles.

91. Terry Louise Fisher, personal interview, January 1984, Los Angeles. Barbara Avedon, personal interview.

92. Exploitation topics use sensational, usually sexual or violent subject material in order to attract an audience.

93. "An Episode of 'Cagney' Under Fire on Abortion," *The New York Times* (November 11, 1985), page unknown, from files of Barney Rosenzweig, Los Angeles.

94. CBS vice president George Schweitzer, cited in Nancy Hellmich, "Daly Defends 'Cagney' Show on Abortion," *USA Today* (November 6, 1985), Section D, p. 1; John Wilke cited on *MacNeil/Lehrer News Hour*, PBS (November 8, 1985).

95. Hellmich, p. 1.

96. Hellmich, p. 1.

97. *MacNeil/Lehrer News Hour* (November 8, 1985).

98. Judy Mann, "Cagney and Lacey, and Abortion," *Washington Post* (November 15, 1985), page unknown, from files of Barney Rosenzweig, Los Angeles; Hellmich, p. 1.

99. Mann.

100. Mann.

101. Teresa de Lauretis, *Technologies of Gender* (Bloomington: Indiana University Press, 1987), pp. 1–30.

102. For more on industry (institution), text, and reception, see Christine Gledhill, "Pleasurable Negotiations," *Female Spectators: Looking at Film and Television* (London and New York: Verso, 1988), pp. 64–77.

103. See Kate Oberlander, "Network Group Hits Boycotts," *Electronic Media*, August 5, 1991, p. 4; and "TV News: New Emphasis on Gay Themes," *TV Guide*, August 17–23, 1991, pp. 25–26. In December 1991, *L.A. Law* featured its bisexual female character in an episode about her lesbian relationship.

Cagney and Lacey

Kate and Allie

Kate and Allie: "New Women" and the Audience's Television Archive
Robert H. Deming

Network television rediscovered the "new woman" *again* in the Fall 1984 season. Several prime-time programs featured female leads in take-charge roles rather than in their usual embourgeoised family roles. The reasons for this rediscovery have to do with the economic goals of the television industry. What this might mean to an audience whose memory extends back at least to *The Mary Tyler Moore Show* and subsequent new-woman programs is not as easy to describe. The project of this essay is to suggest that *Kate and Allie* participates in the displacement, containment and repression which fictions for women often undergo on television. What I find startling to discover in *Kate and Allie* is how the work of ideological, format, and female-character containment continues to be carried out through a proliferation of points of view, a scrambling of codes, and a multiplication of means whereby a spectator is given access to knowledge through a variety of contradictory social positions.

As several critics have recently demonstrated, television works to integrate oppositional and resistant forces, including feminist discourses, by absorbing and naturalizing them, usually into dominant definitions of the family melodrama and heterosexual romance.[1] While various television forms—serials, series, movies, etc.—attempt to express a centrist vision, they also acknowledge the existence of ideas and values which are not part of the dominant vision of things. Television packages oppositional values and repackages them within dominant terms. Yet these "preferred readings" (David Morley's and Stuart Hall's term) always exist within a context of potentially contradictory interpretations. Cultural forms like television are already constituted in ways that limit an audience's ability to appropriate them, but never totally so. The issue for criticism is how to describe the limits of these decodings and, when the text examined is a progressive and in many ways a feminist one like *Kate and Allie*, how to account for the particular critical problematic involved. If, then, there is a "new woman" out there to whom and for whom television wants to speak, how does a program like *Kate and Allie* construct and define forms of female subjectivity?

This essay will argue for the ways in which *Kate and Allie* constructs a form of female subjectivity which is constrained by the new-woman sit-com format, but at the same time, allows for the playing out of cultural and social contradictions. My suggestion is that there is a tension between (format/institutional) constraint and (historical/interpretive) play which allows for multiple points of audience entry and identification. This tension necessarily intersects with a plurality of ideologies and the heterogeneity of the audience's social world. *Kate and Allie* offers various types of involvement for its viewers because it is composed of numerous discourses, ideological propositions and modes of address, which together form a popular, at times progressive, but not necessarily feminist text.

Institutional/Industrial Objectives: The 1984 New Season

It is well recognized that the material practices of the television industry have ideological functions and that those functions cannot be eliminated simply by the subversive readings of audience members. But what did the industry set out to accomplish in the Fall 1984 season? Network executives and programmers were searching for new female audiences and assumed that the new-woman format provided an appropriate vehicle for the task. As Harvey Shepard, then CBS Senior Vice President, claimed, "there is a growing acceptance of the more liberated role of women."[2] This new programming direction is exemplified by the fact that women had leading roles in eight of the twenty-two new prime-time series that fall.[3] Network research had, apparently, discovered that there was a "new woman" out there that television might want to represent and address. That research supported the belief among producers and the creative community that competent dynamic women were needed to ensure a program's success. It also indicated that "women characters make sense for the networks' profitability."[4] After all, in the first weeks of Spring 1984, *Cagney and Lacey* received a respectable 20.9 rating and a 36 share, while *Kate and Allie* received a 21.9 rating and a 33 share. According to David F. Poltrack, CBS Vice President of Research, such programs did especially well among women between the ages of 25–54 in households with incomes of more than $30,000. In addition, a high number of upper-income viewers listed the characters from these two programs to be among their favorites. According to Poltrack's assumptions, only those from lower income households objected to strong women on TV.[5]

The new-woman sitcom's appeal was not limited to commercially-minded network officials. Reform groups embraced these programs for their positive depiction of women. Kathy Bonk, director of the Media Reform Project of the National Organization for Women Legal Defense

Fund, found a "half dozen shows that are nearly ideal for the portrayal of women."[6] In addition, the popular print media, with *TV Guide* leading the way, regularly featured (and continue to print) articles about the new-woman sit-coms. In February of 1985 *TV Guide* gave its "cheers" to the "upgrading of women in prime time this season" because the National Commission on Working Women found that female characters were approaching numerical parity with males (of 143 new characters in prime time that fall, 67 were women) and that 76% of adult females on television held jobs outside the home.[7] John J. O'Connor in his *New York Times* "TV View" column found that "women are getting more sympathetic reading" because "women on television do get to reflect some of the more profound cultural and social changes triggered by the various feminist movements of the past decade." He remarks that *Cagney and Lacey* and *Kate and Allie* inhabit a new terrain of the "woman of independence and ambition, the woman who copes with choices beyond the traditional limits."[8] Finally, Lauren Rabinovitz has recently noted that popular magazines aimed primarily at women, such as *Ms., Vogue, Teen, McCalls,* and *Working Woman,* cited various new-woman sit-coms (*Alice, One Day At a Time,* and *The Mary Tyler Moore Show*) as "exemplary representations of a feminist subject," with *Kate and Allie* being only the latest in a continuous line of such feminist depictions.

Not only did these media discourses applaud the new-woman sit-coms, they also gave female characters a life-like dimension outside of the text. Articles like "I'd Walk Through a Dark Alley with Cagney or Lacey Behind Me," "No Jiggles. No Scheming. Just Real Women as Friends," and "Are *Kate and Allie* Such Good Friends—Off Screen?" were published regularly in *TV Guide.*[10] Of course, this can be seen as the hype of television's promotional industries which try to gather an ever-larger audience for the programs and commercials. But there is another way to view this kind of material. Such articles contribute to what John Langer has called the "embourgeoisement of television's personality system" by making characters in television accessible in terms of the "ordinary" and the "everyday."[11] Such articles contribute to our further intimate and immediate social knowledge of Susan St. James and Jane Curtin. They provide us with a context through which we view the text. They help to make the women less exceptional, less star-like, more like our friends and family. They also tell us how to make sense of *Kate and Allie.*

In addition, publications like *TV Guide,* series like *Entertainment Tonight* and specials like *Don't Touch That Dial,* all give us "behind the scenes" knowledge. These sources create an awareness of the world of sound stages, sets, actresses, technicians; they tell us something about the television apparatus and its institution. This intertextual network forms another context for interpretation.[12]

Finally, industry practices concerning programming for women, both in the past (beginning with *The Mary Tyler Moore Show* in 1971) and in the 1984 season, follow changing demographics. As Serafina Bathrick notes, "between 1950 and 1970 the number of married women who worked doubled, and the percentage of women who made up the work force grew from 34% to 43%."[13] Ten years later, the 1980 Census revealed that only 7% of the 82 million households surveyed fit the traditional description of the typical family; 40.1% of all households contained single, divorced, or widowed individuals.[14] The goals of the television industry in 1984 seem to indicate that programming changed in some ways in order to keep pace with these shifting demographics. (However, many of the programs initiated in that year were cancelled.)

Given these institutional objectives and the enormous range of inter/ extra-textual materials available to the 1984 audience, can we say that the audience understood *Kate and Allie* as the industry wanted it to, as a representation of contemporary "new women"? On the one hand, *Kate and Allie* as a series (as opposed to a single episode) presents its audiences with a range of possible interpretations. This is the result of institutional encoding practices that supposedly ensure the construction of spectator positions which audience members can inhabit comfortably and agreeably, without opposition or resistance. This comes about because so much of the apparatus of *Kate and Allie* is familiar. Like other sit-coms, this program has a limited number of settings and characters, a particular narrative format, and a laugh-track which prompts the appropriate responses to the fiction. However, even if an audience accepts the reading positions offered by a text, it does not necessarily follow that the audience will accept the norms about the social world which are represented (or what David Morley calls the text's "ideological problematic"). Although the spectator may adopt the ideological position(s) inscribed by the text (so as to make sense of it), he/she need not subscribe to it. Still, it is important not to confuse this kind of interpretive play with the absolute "freedom to read oppositionally," for in many cases the range of freedom is limited. Like most other television programming, then, *Kate and Allie* reproduces hegemonic definitions of gender, sexuality, and the gendered patterns of its own consumption, but it also provides for opportunities to resist and subvert these constraints.

Identification and the Television Archive

What can we therefore say about a spectator's identification with these new-women programs, especially *Kate and Allie*? Meaning and pleasure are more likely to be produced in the contextual relationships between texts and their viewers than discovered in a text in isolation. Since, as we have already seen, we are given so much inter/extra-textual information, we can identify with *Kate and Allie* both as "real" people (as actresses) and as characters in the sit-com story. In a letter to the editor of *People Magazine*, one woman claimed that she thought of Cagney and Lacey as "real women [who are] playing characters who are real women." Other viewers see the same characters as housewives who live next door, or else they think the new-woman sit-coms address real problems facing contemporary women, problems like job stress, personal sacrifices and romantic relationships. It is not sufficient for the critic to say that these women are somehow confused or duped by television's conflation with real life. Instead, we need to take these interpretations seriously and to acknowledge that they form another kind of reading context for the series.

Furthermore, since we remember earlier new-woman sit-coms (e.g., *That Girl, The Mary Tyler Moore Show, Rhoda, Phyllis, Alice, One Day at a Time*) we possess knowledge of the so-called "new woman" discourses which have been available on television and in other media for roughly twenty years. Through our own "television archives"—our memories of past programs and surrounding discourses—we are pre-constructed to assume various positions of identification and to accept a range of ideas, actions and behaviors which comprise TV's version of the "new woman." Our past in/of television has also prepared us to see these women eventually contained in the expression of their subjectivity, and especially their sexuality. Again and again, "new women" have had their difference repressed, and their progressive goals displaced onto more acceptable and traditional bourgeois grounds.

From the working girl sit-coms of the 1950s to the 1970s, strong women were featured on television, but usually their strength was figured in stories organized around patriarchal and/or domestic norms. Typically plots focused on the woman's attempt to get even with her dominating husband or boss. By and large, traditional husband-wife roles prevailed. The family remained the chief conduit for social values, and sit-coms presented "healthy" images of domestic life. These programs supported the ideology of "motherhood" and the "family" which were popular in the society at large. They did occasionally raise fears and anxieties about inadequacy, which in early television were sometimes allayed by consumer choices and the acquisition of commodities.[15] Still, the family existed as the site of reception coterminous with the site of dramatic action, and the emphasis on the housewife role meant that socially approved action was confined to the microsocial domestic sphere.

By 1971 *The Mary Tyler Moore Show* supposedly served as the new image of the relevant, contemporary, and innovative woman. Indeed, the innovative content of the program brought about a shift in some of the previous definitions of female experience. On one level, the program can be seen to provoke just that kind of "crisis in the codification and coherency of ideological systems" that Mary Ann Doane sees as a general principle in the female film noir.[16] The new set of meanings in programs like *The Mary Tyler Moore Show* might have opened up a new representational space for female audiences. But at the same time several forces of containment were already in place, working against that space. For example, the ensemble of actors on the program form what has been called the "family work place," which works to condense one dominant institution (the family) with another (the work place). More importantly, the sit-com genre was the likely format for the program because the family work place matched the new cultural mood and also fit with the formal structure of a previously successful program-type.[17] Fredric Jameson suggests that we have a "set" towards the acceptance of repetition of TV formats and genres because we bring a "horizon of expectations" to the reception of programs. This virtually precludes there ever being an "original" program.[18] Repetition also works on the level of content. For example, in the program's continuing episodes, Mary often played a traditional "mother" role or else a female-support role (her bonding with Rhoda), and this kind of female TV character was a conventionalized "type" which could be seen on many other sit-coms. This set toward repetition was already in place by the time *Kate and Allie* appeared on the air.

Kate and Allie: Analysis of Several Episodes

Various episodes of *Kate and Allie* present a range of appropriate roles that women might assume. But the range of female identity is usually constructed through characterizations of social behavior which are "outside" of the *Kate and Allie* family unit itself. The dominant identification structure of the family unit in *Kate and Allie* works to displace any issues of social role, identification or authority which might be sexually defined and assumed. Male and female roles which are "outside-the-white-middle-class-family" (e.g., gay, lesbian, working-class) are rarely given space on television, and when presented in the last few years in sit-coms, made-for-TV-movies, and other series, these characterizations became part of the play of ideological contradictions. None of these "outside" roles are shown to fulfill consumer desire and fantasy, and they often subvert the family narrative and heterosexual romance which television constructs.

In *Kate and Allie* this play of "inside" and "outside" is part of the new-woman sit-com form even when it becomes problematic, as it does in the October 15, 1985 episode. Kate's landlord, Janet, has discovered that Kate and Allie and their respective children have been living illegally in a single-family apartment. After several unsuccessful attempts to locate a new apartment, Kate attempts to solve the dilemma through deception. She tells Janet that she and Kate are lesbians. Kate and Allie then stumble over the reasons why they had been secretive about their affair in the past. Janet herself supplies the reasons in a comic give-and-take: "You were embarrassed . . . ashamed." Kate and Allie respond with great intensity, "So ashamed." Janet says, "you poor little things," and she then introduces Miriam, her lover.

In this short comic segment, Janet articulates through her speech the terms by which she, as an obstacle to representation, can be represented. The lesbian first has to fulfill, it seems, the function of not being a lesbian. She cannot be authentic on any terms because she has to hide her identity. Although Janet is not made into a caricature (this is, after all, 1984), she must first be mistaken for a heterosexual in order for the comedy to work. She has to participate as a "person" on almost a stereotypical level by asking the "straight" questions. Kate and Allie, having perpetuated a lie and a deception, continue to deceive and respond appropriately. Three times the laugh-track deflects us from recognizing the hidden premise of the scene (that Janet is a lesbian). Janet is pushed beyond recognizable limits of believability; Kate and Allie are pushed beyond what they are shown to be in other episodes. All are pushed toward the comic entrance of Janet's lover, Miriam. Still, the comedic situation, timing, and structure of the scene create an oppositional space appropriate to further narrative development.

After Miriam appears, Kate and Allie look astonished. Recognition then leads to further colonization of the "outside" couple. The problem Kate and Allie now face is the dual one of how to acknowledge the existence of the "gay lovers" and how to address Miriam. Janet solves the problem when she introduces Miriam as her lover, but Kate and Allie cannot be allowed to accept that designation, and must resort, again through the conventions of the sit-com genre (especially the vaudevillian over-reactions of characters), to a denial of Miriam and what she actually represents.

Janet then lectures Kate and Allie, reminding them to "never be ashamed of what you are. Have pride." In another context this could be read as good advice, but since it's coming from a lesbian, it brings with it the possibility of contradictory identifications. Although Janet's advice is in line with the bourgeois individualism common to many television sit-coms, its acceptance in this case violates cultural codes. When Miriam presents a pineapple upside down cake to Kate and Allie, even that takes on the threatening meanings associated with the lesbian couple as Kate and Allie initially refuse to accept it. Allie says, "Look Kate, it's a cake from her lover." The cake becomes a site of condensation for the contradictory positions of meaning offered by the narrative. The visual style of the scene, with its rapid point-of-view editing, underlines the crisis in meaning.

As the narrative proceeds, the relationships among the four women become more friendly, intimate, "normal," and family-like. Janet and Miriam decide to initiate Kate and Allie into the wider gay and lesbian society by inviting them to a dance. Eventually, ashamed of the deception, Allie becomes moralistic. She confesses, "We're living a lie," and the land-lord discovers this in the following way:

Landlord: I'm so tired of people who think they have the right to condescend to us just because we're different from them.
Kate: You were willing to penalize us $648 a month just because we're different from you.
Landlord: This apartment is a one-family dwelling.
Kate: As long as you get to say what a family is.
Landlord: Everybody knows what a family is.
Kate: I'm not so sure. Not many people would consider a gay couple a family, but you do. And . . . now . . . so do we.
Miriam: Oh, Janet.
Allie: A family is anybody who wants to share their lives together . . . It's love that defines a family. It could be any kind of love; your kind, our kind.
Kate: You of all people should know that.

Kate and Allie's lecture does not describe relationships between women, but rather it defines what a family is. And this definition is presented by Allie, the female character who most consistently plays the mother role in the program. Using the language of the subcultural group apparently entitles Kate and Allie to their definition of the family. The latter is here presented as a politically and sexually neutral message, but in the context of the society in which this is uttered, it cannot be a neutral statement. Moreover, Janet cannot both assert lesbian rights and accept the definition of the family offered by Allie. A notion of the family predicated on romantic love is not a neutral idea to those whose politics and sexuality have been denied, policed and/or colonized. The oppositional space that had been opened in the episode is closed off by this moral to the tale.

Even the "gay" dance presents the imagery of heterosexual life. The scene includes male partners who promptly exit the frame, as well as Janet, Miriam, Kate and Allie. All the other couples at the dance are straight. As we have learned earlier in the episode, Kate and Allie danced together when they were young girls at summer camp. Kate and Allie's dance in this scene is a reprise of their pre-adolescent schoolgirl days so that their appearance as a couple on the dance floor is presented as female bonding, a socially sanctioned form of non-lesbian female interaction. The dance scene, then, harkens back to an earlier form of girlhood pleasure, and it reaffirms female bonding in this sense. But this form of pleasure is also effectively distanced from lesbian desire.

Kate and Allie, because they belong to the continuing series, have opportunities to transcend the stereotypical, but Janet and Miriam do not. The latter cannot transcend their roles because the sit-com format dictates that minor characters are not allowed the range of character traits that major characters are permitted. These minor characters function to set the sit-com situation, provide the problem, and disappear at the resolution. Janet and Miriam — and lesbianism as a whole — are subsumed in *Kate and Allie*'s overall attempt to provide "relevant" and contemporary meanings. In this episode the creation of an oppositional space — as well as the eventual containment of that space — fits perfectly with the generic limitations of the sit-com form in character, situation, resolution and "problem."

The program, however, does raise questions about alternative female lifestyles. The series, which departs in many ways from traditional family configurations, includes possibilities for a range of interpretations. It presents various definitions of the "new woman" by splitting its two central characters according to two ideals. The program is intertextually associated with the "odd couple" syndrome. Kate is presented as generous, considerate, and sensitive, but she also assumes the role of breadwinner, which is coded in the text as masculine. Allie is shrill, grouchy, obstinate, and she adopts the role of housewife and mother. In one episode Kate and Allie's college professor publishes a novel, and both women fantasize that they are the heroine of his book. Kate's fantasy has her dressed in Joan Collins's excessive garb (white fake fur cloche, clinging white dress). In her dream, Kate sees her boyfriend, Ted, who tells her that she belongs to no man, that she is that "new animal," the "American Woman." In contrast to this notion of the modern woman, Allie's fantasy finds her dressed in frills with an apron covering her outfit. Perhaps it is not too strained to see these contrasts as a continuation of the classic feminine bind, prostitute versus mother/saint. However, Kate and Allie present to their audience their own critical reading of this dilemma when they recognize the contradictions of the fantasy process itself:

> Kate: Look, it's fiction. It isn't real. This is a man's imagination, and we're fantasizing our heads off about it. Listen to us, we're like eight year-olds playing princess. This is fiction. It is not real.
> Allie: I do not need a fantasy life.
> Kate: Everybody needs a little fantasy.
> Allie: Not me.

Multiple definitions of the "new woman" are also provided by the introduction of each episode under which the musical theme is played.

Lauren Rabinovitz has recently examined the introduction to the debut episode (March 19, 1984), demonstrating the way the sit-com relies upon intertextual discourses to ensure identification. As Rabinovitz illustrates, the intro shows us Kate and Allie, who leave a movie theater and stop to chat in front of a poster which advertises the film *An Unmarried Woman*. They take opposing views on the film, especially on Jill Clayburgh's independence, self-assertiveness, and her final decision not to move into Alan Bates's loft apartment. Rabinovitz's analysis turns on precisely the complexity of conflicting and contradictory discourses which is integral to the program. The complexity is brought about by the presentation/representation of the film as a feminist discourse by Kate and Allie's different interpretations of the film (i.e., "feminist" and "romantic" respectively). Although Kate's reading might be seen as the dominant position offered by the film, this does not mean—as this program shows us—that Kate's interpretation is the only one possible. In Kate and Allie's discussion of the film, there is no ideal or correct reading because their dialogue remains, as Rabinovitz notes, empathetic, understanding, and non-competitive.[19] In scenes like this, *Kate and Allie* articulates numerous definitions of feminism and femininity in general.

Closing Comments

Beginning in the 1984–85 season, *Kate and Allie* offered to audiences multiple readings which were themselves constructed by television's signifying practices and by the social constructions of femininity in the culture at large. Yet, as others have suggested, women can interpret texts in ways which are not complicit with the range of meanings offered by those texts. Since there will inevitably be readings which are not anticipated by the program, it is likely that a variety of different and quite contradictory interpretations will be made. Female spectators can read TV programs differently because their own social, political, and historical situations vary. In addition, women have different levels of reading competencies depending on their memories of and familiarity with inter/extra-textual discourses. A distinction must always be drawn between the subject constructed by television and the social subject. The real issue, one that cannot be dealt with here, is whether spectators (male or female) can identify with multiple and contradictory subject positions which are formed by the text and its surrounding social context.

Any position of subjectivity is also a contradictory social position because the social, cultural, and political situations affecting subjectivity are not stable, nor are they fixed. Instead, they change as people become exposed to practices, like televisual practices, which call forth different modes of action. The subject as a discursive position is active in many sites. It is, in Stuart Hall's words, "pluri-centered and multi-dimensional."[20] While the subject might evidence dominant tendencies, it does not slip easily into a single, inscribed unity—female or otherwise.

NOTES

Many thanks to Mary Beth Haralovich for her comments and criticism on earlier drafts of this article.

1. See Laurie Jane Schulze, " '*Getting Physical*': Text/Context/Reading and the Made-for-Television-Movie," *Cinema Journal* 25:2 (Winter 1986), pp. 35–50; Elayne Rapping, "Hollywood's New 'Feminist' Heroines," *Cineaste* 14:4 (1986), pp. 4–9 and the article quoted in Lauren Rabinovitz, below.

2. Cited in Peter Kerr, "Women in Take-Charge Roles Stride into TV's Limelight," *New York Times* (September 26, 1984), p. 29.

3. Kathleen MacKay, "Do Stronger Women Mean Higher Ratings?" *Los Angeles Times* (August 5, 1984), Calendar, pp. 5–6. Of the twenty-two new programs, five were on CBS (including *Murder She Wrote* and *Cover Up*); eight were on ABC (including *Jessie, Paper Dolls* and *Glitter*); and eight were on NBC (including *Partners in Crime, Hot Pursuit* and *Hunter*). Mid-season replacements were *Sara, McGruder & Loud,* and *Moonlighting*. All but two of these programs were cancelled by Fall 1985.

4. Kerr, p. 29.

5. Kerr, p. 30.

6. Kerr, p. 29.

7. *TV Guide* (February 2, 1985), p. 22.

8. John J. O'Connor, "Women are Getting a More Sympathetic Reading," *New York Times* (October 14, 1984), p. 27. O'Connor's memory of television programing extends back far enough to remind us that this does not mean that "sensitivity is in and exploitation is out."

9. Lauren Rabinovitz, "Sit-coms and Single Moms: American Television and the Feminist Subject," paper delivered at the 1986 International Television Studies Conference, p. 1.

10. *TV Guide* (February 2, 1985), p. 407; *TV Guide* (November 24, 1984), pp. 6–8, 10; *TV Guide* (April 26, 1986), pp. 26–27.

11. John Langer, "Television's 'Personality System'," *Media, Culture & Society* 3:4 (October 1981), p. 354. Langer suggests that a tension is created by publicizing the intimately known television personality in TV magazines, etc.,

and the effort to create the "exceptional" new woman and new family as "ordinary," "familiar," and "natural" in an ideological sense.

12. To this I would only add Nick Browne's notion of the "supertext," which consists not just of the program and its related commercials but the program's specific position in the daily schedule. He proposes that the proper context for the analysis of television is the text itself, its commercials, its relation to the schedule and its relation to the "structure and economics of the work week of the general population." See "The Political Economy of the Television (Super)Text," *Quarterly Review of Film Studies* 9:3 (Summer 1984), pp. 74–82.

13. Finding of Fabian Linden cited in Serafina Bathrick, "*The Mary Tyler Moore Show*: Women at Home and at Work," in *MTM: "Quality Television"*, eds. Jane Feuer, Paul Kerr and Tise Vahimagi (London: BFI, 1984), p. 100.

14. Valerie A. Zeithmal, "The New Demographics and Market Fragmentation," *Journal of Marketing* 49 (Summer 1985), pp. 64–75.

15. See George Lipsitz, "The Meaning of Memory: Family, Class and Ethnicity in Early Network Television Programs," in this issue.

16. Mary Ann Doane, "*Gilda*: Epistemology as Striptease," *Camera Obscura* 11 (Fall 1983), p. 23.

17. Todd Gitlin, *Inside Prime Time* (New York: Pantheon, 1983), p. 215. See a fuller discussion of *The Mary Tyler Moore Show* in Bathrick.

18. Fredric Jameson, "Reification and Utopia in Mass Culture," *Social Text* 1:1 (Winter 1979), pp. 130–148.

19. Rabinovitz, p. 4.

20. Stuart Hall, "Signification, Representation, Ideology," *Cultural Studies in Mass Communication* 2:2 (June 1985), pp. 91–114.

The Mary Tyler Moore Show

General Hospital

All's Well that Doesn't End—Soap Opera and the Marriage Motif
Sandy Flitterman-Lewis

It is a well-known fact that the desire for narrative closure—the resolution of a fiction's complications—is the mainstay of classical Hollywood cinema. Raymond Bellour has effectively demonstrated, in fact, that a "slide from the familial into the conjugal," with its constitution of the couple and harmonious institution of closure, structures the *cinematic* narrative from start to finish.[1] But television soap opera—that quintessential *televisual* form, whose very definition as a "continuing drama" implies the perpetual frustration of an ending—regards its "endings" in quite a different way. Where it might be said that all Hollywood movies lead us inevitably toward marriage, the daytime serials, by contrast, conceive of weddings as starting points, highly dramatic moments which function to provide crisis rather than resolution, complication rather than closure.

The reason for this is double-edged, having to do with the soap opera as a form (its conventions, both dramatic and videographic) and with soap opera as a *televisual form* (television's specificity, its particular mode of meaning production). These two factors are interactive: because soap opera is a highly segmented structure whose essential fracture of narrative produces a dispersed subjectivity, it is perfectly suited to the type of distracted viewing which characterizes television as an institution. As John Ellis points out, television is a medium which "engages the *look* and the *glance* rather than the gaze."[2] The necessary profusion and dispersal of narrative elements at the heart of soap opera's organization goes hand in hand with the varied and casual attention which distinguishes television from film.

The consequences of this for television narrative are crucial. For one thing, from genre to genre (but most particularly in the soap opera), the televisual style contradicts the most fundamental of narrative film's principles—the harmonizing function of textual effects in the production of a coherent resolution. The film audience is conditioned to watch a film within the context of its completion. On the other hand, the unstable, reversible, and often repetitive form of the soap opera narrative embeds interruption deep within its discursive structure. This fragmentation—so central to the televised daytime drama—contrasts with classical cinema's unified form,

217

for, as Jeremy Butler points out (in his extremely cogent and useful article on the "soap opera apparatus"), the "audial and visual style of soap operas [is] uniquely adapted to the preservation of enigmas rather than their resolution."[3] Based on ambiguity and lack of closure, segmented both diegetically (within the narrative) and intertextually (the commercials, the different programs), the soap opera, as TV's own apotheosis, has openness, multiplicity, and plurality as its aims. As a result, as I point out in another context, the quality of televisual "viewer involvement . . . is one of continual, momentary, and constant visual repositioning, in keeping with television's characteristic 'glance'."[4] In TV, vision is dispersed, fragmentary, amplified, and thus indicative of the peculiar kind of spectatorship so different from that of film.

Since TV's fragmented viewing experience is so emphatically reinforced on the level of narrative in the soap opera, the wedding episode is a privileged site of complication. Rather than resolving weeks of conflict which it has been the serial's function elaborately to spin out, the wedding provides a complex and fertile textual "knot," a matrix of disruption which instigates further narrative problems. In the wedding, new configurations of character temporarily align as each "knot" reveals new obstacles, new reasons for the deferral of completion. Underlying each wedding is thus a substratum of impermanence, a foundation of uncertainty reflecting the perpetually shifting complexities of soap opera relationships. In many cases, what often disturbs the marital moment is the irruption of an enigma, a riddle which has been haunting the characters throughout the prior episodes and which now must seek an outlet in whatever form. It is the enigma that then becomes the catalyst for new enigmas and situations, as consequences (of past actions, memories, desires) become the point of crisis in the wedding. In the soap opera, as a result, our need for completion and satisfaction, our desire for narrative closure—so fundamental to the fictions of Hollywood cinema—becomes *reorganized*. Elements of the story are here only *partially* resolved, and resolved in ways which inevitably permit the further elaboration of the text. The soap opera, motivated as it is by an endless continuity, uses the wedding to *contribute to,* rather than resolve, the flow (of narrative actions, or programming). As TV viewers, then, we crave the perpetual continuation which the disrupted wedding provides.

My analysis focuses on two weddings that took place on *General Hospital,* that of Kevin O'Connor and Terry Brock broadcast in February of 1986, and that of Duke Lavery and Anna Devane broadcast in May of 1987. The weddings have this in common: both were haunted from the start by a secret from the past, a secret involving memory, transgression, female sexuality and death. Each ceremony is interrupted at a critical moment, and while the immediate consequences differ, the long-term effects are the same. Kevin and Terry are finally married after Terry, reliving her traumatic past, comes to terms with her personal disgrace by triumphantly singing a hymn down the town's main street as she goes to meet her groom. An expressionistically stylized flashback provides the disruption—the return of the repressed—which triggers the suspenseful question: will this hysterical rupture, in fact, prevent the wedding from taking place at all? The emergence of the past takes a different form for Anna and Duke—more concrete, less fantasmatic—but this, in this case, succeeds in stopping the wedding altogether before it can begin. Here, too, a crime has been committed in secrecy and mystery, but an assiduous and bloodthirsty reporter has succeeded in bringing forth damning information at the very moment the vows are to be said. In both cases, the weddings, whether accomplished or not, yield complications that stretch far beyond the moment of the nuptials themselves and well into the complex web of soap opera relationships.

In the case of Kevin and Terry, two clouds hang over the prospective marriage and thereby threaten the coming wedding: 1) an undefined and unnameable crisis of three years earlier—deeply repressed in Terry's psyche—which involves Terry and her entire hometown (Laurelton, where the wedding is to take place), and 2) two unsolved murders of Laurelton men which occurred in Port Charles (the regular setting of *General Hospital*) only recently. While all of Kevin and Terry's close friends from Port Charles are at the wedding, police chief Anna Devane continues her murder investigation; she too arrives in Laurelton, suspecting both O'Connor brothers as possible murderers, and as the wedding is about to begin, she rushes frantically to prevent it from happening. Some fifteen months later (in viewer time, i.e., real time as opposed to diegetic time)—and this effectively illustrates the soap opera's characteristic intricacy of permutation and variation on the level of the plot—it is Anna herself, about to be married to Duke, who is subjected to the same desperate rush against time as someone seeks to interrupt the wedding in the name of a crime committed in the past. As a police chief whose lover is a former mobster, it is now Anna herself who is accused of covering up a murder, also committed several years earlier (four, to be exact), and also shrouded in mystery—"The Secret of L'Orleans." This time, however, both the viewers and some of the characters know exactly what happened—Duke's "sister" Camelia, having been attacked by the brutal Evan Jerome and having subsequently killed him with a candlestick, has hysterical amnesia while Duke and his father Angus McKye bury the body and disguise the crime. Now, at the precise moment of Anna's marriage to Duke, Camelia remembers what happened while Marc Carlin, a reporter on the *Port Charles Herald,* seeks to expose Anna's complicity in obstructing justice. Thus, whereas Terry's wedding is interrupted by her own recognition of the past,

Anna's is halted entirely—by forces beyond her control. Deceived, humiliated, and deluded, she must pay for a crime she neither knew about nor committed. Thus from one wedding to the next, a significant displacement has occurred, while the primary terms of memory, desire, and death—reorganized into new configurations—remain undeniably the same.

But even beyond the complicating function of the wedding—so in keeping with the soap opera's patterns of looking, narrative, and address—I maintain that it is precisely these configurations of sexuality and the past (which erupt onto the matrimonial scene) that represent a "memory of the cinema" coming to haunt the televisual text. For, both of the weddings under analysis are disrupted by the past, and this, in the form of a flashback (immediate or not), involves structures traditionally associated with the classical cinema (the subjective point-of-view and reverse-shot figures, systems of continuity and alternation, a focus on the image over sound [remember that soap opera's conversational mode makes it usually foreground spoken dialogue], and special attention to the figure of the woman-as-display). I have dealt elsewhere[5] with the particular variation of the point-of-view shot that occurs in Terry's wedding episode, and with the TV text's inability to master or control such uncharacteristic evidences of interior perception and subjective vision. Here I would like to discuss the way in which the fantasm of the past is intimately—and voyeuristically—associated with female sexuality. My discussion of the disruption of Anna's wedding, on the other hand, will focus on the link between a peculiarly *cinematic* mode of narration—alternation—and its critical position in the soap opera text.

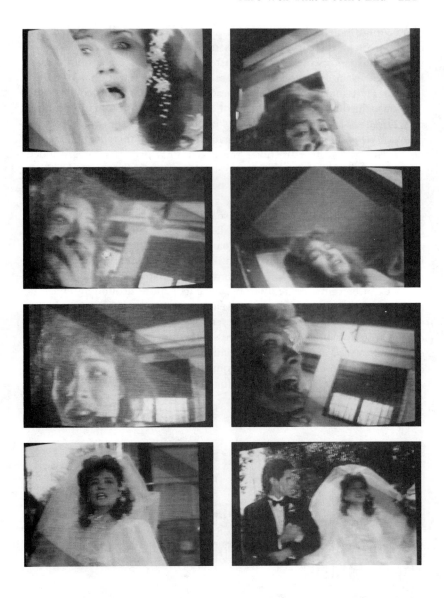

Terry's ride to the church (accompanied by Jake Meyer, who will give her away) is interrupted by a flashback. The sight of a motel sign activates a memory of its neon glow, which in turn brings the recollection of the night when Terry—dazed, hysterical, and naked—staggered down the main street of Laurelton, sobbing, half singing and half praying. A conventional fantasy/nightmare of exhibitionism, Terry's emotionally-charged and highly erotic spectacle distinguishes itself from the more domesticated versions of soap opera sexuality (chaste or not-so-chaste bedroom scenes, furtive kisses in seclusion, passionate embraces in traditional romantic locales). Here such a *public* performance, and indeed it is, of female desire (the masochistic component of identification with her humiliation cannot be ignored) is framed by the glances of spectators on the street. But the point-of-view shots are all mis-aligned, the angles unmatched; there are no "fictive alibis" to narrativize the gaze. What becomes foregrounded instead is the very act of looking itself, the undeniable fact of watching the woman as spectacle in a virtual performance of sexual transgression and excess.

Even as she recovers into the present, Terry remains a focal point for the gaze. For as she suddenly "awakes" and expiates her past by now marching triumphantly down this same street—clothed in the garb of legitimized sexuality and sanctioned display (the wedding portrait)—she is offered as a spectacle in ways seldom seen in soap opera. While classical cinema can be said repeatedly to organize its fictions around an image of the woman, object of desire for the masculine pursuit, the soap opera maintains no such hold on its representations of the feminine. The gaze on the woman's body is much more subtle and diffuse. Yet here, in the episode of a wedding, traces of the cinema erupt specifically in this gaze, erupt precisely to disturb, if only momentarily, the soap opera text, with a memory of the cinematic and its fundamental forms.

The disruption of Duke and Anna's wedding makes use of another strategy historically associated and strongly aligned with filmic narration. The entire episode is structured around a series of alternations—interrelated sequences which grow more and more urgent as the time for the wedding approaches. For weeks the various narrative threads have been elaborated: Marc Carlin's investigation into Anna as a corrupt police chief, Duke's withholding of information about the secret of L'Orleans (and Anna's trusting acceptance of this), Camelia's progressive recollection of the events of four years ago and her ensuing panic about the disaster she's instigated by trying to probe the past. Now the intercutting rhythm of this single episode builds (the wedding preparations and beginning of the ceremony, Camelia's recognition spurred by the mysterious arrival of the murder weapon, a candlestick, and the calling of a press conference with the incendiary news of the coverup) until the agitated reporters at Marc Carlin's press conference burst into the room as the wedding is about to begin, their accusations making the marriage of Duke and Anna impossible.[6] What marks this episode, then, is a form of alternating parallelism very common in the cinema but rare in the daytime television text. The "meanwhile effect" of cross-cutting in classical cinema—whose simultaneous representation of different but related actions has made it the foundation of cinematic storytelling—is most usually absent from daytime drama, whose structure requires the articulation of several *autonomous* episodes held in suspension. Ever since Griffith, classical cinema has relied on a cause-effect chain, traditionally heightened by just the sort of alternating montage intended to build suspense through parallel organization.

But soap opera only rarely relies on the *mutually consequential* implications of such consecutive sequences, for the soap opera usually proceeds in terms of simple succession rather than causality. Unlike film, it has no single, linear flow of time which moves its sequences inevitably toward a climax. Instead, there are (conventionally) numerous simultaneous "present-tenses," each existing in its own sphere of activities, discrete and relatively self-contained. Thus it is here, at the crisis of Duke and Anna's wedding, built, as it is, on precisely the effect of alternation which we find so prevalent in film, that *cinematic* organization erupts into the fragmentary discourse of the soap opera. And in keeping with the association of feminine sexuality and the cinema which I have suggested, this "cinematic" past is tied to sexual transgression and the female body, for it is Camelia's crime—connected, as it is, to seduction and violation—which provides the motive for this disruption. Here, at Duke and Anna's wedding, since the emergence of the cinematic is discussed in terms of narrative structure, the sexual is tied to one of the alternating threads which build to the episode's climax—the traumatic memory of sexual violence and its eruption into the present. And it is thus, once again, an excess of "femininity" which marks the peculiar status of the soap opera's interrupted wedding.

I began by asserting that the fragmentation of sequences and the dispersal of narrative elements so fundamental to soap opera structure are compatible with the ways in which all material on television is organized. As a consequence, because of soap opera's conventionally disrupted narrative form and its avoidance of narrative closure, it adapts the wedding—that hallmark "happy ending" of the cinema—to its own televisual ends. To the cinema's totalizing conclusions, soap opera responds with the perpetual frustration of an ending—its peculiar use of the wedding reminds us of this. However, the wedding sequence is both characteristic of the soap opera and not. For it is precisely in these episodes of narrative complication, episodes in which "pseudo-endings" are meant temporarily to disguise their inevitable "initiating" function, that the cinema makes its return. In the daytime drama, in fact, weddings function to remind us of a cinematic past. But since the wedding's resolving status in film is *inverted* by the soap opera's use—it functions to prolong events rather than conclude them—the cinema must make its appearance in quite another way. The marriage motif in soap opera, then, provides us with displacements, *traces* of the cinematic in a structure that never ends.

NOTES

1. Raymond Bellour, "Segmenting/Analyzing," in *Genre: The Musical,* ed. Rick Altman (London: Routledge and Kegan Paul, 1981), p. 118. The present article is a version of a paper delivered at the Society for Cinema Studies Conference, Concordia University, Montreal, Quebec, Canada, May 21–24, 1987. Many thanks to Joel Lewis.

2. John Ellis, *Visible Fictions: Cinema, Television, Video* (London: Routledge and Kegan Paul, 1982), p. 128.

3. Jeremy Butler, "Notes on the Soap Opera Apparatus: Televisual Style and *As the World Turns,*" *Cinema Journal* 25, no. 3 (Spring 1986), p. 67.

4. Sandy Flitterman-Lewis, "Psychoanalysis, Film and Television," in *Channels of Discourse: Television and Contemporary Criticism,* ed. Robert C. Allen (Chapel Hill: University of North Carolina Press, 1987), p. 195.

5. See the chapter in *Channels of Discourse* noted above.

6. This is, in fact, carried over a weekend, for the episode broadcast on Friday, May 1, 1987, concerns precisely this acceleration of tension while that of Monday, May 4, 1987, opens with the wedding itself, its interruption, and its aftermath. I will only suggest here the extreme difficulties encountered in television scholarship due to the ephemeral nature of the television text and the general indifference of network officials.

All That Heaven Allows (Douglas Sirk, 1955)

All that Television Allows: TV Melodrama, Postmodernism, and Consumer Culture
Lynne Joyrich

I. Drama at Our Fingertips

In an emotionally charged scene in Douglas Sirk's 1955 melodrama *All That Heaven Allows*, the protagonist (Jane Wyman) receives a TV set as a gift. Wyman plays Cary Scott, a middle-aged and upper-middle-class widow in love with a man who is not only younger than her, but of a lower social class—she first meets Ron Kirby (Rock Hudson) when he's pruning her trees. In the course of the narrative, Cary faces increasing social and familial opposition to the romance and is forced to leave Ron. She receives the present from her two grown children who offer it as an affirmation of her continued bourgeois status (her decision not to marry and leave the family home) and as a substitution for the love she has renounced. She is, in other words, given a typical media solution to the problems inherent in her gender and class position—consumer compensation in exchange for an active pursuit of her desire. As the TV salesman explains that "All you have to do is turn that dial and you have all the company you want right there on the screen—drama, comedy, life's parade at your finger tips," there is an image of Cary's face, framed and reflected in the TV screen as she realizes the futility of her actions and the impossibility of her situation. Figured as the ultimately passive spectator, so tangled in the web of bourgeois culture that she is literally collapsed onto the picture of her misery, Cary's very subjectivity is incorporated into television.

In a recent article detailing the path of melodrama ". . . from its birth in the crowded city streets to its death in the television dominated home," Laura Mulvey refers to this same cinematic scene.[1] In the late 1950s, television erupted in the American home and placed itself firmly within the realm of family, domesticity, and consumerism, the ground of the family melodrama. Noting Hollywood's response to this invasion, Mulvey writes, "It is as though, at the moment of defeat, Hollywood could afford to point out the seeds of decay in its victorious rival's own chosen breeding ground."[2] Yet these seeds of decay were not enough to overthrow the new

All That Heaven Allows

medium or its familial base. Instead, the consolidated family, with TV as its tool, seemed to triumph over critical melodramas. Mulvey concludes that the swing to political conservatism and the repositioning of women in the home gave order to the oppositions public/private, production/reproduction, and inside/outside whose tensions had propelled melodrama and allowed it a political dimension. The birth of television thus displaced, and seemingly even resolved, the genre's animating force. As TV brought popular entertainment into the home, national consensus triumphed over a potentially oppositional melodrama.

But has melodrama died? Or has it been subsumed into television, engulfing the medium as it engulfs its spectators and precluding its location as a separate category? This possibility is strikingly figured in *All That Heaven Allows* as the TV screen takes over the cinematic frame, enclosing Cary and the entire melodramatic mise en scène in a haze of consumerism, impotent spectatorship, and hyperreality associated with television. These are the terms of postmodern American culture in which history, subjectivity, and reality itself flattens out into a TV image and we are left searching for signs of meaning within an endless flow of images — a situation leading to nostalgia for past traditions and what may be a backlash against women's social and political gains.[3] In this historical scenario, television draws us all, women and men, into a shared bond of consumer overpresence and powerless spectatorship as melodrama becomes the preferred form for TV, the postmodern medium *par excellence*. In other words, rather than eclipsing melodrama, television incorporates it so as to bring the strands of passivity and domesticity associated with both melodrama and TV together in a simulated plenitude, thereby positioning all viewers as susceptible consumers. At the same time, the "feminine" connotations traditionally attached to melodrama—and to both consumerism and television viewing—are diffused onto a general audience, opening up contradictions of gender and spectatorship in the TV melodrama which invite further investigation. In this article, I want to explore such questions of TV melodrama and to map out the discursive connections forged between melodrama and postmodern consumer culture, focusing on the problems of gender constituted within this field.

II. Television: The Melodramatic Screen

With a broadening appeal to a general audience of viewer-consumers, melodrama moves to television and so dominates its discourse that it becomes difficult to locate as a separate TV genre. Of course, there are some television forms that are clearly marked as melodrama. Both the daytime and prime-time soap opera, for example, seem to employ many of the characteristic devices of the film melodrama. The use of music to convey emotional effects defines the basic attribute of melodrama in all its forms, and this same trait defines the soap opera. Music orchestrates the emotional ups and downs and underscores a particular rhythm of experience. This rhythm, in film melodrama and the TV soap opera, is one of exaggerated fluctuations, marking the discontinuities of emotional experience as the plots slowly build, amidst much delay, to dramatic moments of outbreak and collision before sudden reversals of fortune begin the movement again.

Dramatic intensification is also heightened by concentrated visual metaphors—the repetition of configurations of actors from one scene to the next, for example, to indicate similar or contrasting emotional relations, the references to visibly different styles of dress or color of hair to signify opposing positions within the program's familial schemes, or the externalization of emotion onto representative objects that act as stand-ins for human contact. The meaning of everyday action, ordinary gesture, and standard decor is thus intensified so that the psychic strains and breaks or rise in feeling are made manifest. Like the film melodrama, soap opera expresses what are primarily ideological and social conflicts in emotional terms. Action then largely takes place within the context of the home or in sites at the intersection of public and private space that are central to personal concerns (the hospital room, a hotel, the private office available for intimate conversations, etc.). The intensification of the significance of mundane objects and locations—the doorbells and telephones, doctor's offices and bedrooms so charged with connotations in the soap opera—works to displace the emphasis from social relations to material objects even as they express an anxiety about the uncertainties of daily American life.

While such patterns drawn from the cinematic conventions of the family melodrama seem appropriate for the typically domestic interiors of the soap opera, soap opera has lately expanded to include broader and more diverse settings while extending melodramatic conventions to a wider scope. Soap opera now combines with other genres—police, crime and spy dramas have been popular on *General Hospital,* for example, the world of big business has been taken on by prime-time soap operas such as *Dynasty* and *Dallas* (which also employs elements of the Western), and soap opera has even combined with elements of science fiction (seemingly the last domain of wide open space) in recent episodes of *One Life to Live* and last season's finale of *The Colbys.* It seems as if soap operas have been able to move into realms not usually associated with the melodrama, while at the same time, TV forms not typically seen as melodrama have become more and more melodramatic.

The made-for-TV movie, for example, is often marketed as a form particularly suited for dealing with contemporary social issues. Yet like the fifties film melodrama, it manages these issues by inserting them into a domestic framework in which the family functions as the sole referent. Police and detective dramas also purportedly deal with the social issues of crime, drugs, prostitution, and so on, yet even while their emphasis on action seems to remove them from the domain of the melodrama, they exhibit many of its characteristics. Although they allow their protagonists to act freely against the criminals, the heroes of TV cop shows are still trapped within a confined world in which emotional pressure, familial concerns, and gender or class position take on heightened importance. Because of the economic and institutional demands of television, the good guys are never fully allowed to conquer their enemies—instead they are forced to repeat their actions week after week, trapping them within a restricted world of perpetual victimization and thereby lessening the gap between these dramas and the soap operas where perpetual suffering is the rule.

As direct action proves futile, the emphases of even the crime series shift to the more personal issues traditionally associated with the melodrama. In many cop or detective shows, the audience's emotional involvement is induced by a focus on the family in danger of dissolution. The officer or detective then must strive to save the family—either his own (*Heart of the*

City, Hill Street Blues), those of his clients (*The Equalizer, Stingray* and *Spenser: For Hire,* among many other shows, have featured such plots), or that of the police force itself. Very often the strains and tensions that exist between members of the police "family" are investigated, and the contrasts drawn between members of the team are used to explore issues of class, racial, or gender dynamics. For example, *Spenser: For Hire* can be seen as mapping out relations (and exposing contradictions) of race and class in the contrasts made evident between Spenser and Hawk, his "street-smart" black buddy who assists him with his cases. Gender, on the other hand, is made central on *Magnum P.I.*, *Miami Vice*, and other shows in which the attempt to define masculinity is a crucial issue, often taking precedence over the specific crimes portrayed.[4] As the focus shifts from problems of crime to questions of identity within familial and social roles, these television series move into the realm of melodrama.

Crime and social crises are the mainstay of network news programming as well, yet these shows too turn to melodrama to handle such "stories." Peter Brooks concludes his study of the melodramatic imagination by noting its persistence in today's dramas of natural disasters and political personalities, the stuff of newscasts "homologous to the dramas played out every day on television screens."[5] Like the cop/detective shows, news stories are often framed in personal terms as a way of avoiding the larger institutional, political and ideological issues they raise. By employing conventions taken from narrative TV melodrama (including a focus on the family—the news "family" and the families investigated), news programs can achieve the emotional intensification and moral polarization associated with dramatic serials.[6]

In other words, even programs or genres that seem far removed from the melodramas of the cinema employ devices that link them together. The series *Max Headroom,* for example, has been seen as TV's most innovative and "televisual" show in its self-reflexive use of video and computer technology, innovative sets and costumes, distorted visuals and unusual camera angles, fast-paced editing, and up-to-date language (dialogue that only a techno-whiz-kid can fully understand). Yet even this "postmodern" program ultimately resorts to melodrama as it collapses back into a standard representation of good vs. evil. The good guys are, of course, hard working independent men and women who care about the common folk while the bad ones are associated with a powerful bureaucracy that feeds off human suffering. Such oppositions are made visible through contrasting clothing, styles, manners and possessions: the wealthy villains are well-groomed smooth talkers in black suits who guard their rare possessions while likable characters wear casual clothes, understand street talk, and treasure their old stuffed animals. In providing this typically melodramatic scenario, even while attempting to remain informed and self-aware concerning television's power to construct identity, history and reality, *Max Headroom* exists in the tension between modern and post-modern forms. It solves this contradiction by splitting its protagonist into two—we have both the tough and dedicated TV journalist Edison Carter and his video-generated alter-ego Max Headroom who was created by a young computer genius while Carter battled crime. By so splitting the character, the program is able to displace all the cyborgian elements of postmodern subjectivity onto Max, leaving Carter free to play the role of hero who is nonetheless caught in a limited world—his actions, risks and sacrifices will never really free society of its problems or contradictions.

Max Headroom

Max Headroom thus fully demonstrates the extent to which television still relies on melodrama, even in TV's most "advanced" forms. Like the strategy employed by this show, it is as if we turn to melodrama to ward off the threat of a new form of culture and to buttress ourselves against a postmodern world in which even the distinction between video image and human identity becomes blurred. Despite Mulvey's claim that melodrama (or at least its potentially subversive mode) has died in the TV-dominated home, television melodrama stands strong. Its conventions are employed in a wide range of texts as television attempts to maintain the clarity melodrama provides through its strongly marked oppositions and heightened moral register. Yet as it spreads out across a number of TV forms from the soaps to the police dramas of masculinity, the news to the commercials, melodrama loses its specificity, becoming diffuse and ungrounded in its multiple deployments in the flow of TV.

III. Simulated Sentiment

It is not surprising that today's media-saturated society has been linked, in Mulvey's analysis for example, to the end of melodrama. As Fredric Jameson remarks, postmodernism is repeatedly marked by such "senses of the end of this or that . . . the hypothesis of some radical break or *coupure*, generally traced back to the end of the 1950s or the early 1960s," the death of melodrama in the TV-centered home being one more example of this phenomenon.[7] Yet melodrama's popularity has historically coincided with times of intense social and ideological crisis, and the postmodern age is certainly characterized by its many theorists as *the* age of crisis.[8] Aligned with the rise of multinational and consumer capitalism, it replaces determining machines of production with weightless models of reproduction, dissolving any possible distinction between aesthetic and commodity production and proclaiming the end of meaning, the liquidation of the referential, and the dissolution of identity. With this crisis in representation comes a crisis in power, authority and legitimation as the traditional "master narratives" fail to function. It would then seem that postmodernism multiplies the contradictions that animate melodrama—contradictions between production and reproduction, average and excess, topicality and timelessness, public and private, the Law and desire, masculine and feminine—further dissolving the stability of Western culture. Given this state, Jean-François Lyotard announces that "[t]he narrative function is losing its functors, its great heroes, its great dangers, its great voyages, its great goal. It is being dispersed in clouds of narrative language elements."[9] In other words, we face the death of the great male story. As Lyotard claims, all is dispersed in a cloud of dramatic fragments held together through only surface relations and tensions — a description corresponding remarkably well to both melodrama and network television.

Other critics have recognized the ties between contemporary media culture and melodramatic form. David Thorburn, for example, claims that "television melodrama has been our culture's most characteristic aesthetic form," and in his discussion of this broad category — encompassing made-for-TV movies, westerns, lawyer, doctor, cop and adventure shows as well as the more easily recognized daytime and prime-time soap operas — Thorburn argues for the specific suitability of melodrama for television.[10] Like television, melodrama is scorned for its moral simplification, reassuring fantasies, and immediate sensation in its effort to portray behavior shocking to its time. TV parallels melodrama in its form as well as content as it centers on familial space, a situation fostered by the size of the screen and its location in the home. Together with the low visual intensity of the medium and the smaller budget of its productions, these factors encourage television's reliance on background music, the close-up, confined interior, and intimate gesture rather than action — elements that resonate with melodramatic conventions.

TV melodrama is then ideally suited to reveal the subtle strains of bourgeois culture with all the contradictions it entails. As market commodities structured according to rigid schedules and commercial interruptions, such strains include the tensions that emerge in the juxtaposition of the drama proper and the mini-melodramas seen in the commercials — stories which convey the hopeful sensibility of advertising (even as they reveal the daily problems of dirt and stress) and jar with the claustrophobic and pessimistic worlds of prime-time soap operas (which nonetheless mask the labor required to maintain their luxury). Yet Thorburn claims that such commercial limits are merely formal conventions guiding the genre. While he notes that as both aesthetic and commodity creations, TV melodramas may reveal the ambivalence of industrial society, Thorburn does not fully explore the discord expressed by this form — contradictions grounded in consumer culture and tied to the shifting gender and class relations of postmodern America. In fact, Thorburn argues that television resolves melodrama's basic conflict: TV's ability to present intimate detail and intense emotion in a small and familiar space minimizes the tension between ordinary reality and an excessive emotional heightening brought together in the genre.[11] Yet as the medium which best illustrates the fluctuating ground of a media-created world, TV cannot resolve the contradictions of postmodern culture. It may be a desperate attempt to evade these tensions by reclaiming meaning and tradition, but this attempt is doomed to failure and TV melodrama is forced endlessly to replay its contradictions — contradictions which must be investigated so as to open a space for renewed feminist analyses and politics.

According to Jean Baudrillard, the discord of contemporary culture infects even the "certainties" of rational discourse, meaningful history, and coherent reality. Postmodernism is "hyperreal"—an age characterized by simulation. No longer tied to origin, reference, or identity, our culture is ruled by simulacra—copies without originals. Not only are objects and texts reproduced, their very production is governed by demands of reproducibility. In this case, the territory of the real is no longer mapped onto a representation, but the map precedes the territory—events are already inscribed by the media in advance as television is diffracted into reality and the real is diffracted into TV. With the breakdown of the distinction original/copy comes the breakdown of other such polarities—real/imaginary, true/false, cause/effect, subject/object—and according to Baudrillard, the subversion of Western logic, historical determination, and meaningful identity entirely. Simulation is thus the ruin of representation, giving the lie to our faith that a sign can exchange for meaning since it only exchanges in itself—we find only more signs and images in a circuit without reference or direction.

Paradoxically, while capitalism was the first system to destroy the referential by establishing a law of equivalence in which all is exchanged in the medium of money, it must now protect itself from the subversion of order inherent in the simulacrum. America has thus hardened itself against its own hyperreality—a weightless play of signs which decenters power as it destroys the gravity of rational discourse and grounded meaning. As Baudrillard remarks, a "panic-stricken production of the real and the referential" today overtakes even the drive toward material production. We exhibit an obsession with signs of reality, tradition, and lived experience as nostalgia engulfs us in an hysterical attempt to find stakes of meaning. Thus we stockpile the past to guarantee authenticity, and we create fantasies (Disneyland is his example) to convince ourselves that a separate imaginary is possible—to assure ourselves, in other words, that the real exists apart and distinguishable from Disneyland.[12] The production of such fictions of the real defines the role of TV in both its "realistic" (news, live television) and imaginary (narrative) forms—both provide the illusion of actuality and bolster our sense of the reality of the stakes.

Melodrama might at first appear to be an odd form in which to search for signs of the real. But as Peter Brooks has argued, the melodramatic mode, above all, expresses the desire to find true stakes of meaning, morality, and truth. It thus emerges in times of doubt and uncertainty, employing signs which may seem overdetermined and excessive in order to mark out values left cloudy by a disintegrating sacred system. Combating the anxiety produced by a new order which can no longer assure us of the operation, or even existence, of fundamental social, moral, or "natural" truths, melodrama "arises to demonstrate that it is still possible to find and to show the operation of basic ethical imperatives, to define, in conflictual opposition, the space of their play. That they can be staged 'proves' that they exist."[13] That is, moral struggle is made visible, announcing itself as an indisputable force. By enacting irreducible imperatives, melodrama serves to reassure a doubting audience of essential truths while its "logic of the excluded middle" acts to focus feeling into pure and immediate knowledge.[14]

The staging of melodrama's Manichean conflicts as a strategy to counter the decentered consciousness arising in a society in which fundamental meaning and morality have been thrown into question, then, sounds strikingly like the strategies Baudrillard outlines for the postmodern world. Both may be seen, in other words, as desperate attempts to map out artificially a real which is in danger of being lost in the shift to a new social and discursive field. While Brooks calls melodrama "a peculiarly modern form," it is also particularly suited to our postmodern sensibility. As the political, social, and aesthetic representations of modern society lose their legitimacy, we are forced once again to find new stakes of meaning, and melodrama is the form to which we turn. In a simulated society which typically stages reality in order to "prove" its existence, melodrama offers a way to assert the "actual" drama of life.

In order to find such meaning and make it universally legible, melodrama leaves nothing unsaid. Its hyperbole and emotional heightening correspond to the difficulty of naming the reality it strives to locate. But with the loss of traditional guarantees, meaning becomes sentimentalized and individual. As Brooks explains, "melodrama represents both the urge toward resacralization and the impossibility of conceiving sacralization other than in personal terms. . . . The decision to 'say all' . . . is a measure of the personalization and inwardness of post-sacred ethics, the difficulty of their location and expression."[15] Personality becomes the new value and sole referent—a condition central to today's consumer culture in which TV takes the leading role. Personality is one of the primary selling points of television, the basis of its performers' appeal. Producing a sense of intimate contact, personality on television is an effect of TV's fiction of presence. Unlike the enigmatic aura of the cinema star (who is desirable insofar as he/she is distant, absent, and mysterious), the television personality seems immediately available to us.[16] Personality is then constructed as an outer layer, readable to all and there for us to have—or, as the commercials imply, to buy. In this way, it becomes a key element in the marketing of almost all commodity goods.

Americans' preoccupation with personality in the form of emotional satisfaction, psychic health, and images of well-being is tied to the rise of a therapeutic discourse that is central to media culture and consumer society. Like the melodrama, this therapeutic ethos is "rooted in peculiarly modern emotional needs—above all the need to renew a sense of selfhood that had grown fragmented, diffuse, and somehow 'unreal.' "[17] While the growth of the therapeutic ethos and a consumption-oriented secularism has been linked by T. J. Jackson Lears to a sense of weightlessness found in the late nineteenth and early twentieth centuries, these are today almost fully institutionalized.[18] Yet rather than fulfilling the need for self-realization and the experience of "real life," the therapeutic prescriptions offered by advertising and the "leisure industry" have exacerbated the problem, further enmeshing us in a web of consumer interdependence and ego diffusion. As consumers continue to search for the path to the "real" self, they are led in circles, a situation which reinforces rather than resolves this sense of weightlessness and the process of rationalization. The same sense of unreality that nourishes the melodramatic imagination, then, fosters a consumer culture bent on supplying a simulated image to make up for our sense of loss of place and identity.

IV. The Space and Time of Consumerism

While melodrama, like advertising, figures social turmoil in the private, emotional terms of self and experience, it rejects the psyche as a realm of inner depth. As both Brooks and Elsaesser point out, psychological conflicts are externalized so that they may be clear as fundamental forces. It is in the clash and play of their visible oppositions that melodrama's meaning becomes both legible and consumable. Elsaesser thus emphasizes the genre's "non-psychological conception of the *dramatis personae,* who figure less as autonomous individuals than to transmit the action and link the various locales within a total constellation." Charting a relational field, melodrama may be seen as architectural rather than literary, "a combination of structural tensions and articulated parts."[19] It is through its connecting points, rather than the interior depth of its characters, that melodrama expresses a particular historical consciousness.

Television has also been criticized for its failure to portray fully rounded characters, and as a medium composed of disjointed parts that are only held together in overlapping networks of shared commercial time, TV creates a constellation of consumption. Postmodern culture in general has been linked to such a space—a hyperspace of "constant busyness" suppressing depth, a packed emptiness "without any of that distance that formerly enabled the perception of perspective or volume."[20] Depth is replaced by multiple surfaces across which codes play and flow. In the words of Baudrillard, the psychological dimension has given way to the "forced extroversion of all interiority, this forced injection of exteriority."

Even the fiction of autonomous subjectivity vanishes as our sense of inner space collapses. Identity is instead caught up in the circuit of "connections, contact, contiguity, feedback and generalized interface that goes with the universe of communication. With the television image — the television being the ultimate and perfect object for this new era — our own body and the whole surrounding universe become a control screen."[21]

The spatial logic of postmodern culture has its counterpart in a weightless relation to time, history and memory — a construction also found in television melodrama. As images and narratives become fragmented and spectatorship more and more dispersed, we begin to inhabit "the synchronic rather than the diachronic," leading to what has been described as a crisis in historicity. To paraphrase Fredric Jameson, our relationship to the past is one of "historicism effacing history" — as even the illusion of a full or authentic relation of lived experience to history dissolves, we are left with a random collection of images to which we turn in a frantic effort to appropriate a collective past.[22] In its endless replaying of yesterday's shows, nostalgic fondness for former styles, and obsessive announcements of its own historical weight, television contributes to both the dissolution of the aura of tradition and the attempt to reformulate a new historical connection. History is constantly invoked as a reassuring anchor, but as it is dispersed in a pastiche of partial testimony and resituated in the flux of media production, it is deflated and eclipsed in a frame of eternal "nowness."[23] TV narrative provides a present method of consuming the past.

Television melodrama in particular plays on this hollow sense of time — its artificially contrived plots vacillate between both the compression and extension of time as old plots and stereotypes are recycled or rehearsed rather than fully developed. By replaying its own formulas, TV fosters a sense of living tradition, a continuously available history that appeals to the nostalgic mode of postmodern culture. With no agreed transcendental value to be achieved, melodrama can offer no final closure, and thus its narratives — in both continuing serials and episodic series — are circular, repetitive and unresolvable. This is clear in the case of melodramatic series — weekly doctor or detective dramas, for example — in which characters are doomed endlessly to re-enact the dilemmas propelling their shows. Daytime and prime-time soap operas, on the other hand, provide continuing stories that seem to demand a historical sense of time. Yet comparable to the series, soap operas ultimately reject the notion of progress, the belief in a visible difference between past and future. In a genre whose form has been described as "an indefinitely expandable middle" lacking beginning or end, the viewers as well as the characters are trapped in an eternally conflictual present.[24] Such melodramatic serials thus create a strange sense

of time as they run vaguely along "real" time, stretching it at some points—
when a climactic diegetic moment fills up several episodes or time freezes
to hold a tableau—while compressing it in others—when young children
leave for boarding school, for example, and return in a season or two as
teenagers. Noting this "curious holding of memory and forgetfulness" that
is specific to television narration, Rosalind Coward exclaims, "if these
programmes require such feats of memory, how is it that they also require
equally spectacular acts of forgetfulness?"[25] Invoking history and memory
even as they refuse historical grounding, TV melodramas deny the spectator
any sense of coherent time, position, or identity, thereby allowing the
manipulation of past TV history to instigate present viewing and consumption.

The oddest case of TV's deployment of history, memory, and time,
examined in a provocative paper by Mimi White, is the 1986–87 season
premiere of *Dallas* in which the character Bobby Ewing—who had been
hit by a car in the final episode of the 1984–85 season and lay dead and
buried in 1985–86—returns through an incredible rewriting of diegetic
history.[26] The explanation tested even viewers accustomed to soap operas'
ability to resurrect dead figures. In the new diegetic "reality," Bobby's
accident and death did not really happen—the fatal episode, with all the
other episodes in the 1985–86 season, was merely Pam Ewing's bad dream.
Here the demands of demographics (Bobby was an extremely popular
character) overruled any sense of rational history, and the *Dallas* spectator,
not to mention the viewer of the *Dallas* spin-off *Knots Landing,* is left
with some troubling but unanswered questions: Did Pam dream *all* of the
events, involving all of the characters, in 1985–86? Why haven't the characters in *Knots Landing* (who mourned Bobby in 1985 but haven't yet
realized their mistake) awakened from Pam's dream? Whose dream is this
anyhow? If anything, it is the dream of postmodern culture in which
consumer desires can alter history while providing present pleasures. In
fact, "Pam's dream" has been used to sell programs other than just *Dallas*—
rival series *Dynasty* and *The Colbys* ran ads in *TV Guide* and other
magazines in the fall of 1986 stating, "This is no dream" and "What we
dream, they live," in an attempt to play off the viewer's knowledge of
events on *Dallas.*

V. Consumer Closeness and Constructions of Femininity

History and memory are allowed to wander as emotion provides the only
stake, a situation giving free rein to consumer fantasies. With the elision
of history comes the promotion of the image (of both the commodity and
the self) which is now personal and self-referential. Space flattens out and

TV Guide (Jan. 14, 1987), pp. 17–18

history dissipates, making it difficult to ground any unified position. It is then no surprise that melodrama, television and postmodernism, which all share this particular construction of flattened space and weightless time, have been linked to the dissolution of a stable site of mastery, the ideal of masculinity. They are thus aligned with the threat of the feminine, the gender assigned to consumer passions.

The melodrama, for example, seems to disallow the achievement of a masculine ideal even as it reflects the lack of such mastery—not only is melodrama motivated by the anxiety of a decentered existence (as Brooks argues), but it lacks powerful protagonists with whom to identify, thus maintaining the spectator in a powerless position. As film theorists have noted, there is a split in the American cinema between those forms considered "feminine" in which a passive heroine or impotent hero suffers (the melodrama) and those deemed "masculine" (by both critics and audiences) which feature an active hero immune to suffering (typified by the western).[27] Placed on the side of femininity since its claustrophobic and implosive world precludes the direct action of a masterful ego, melodrama has been noted for its exploration of feminine subjectivity and its appeal to a female audience.

Yet like Cary in *All that Heaven Allows,* the female viewer thus addressed can become only a "spectacle of the impotent spectator."[28] While the spectator may have greater knowledge than any of the characters, she is still unable to determine the course of the narrative and is thus helpless. With no controlling protagonist to provide her with a lead, the spectator is at the mercy of the story and must simply wait (as is so common for the characters) for time to unfold. According to Steve Neale, it is this powerlessness that drives melodrama's viewers to tears—we cry from the lack of coincidence dramatized on the screen, a lack we are powerless to change: the gap between our knowledge and that of the characters, between what should happen and what actually does, between the "rightness" of a union and its delay. Invoked in these gaps are deep-rooted fantasies of fusion, of a perfect coincidence of both communication and desire—yearnings related to the nostalgic fantasy of union with the mother, the wish for maternal plenitude.[29]

By engaging such wishes, melodrama is able to *move* the spectator, to manipulate emotions to a degree that seems to many critics to go beyond aesthetic or rational justification. This assessment is conveyed even in the labels commonly applied to melodrama: "weepies" and "tearjerkers"—terms that imply the strength of the genre (powerful enough to shake emotion out of the viewer) even as they discredit the presumed female spectator. This spectator, overinvolved and displaying an excess of feeling, is figured as powerless to attain any distance from the sentimental fantasies portrayed. In the popular imagination then, the woman's relationship to the screen is an overly close one—she is so bound to the drama, so susceptible to the image, that it can even evoke a physical reaction in her tearful response.[30] What the female spectator lacks is the distance necessary for "proper" viewing and judgment. As Mary Ann Doane has argued, while the cinema appears to offer a plenitude of sensory experience, it necessarily depends upon an absence and the irreducible distance between viewer and object. Yet the cultural place assigned to women as viewers acts against the maintenance of such distance:

> A distance from the image is less negotiable for the female spectator than for the male because the woman is so forcefully linked with the iconic and spectacle or, in Mulvey's terms, "to-be-looked-at-ness." Voyeurism, the desire most fully exploited by the classical cinema, is the property of the masculine spectator. Fetishism—the ability to balance knowledge and belief and hence to maintain a distance from the lure of the image—is also inaccessible to the woman, who has no need of the fetish as a defense against a castration which has always already taken place. Female spectatorship, because it is conceived of temporally as immediacy . . . and spatially as proximity . . . can only be understood as the confounding of desire.[31]

For the female spectator, there is an overpresence of the image—she is supposed to *be* the image—and her desire thus seems to be trapped within the confines of narcissism (as she becomes the object of desire) or masochism (as she overidentifies with the passive character). Unlike the man, whose voyeuristic and fetishistic distance allows him to master the image and whose cinematic counterparts control its flow through time, the female spectator is cast as too close to the image to achieve such mastery, and melodrama, the genre most often addressing a female audience, exploits this closeness through its tearful fantasies of (maternal) union.

The image of the overinvolved female spectator not only occurs in the popular imagination, but can likewise be found in theoretical accounts of feminine desire—there is a convergence, in other words, between the popular and the critical discourses on femininity. Tropes of proximity and overpresence have been used by feminist and psychoanalytic theorists to explore basic constructions of feminine subjectivity and sexuality, particularly in relation to the maternal origin and object of desire. Just as film theory posits the female spectator as "too close" to the cinematic image to adequately command the text, psychoanalytic theory represents women as too close to the maternal and their own bodies to claim the gap required for mastery of signification and desire that is granted men by the phallic signifier (representing the possibility of loss). Within this discursive field (and aligned with popular representations of femininity), women are seen as suffering the lack of a firm subject/object dichotomy. Michèle Montrelay, for example, describes femininity as "one chaotic intimacy . . . too present, too immediate—one continuous expanse of proximity or unbearable plenitude. What [is] lacking [is] a lack, an empty 'space' somewhere."[32] Similarly, Luce Irigaray describes female subjectivity as that which resists a separation of isolated moments and locations, thereby allowing woman a self-caressing eroticism in which she can touch herself without mediation. Again the notion of an overpresence that disallows mastery over discourse and the object is suggested (even though Irigaray offers her constructions in resistance to traditional psychoanalytic theories of femininity): "Nearness so pronounced that it makes all discrimination of identity, and thus all forms of property, impossible."[33] In the discourses of psychoanalysis and feminism, woman is figured as too close to the object to become a full subject.

While feminist theorists may posit such nearness as a subversive alternative to the male model, proximity is also bound to consumer desires. The same closeness that ruptures the boundary between subject and object, allowing women a multiplicity of identifications and a self-embracing eroticism, also makes the female subject susceptible to the lure of consumerism which plays on her fluctuating position and the narcissism it implies. It is the focus on self-image that invites the consumer to attend to the images of advertised products, and the woman, whose role is to purchase in order to enhance her own status as valued item, becomes the prototypical consumer—the same overpresence that ties her to the image allows her to be situated as both the subject and the object of consumerism at once. As Mary Ann Doane writes, "the increasing appeal in the twentieth century to the woman's role as perfect consumer (of commodities as well as images) is indissociable from her positioning *as* a commodity and results in the blurring of the subject/object dichotomy. . . ."[34] The proximity that defines femininity in psychoanalytic discourse then corresponds with women's social position under capitalism—women are assumed to be the perfect consumers, devouring objects, images, and narratives just as they have been said to "devour" their loved ones.

Yet the discursive link forged between consumerism and femininity, both related to an overidentification with the image or commodity object, affects the whole of Western culture. Not only are women presumed to be the best of consumers, but all consumers are figured as feminized—a situation yielding tension in a culture desperately trying to shore up traditional distinctions even as its simulations continue to destabilize such attempts. As the distance between subject and object diminishes in the weightless space of postmodern culture, the threat of feminization as well as an all-encompassing consumerism hangs over all subjects. This relationship between the hyperreality of the simulacrum and consumer overpresence is prefigured in the theory of Walter Benjamin who, in the essay "The Work of Art in the Age of Mechanical Reproduction," explores the rise of a society geared toward mass reproduction, a condition fully realized by our own society of simulation. In this mass-mediated world, the aesthetic object, just like the commodity, loses its unique presence—what Benjamin calls the "aura"—and thus its claim to autonomous existence, historical testimony, and traditional value.[35] The aura is defined as "the unique phenomenon of a distance, however close it may be," and its destruction is linked to a particular historical consciousness, a consumer subjectivity that resonates with femininity:

> Namely, the desire of contemporary masses to bring things 'closer' spatially and humanly, which is just as ardent as their bent toward overcoming the uniqueness of every reality by accepting its reproduction. Every day the urge grows stronger to get hold of an object at very close range by way of its likeness, its reproduction.[36]

Here then, the closeness and empathy traditionally associated with femininity is tied to the liquidation of the referent found in postmodern culture and key to consumer consciousness.

With the media now indissociable from consumerism, the discursive equation established between consumer and feminine subjectivity produces curious tendencies in the way media culture is represented. Symptomatic of this discursive conflation of femininity and consumerism is the way in which both postmodernism, the cultural dominant of consumer capitalism, and television, so central to consumer culture, are themselves often figured as feminine. Just as melodrama is seen to collapse distance, particularly as it appeals to the female spectator, tropes of proximity have also emerged in discussions of television viewing and postmodern culture in general, implying that TV places all viewers in a position traditionally associated with women. Building on this link, for example, TV theorist Beverle Houston argues that television situates all spectators as feminine.[37] Yet even critics not explicitly making this claim often allow gendered imagery to creep into their analyses, thereby also figuring TV as somehow "feminized."[38] Comparing television to film, for instance, John Ellis argues that while cinematic narration constructs a scenario of voyeurism, centering the look on the female body and granting the spectator power over the image, TV offers itself as an immediate presence, lacking the "present absence" central to cinema's voyeuristic regime. Rather than the cinematic gaze, TV involves what Ellis calls "the glance," a domestic, distracted, and powerless look. The TV viewer then delegates his or her look to television itself, forging a sense of intimacy and co-presence as events are shared rather than witnessed.[39] Television's inclusive space spills over to media culture as a whole, involving all of us in an implosive sphere of consumer overpresence. As the media now create what count as "real events," we can no longer fully separate the image from our own position of viewing. Describing this hyperreality in which television functions as almost our genetic code, Baudrillard writes:

> We must imagine TV on the DNA model, as an effect in which the opposing poles of determination vanish according to a nuclear contraction or retraction of the old polar schema which has always maintained a minimal distance between a cause and an effect, between the subject and an object: precisely, the meaning gap, the discrepancy, the difference. . . . [40]

The operations of postmodern culture—with TV as its exemplary mode— thus seem generally to involve the overpresence and subject/object confusion that have been linked to consumerism and "feminine" cultural forms. Dissolving classical reason, decentering identity, and abolishing the distance between subject and object, active and passive, that upholds the masculine gaze and the primacy of the male subject, postmodern culture threatens to draw all viewer-consumers into the vacuum of mass culture— an irrational and diffuse space coded as feminine.[41]

The "threat of feminization" lurking over all American culture, now fully implicated in consumerism, poses serious problems for a culture desperately trying to retrieve and maintain its traditional distinctions. Postmodern culture decenters oppositions even as it attempts to resuscitate them (feminization "infects" everyone just as renewed efforts to define sexual difference are launched across the political spectrum) and in this swirling movement, strains and contradictions emerge in both media criticism and media texts. Such stress must then be managed, and the melodramatic mode is once again employed to ease these tensions. Melodrama is then a privileged forum for contemporary television, promising the certainty of clearly marked conflict and legible meaning even as it plays on the closeness associated with a feminine spectator-consumer. Melodrama allows us both closeness and certainty through its appeal to a prelinguistic system of gesture and tableaux that aims beyond language to immediate understanding.[42] In its attempt to render meaning visible and recapture the ineffable, melodrama emphasizes gestures, postures, frozen moments and expressions. Television strengthens these conventions as it clearly directs attention to the revelations of facial expression, providing close-ups that disclose "what before . . . only a lover or a mother ever saw."[43] TV melodrama, like its precursors in the theater and cinema, thus tends to deny the complex processes of signification and to collapse representation onto the real, assuring its audience of firm stakes of meaning.

This assurance, however, comes with a price. Melodrama has historically been associated with female audiences who are figured in popular and critical discourses as unsophisticated viewers. "For there is a certain naiveté assigned to women in relation to systems of signification—a tendency to deny the processes of representation, to collapse the opposition between the sign (the image) and the real."[44] Yet the attractions of the melodramatic mode need not be judged so negatively, and the security it provides today appeals to men as well as women. Melodrama helps us place ourselves in a confusing world—its insistence on the validity of moral or experiential truths and its faith in the reality of the stakes creates a space from which to act. The "naiveté" associated with a feminized spectator may in fact reflect melodrama's suspicion of linguistic and cultural codes, a suspicion that is now well-founded in today's flood of mobile signs and codes. While melodrama—and its female viewers—have been seen as suspect, there is something offered in this stance. Melodrama's promise of universally legible meaning seems to be particularly compelling in the postmodern era, experienced by many as desperately in need of some kind of grounding. It is the panic provoked by this sense of weightlessness that adds to the mode's present appeal—a panic which may serve the political right as much as it does consumer capital.

VI. Envisioning "Another World" of TV Melodrama

Melodrama is thus an ideal form for postmodern culture and for television—a form which arises from a fragmented network of space and time yet still seems to offer a sense of wholeness, reality, and living history. Raising conflict to the level of fundamental ethical imperatives, melodrama provides a world into which we can fully immerse ourselves and evokes emotions with which we can immediately identify. In the struggles it presents, there is no doubt that real forces are at stake. As Ien Ang explains in connection to the prime-time melodrama *Dallas*:

> The melodramatic imagination is therefore the expression of a refusal, or inability, to accept insignificant everyday life as banal and meaningless, and is born of a vague, inarticulate dissatisfaction with existence here and now. . . . In a life in which every immanent meaning is constantly questioned and in which traditions no longer have a firm hold, a need exists for reassurance that life can in fact have meaning and therefore life is worth the trouble, in spite of all appearances to the contrary.[45]

While the banality and meaninglessness of everyday life might historically be most pronounced for women (given the material conditions of their labor in the home and workplace), the frustration provoked by a shallow ungrounded existence is one that seems quite common today. Lacking a sense of tradition, place, and meaning in their own lives, many Americans turn to the media to find such values.

Making up for our want of these certainties is TV melodrama which plays on and profits from our shifting reality. But also profiting from this lack of stable ground are neo-conservative politics and multinational capitalism, both of which have been linked to postmodern culture. Simply because melodrama has been seen as emblematic of feminine subjectivity is no reason for contemporary feminists uncritically to applaud its rise on American television. We are reminded by Thomas Elsaesser of the "radical ambiguity attached to the melodrama" which may "function either subversively or as escapism—categories which are always relative to the given historical and social context."[46] It is often the status of the "happy ending" which determines melodrama's political meaning—whether the ending convincingly solves all the problems and closes the issue, or on the other hand, whether conflicts remain a bit open, leaving the viewer to consider their import. This ambiguity is even more apparent in regard to television melodramas—lacking the "happy ending," in fact never really ending at all, TV melodramas may not have the ability to draw attention to unresolved contradictions and excess, the key to film melodramas' subversive potential.[47] While melodrama has at times functioned as a politically progressive form, it is not clear that TV melodrama allows for this possibility.

Yet it is also not clear that TV melodrama has precluded this potential. Peter Brooks remarks that melodrama has been such an enduringly popular form because it is both "frightening and enlivening" as it exists on the "brink of the abyss," allowing us the comfort of belief in the importance of our lives as well as the challenge this entails. As such, it may give a false sense of strength, but it also "works to steel man for resistance, it keeps him going in the face of threat."[48] As a feminist concerned with the historical connections between women, melodrama, and consumerism, I hope it may work to steel women for resistance too. Film melodrama has been able to call attention to the contradictions in our class and gender system through its use of formal conventions which stand as ironic commentaries on otherwise conventional narratives. By reading TV melodramas against the grain and providing our own ironic commentaries, feminist criticisms may continue to bring out the contradictions of the TV age so that these issues do not get lost in the flow of media images. Such work might then make more apparent the sites of stress and contradiction in postmodern culture, its construction and deconstruction of the terms of gender and consumption, so that the boundaries thus drawn may be stretched in new directions. To define these directions, we too may turn to the melodramatic mode. But by recognizing the provisionality of these heightened dramas even as we play them out, we open up the space for both pleasure and resistance, activating melodrama's contradictions in our struggle for new meanings.

NOTES

1. Laura Mulvey, "Melodrama In and Out of the Home," *High Theory/Low Culture: Analysing Popular Television and Film,* ed. Colin MacCabe (New York: St. Martin's Press, 1986), p. 82.

2. Mulvey, p. 82.

3. For a discussion of postmodernism, nostalgia, and tradition, see Andreas Huyssen, *After the Great Divide: Modernism, Mass Culture, Postmodernism* (Bloomington: Indiana University Press, 1986). Huyssen mentions the relationship of postmodernism to the "emergence of various forms of 'otherness,' " including feminism, which are perceived as a threat to cultural tradition and so provoke nostalgic reactions, see pp. 199 and 219–220. Also raising this issue is E. Ann Kaplan who suggests that certain critics have been drawn to postmodernism because "it seems to render feminism obsolete" precisely when women have begun to win demands in this system. E. Ann Kaplan, "Television/Feminism/Postmodernism," paper presented at the Society for Cinema Studies Conference, Montreal, May 21, 1987.

4. For a discussion of this issue, see, for example, Sandy Flitterman, "Thighs and Whiskers: the Fascination of *Magnum, P.I.*," *Screen* 26:2 (March-April 1985), pp. 42–58 and Jeremy Butler, "*Miami Vice*: The Legacy of Film Noir," *Journal of Popular Film and Television* 13:3 (Fall 1985), pp. 127–138.

5. Peter Brooks, *The Melodramatic Imagination: Balzac, Henry James, Melodrama, and the Mode of Excess* (New Haven: Yale University Press, 1976), pp. 203–204.

6. For analyses of the news, see, among others, Margaret Morse, "The Television News Personality and Credibility: Reflections on the News in Transition," *Studies in Entertainment: Critical Approaches to Mass Culture,* ed. Tania Modleski (Bloomington: Indiana University Press, 1986), pp. 55–79; Robert Stam, "Television News and Its Spectator," *Regarding Television: Critical Approaches—An Anthology,* ed. E. Ann Kaplan (Frederick, MD: University Publications of America, 1983), pp. 23–43; and Jane Feuer, "The Concept of Live Television: Ontology as Ideology," *Regarding Television,* pp. 12–22. All of these articles indicate the ways in which news shows promote a sense of familial unity—a news "family," which extends to the viewer, linked together by the anchor's glances and a sense of shared space and time.

7. Fredric Jameson, "Postmodernism, or The Cultural Logic of Late Capitalism," *New Left Review* 146 (July-August 1984), p. 53.

8. On the relationship between melodrama and periods of ideological crisis, see Thomas Elsaesser, "Tales of Sound and Fury: Observations on the Family Melodrama," *Monogram* 4 (1972), particularly p. 3. For an account of postmodernism as crisis-ridden see Jean Baudrillard, *Simulations* (New York: Semiotext(e), 1983) and *In the Shadow of the Silent Majorities . . . Or the End of the Social and Other Essays* (New York: Semiotext(e), 1983).

9. Jean-François Lyotard, *The Postmodern Condition: A Report on Knowledge,* trans. Geoff Bennington and Brian Massumi (Minneapolis: University of Minnesota Press, 1984), p. xxiv.

10. David Thorburn, "Television Melodrama," *Television: The Critical View,* ed. Horace Newcomb, 4th ed. (New York: Oxford University Press, 1987), p. 628. For an elaboration of this argument, see pp. 630–631 and 638–641.

11. For these arguments, see Thorburn, pp. 631–634, 638.

12. On the production of the real see Baudrillard, *Simulations,* particularly pp. 13, 23–25, 71. For his discussion of capitalism, see pp. 43–44.

13. Brooks, pp. 200–201.

14. Brooks, particularly pp. 15–18.

15. Brooks, p. 16.

16. On the distinction between the cinema star and the TV personality, see John Ellis, *Visible Fictions: Cinema, Television, Video* (Boston: Routledge and Kegan Paul, 1982), pp. 91–108.

17. T. J. Jackson Lears, "From Salvation to Self-Realization: Advertising and the Therapeutic Roots of Consumer Culture, 1880–1930," *The Culture of Consumption: Critical Essays in American History, 1880–1980,* eds. Richard Wightman Fox and T. J. Jackson Lears (New York: Pantheon Books, 1983), p. 4. Also providing a cogent account of therapeutic discourse in American television is Mimi White who argues that while "therapeutic and confessional modes of discourse have frequently been affiliated with female audiences, especially in forms of melodrama and 'woman's fiction,' . . . they figure as pervasive influences on prime time television in general." I would argue that this is in part due to the fact that melodrama has engulfed much of television's discourse. Mimi White, "Mediating Relations: Therapeutic Discourse in American Prime Time Series," paper presented at the 2nd International Television Studies Conference, London, July 1986, p. 31.

18. T. J. Jackson Lears, *No Place of Grace: Antimodernism and the Transformation of American Culture, 1881–1920* (New York: Pantheon Books, 1981).

19. Elsaesser, pp. 2, 13.

20. Jameson, pp. 82–83.

21. Jean Baudrillard, "The Ecstasy of Communication," *The Anti-Aesthetic: Essays on Postmodern Culture,* ed. Hal Foster (Port Townsend, Washington: Bay Press, 1983), pp. 132, 127.

22. Jameson, pp. 64, 65.

23. Mimi White has provided a compelling account of TV's invocation of history in "Television: A Narrative Ahistory," paper presented at the Television and History Symposium, National Humanities Center, Research Triangle Park, North Carolina, March 1987.

24. Dennis Porter, "Soap Time: Thoughts on a Commodity Art Form," *College English* 38:8 (April 1977), p. 783. See also Ien Ang, *Watching Dallas: Soap Opera and the Melodramatic Imagination* (New York: Methuen, 1985), p. 75.

25. Rosalind Coward, "Come Back Miss Ellie: On Character and Narrative in Soap Operas," *Critical Quarterly* 28:1–2 (Spring-Summer 1986), p. 172. In this article, Coward deals with the phenomena of actor substitution in the roles of continuing characters, a situation producing many unusual memory effects. Similarly, adding actors who are well-known for earlier roles may also play with TV history and viewer memory in order to promote further viewing and consumption. Note, for example, the recent *TV Guide* ads featuring Genie Francis, famous for her role as Laura on *General Hospital*: "What do you do when you've had it with doctors in white, white hospital walls, and a white wedding to end all weddings? . . . You switch to *Days of Our Lives.*" Here the ads play with the viewer's memory of Francis' previous role in order to promote present viewing.

26. White, "Television: A Narrative Ahistory."

27. Geoffrey Nowell-Smith, "Minnelli and Melodrama," *Screen* 18:2 (Summer 1977), p. 115.

28. Griselda Pollock, "Report on the Weekend School," *Screen* 18:2 (Summer 1977), p. 111. Also on the disempowerment of the female spectator due to this lack of a single controlling protagonist, see Tania Modleski's chapter "The Search for Tomorrow in Today's Soap Operas" in *Loving With a Vengeance: Mass-Produced Fantasies for Women* (Hamden, Connecticut: Archon Books, 1982), particularly pp. 91–92.

29. Steve Neale, "Melodrama and Tears," *Screen* 27:6 (November-December 1986), pp. 11, 17, 19.

30. See Mary Ann Doane, *The Desire to Desire: The Woman's Film of the 1940s* (Bloomington: Indiana University Press, 1987), particularly the chapter "The Desire to Desire," and Mary Ann Doane, "Film and the Masquerade—Theorising the Female Spectator," *Screen* 23:3–4 (September-October 1982), pp. 74–88.

31. Mary Ann Doane, *The Desire to Desire*, pp. 12–13.

32. Michèle Montrelay, "Inquiry Into Feminity," *m/f* 1 (1978), pp. 88, 91.

33. Luce Irigaray, *This Sex Which Is Not One*, trans. Catherine Porter (Ithaca: Cornell University Press, 1985), p. 31.

34. Mary Ann Doane, *The Desire to Desire*, p. 13.

35. Walter Benjamin, "The Work of Art in the Age of Mechanical Reproduction," *Illuminations*, ed. Hannah Arendt (New York: Schocken Books, 1969), pp. 220–221.

36. Benjamin, pp. 222–223.

37. Beverle Houston, "Viewing Television: The Metapsychology of Endless Consumption," *Quarterly Review of Film Studies* 9:3 (Summer 1984), pp. 183–195.

38. Accounts that figure television as somehow "feminine" include: Marshall McLuhan, *Understanding Media* (New York: McGraw-Hill, 1964); John Fiske and John Hartley, *Reading Television* (New York: Methuen, 1978); and Joshua Meyrowitz, *No Sense of Place: The Impact of Electronic Media on Social Behavior* (New York: Oxford University Press, 1985). Analyses of gendered rhetoric in TV studies are provided by Patrice Petro, "Mass Culture and the Feminine: The 'Place' of Television in Film Studies," *Cinema Journal* 25:3 (Spring 1986), pp. 5–21, and Lynne Joyrich, "Good Reception? Gender Inscription in American Television," paper presented at the Society for Cinema Studies Conference, Montreal, May 21, 1987.

39. Ellis, pp. 131–132, 137–139, 141–143.

40. Baudrillard, *Simulations*, p. 56.

41. See Jean Baudrillard, *Simulations,* particularly pp. 30–31 and 49–58, and *In the Shadow of the Silent Majorities,* particularly pp. 9 and 30–33. For an analysis of the historical alignment of mass culture and femininity, see Andreas Huyssen, "Mass Culture as Woman: Modernism's Other," *After the Great Divide*; and Tania Modleski, "Femininity as Mas(s)querade: A Feminist Approach to Mass Culture," *High Theory/Low Culture: Analysing Popular Television and Film,* which includes a reading of Baudrillard's use of feminine imagery.

42. Peter Brooks discusses the importance of gesture and tableaux for the melodrama in terms of a crisis in meaning in which language is inadequate, fueling the desire for a primal and immediate expression which melodrama's visual composition seems to provide. See Brooks, pp. 66–67. While TV melodrama similarly employs facial expression, gesture and tableaux to crystallize meaning, there is nonetheless a complexity of dialogue, particularly in the soap opera, which is polyvalent. The soap opera then seems to exist in a certain tension, exhibiting both the urge to express the essence of experience through direct expression (the summarizing close-ups held at the end of every scene) and the recognition that meaning is often veiled or ambiguous (when characters refuse to say all, say more than they intend, or mask their "true" feelings as they play with the network of meaning and its failures).

43. Porter, p. 786.

44. Doane, pp. 2, 1.

45. Ang, pp. 79–80.

46. Elsaesser, p. 4.

47. For a discussion of the difference between television and film in terms of the status of "the ending," a summary of the debate regarding melodrama's subversive force, and an analysis of the political significance of television melodrama, see Jane Feuer, "Melodrama, Serial Form and Television Today," *Screen* 25:1 (January–February 1984), pp. 4–16.

48. Brooks, pp. 205–206.

The Adventures of Ozzie and Harriet (courtesy of the
Wisconsin Center for Film and Theater Research)

Source Guide to TV Family Comedy, Drama, and Serial Drama, 1946–1970

UCLA Film and Television Archive: Dan Einstein and Nina Leibman
Wisconsin Center for Film and Theater Research: Randall Vogt
Museum of Broadcasting: Sarah Berry
Museum of Broadcast Communications at River City: Jillian Steinberger
Alternative Sources/Anthology Drama: William Lafferty

This source guide is designed to help researchers locate television programs, produced between 1946 and 1970, that featured plots about domestic life and family romance. The first section of this guide presents family situation comedies, dramas, and soap operas that are located at major archives across the country, including the UCLA Film and Television Archive, the Museum of Broadcasting, and the Wisconsin Center for Film and Theater Research. It reflects holdings as of 1987, the time at which the guide was first compiled for *Camera Obscura* 16. To that original list, we have added the holdings at the Museum of Broadcast Communications at River City, which was founded in 1987. These holdings are presented separately, in the section immediately following the original guide to archival programs. The final section of the source guide contains information on anthology dramas that featured family-oriented plots, and it also lists alternative sources for early programming, including retail outlets and collectors.

The UCLA Film and Television Archive
1438 Melnitz Hall
405 Hilgard Avenue
Los Angeles, CA 90024
(213) 206-8013

The UCLA Film and Television Archive is one of the nation's preeminent centers for the preservation and study of motion pictures and the broadcast media. With nearly 100,000 films, videotapes, kinescopes and radio transcriptions, the Archive is second only to the Library of Congress in the size and scope of its collection. The Archive's television collection was founded in 1965 under the joint auspices of the Academy of Television Arts and Sciences and the University of California. In its collection of over 25,000 broadcasts, virtually every aspect of American television from 1946 to the present is represented. The collection contains extensive holdings in the area of domestic comedy and family drama, ranging from such early series as *Jackson and Jill, Wren's Nest* and *The Marriage,* to such classic comedies as *I Love Lucy, The Honeymooners, Father Knows Best* and *Leave it to Beaver,* to soap operas including *One Man's Family, As the World Turns,* and *The Guiding Light,* to more contemporary classics like *All in the Family, Soap, Family Ties, The Cosby Show* and *Golden Girls.* Access to the collection is available in our on-site viewing rooms and is by advance appointment only.

The Wisconsin Center for Film and Theater Research
6039 Vilas Communication Hall
University of Wisconsin-Madison
Madison, Wisconsin 53706
(608) 262-9706

The Wisconsin Center for Film and Theater Research is co-sponsored by the University of Wisconsin-Madison and the State Historical Society of Wisconsin. The Center holds filmed copies of a broad range of television programs. Its largest television collection is the Ziv Library, part of the United Artists collection. Other extensive holdings include the Fred Coe collection, the Nat Hiken collection and a sampling of episodes from series produced by MTM including 1970s sit-coms like *The Bob Newhart Show, Rhoda,* and fifty-six episodes of *The Mary Tyler Moore Show.* Examples of television situation comedy and family drama are also available. The Center's Film Archive at the Historical Society, which is open from 1:00 PM to 5:00 PM on Monday through Friday, holds the television collections. Those interested in obtaining general information should write to, telephone, or visit the Center's administrative offices. Researchers are urged to contact the Center in advance because some materials may be temporarily unavailable and some donors have placed restrictions upon use of portions of their materials.

The Museum of Broadcasting
1 East 53rd Street
New York, NY 10022
(212) 752-7684 (information)
(212) 752-4690 (offices)

The Museum of Broadcasting is a non-profit archive of radio and television programming that is open to the general public. Founded in 1975 by William Paley, Founder/Chairman of CBS, Inc., the Museum houses programs from the three commercial networks and the Public Broadcasting Service, and also includes collections from corporations, individuals and producers. The Museum's operations are supported by the networks, foundations, corporations, and members. The collection includes a good selection of family drama and domestic comedy from the 1950s and 1960s. In general, entire runs of series are not available, but the selected shows are often premiere, final, or transitional episodes. The Museum of Broadcasting is open from 12:00 PM to 5:00 PM on Wednesday through Saturday and from 12:00 PM to 8:00 PM on Tuesday. Researchers should contact the Museum in advance to set up viewing appointments.

The Addams Family

Holdings:

Addams Family, The. ABC; 1964–1966. This sit-com is based on the bizarre family of cartoon characters created by Charles Addams. John Astin and Carolyn Jones star as the mother and father of a strange, yet ultimately conventional nuclear family. Episodes generally revolve around the reactions of outsiders to this highly unusual group of individuals who believe they are normal. UCLA: 2 episodes; 1964, 1965. MOB: 1 episode; 1964.

Adventures of Ozzie and Harriet, The. ABC; 1952–1966. One of TV's longest running sit-coms, this series began on radio in 1944 and starred the real-life family of bandleader Ozzie Nelson and his wife, former singer Harriet Hilliard. Early episodes generally concern the four Nelsons (Ozzie, Harriet and sons David and Ricky) at home, but later, episodes deal with the boys' girlfriends, college life and eventual marriages. UCLA: 24 episodes; 1952–1966; some with commercials and some miscellaneous promos. MOB: 2 episodes; 1952 (premiere), 1966 (final); one with commercials.

Aldrich Family, The. NBC; 1949–1953. A radio favorite since the 1930s, this television series was NBC's first successful TV sit-com. Episodes revolve around "typical" teenager Henry Aldrich, his family, his high school chums and girlfriends. Five actors portray Henry during the show's run: Bob Casey, Richard Tyler, Henry Girard, Kenneth Nelson and Bobby Ellis. UCLA: 2 episodes; 1950, 1951. MOB: 1 episode; 1953; with commercials.

All My Children. ABC; 1970–present. This popular daytime soap opera was created by Irna Phillips's protegé, Agnes Nixon. UCLA: 8 episodes; 1983.

Amos 'n' Andy. CBS; 1951–1953. Based on the long-running radio show created by white dialecticians, Freeman Gosden and Charles Correll, this sit-com was produced for television with an all black cast. Set in Harlem, the series centers on the activities of George "Kingfish" Stevens, a scheming con man who is always looking for a quick dollar. The series lasted two years as a first-run show and remained in syndication until 1966 when pressure from various civil rights groups (which always felt the show had racist overtones) finally prompted CBS to withdraw *Amos 'n' Andy* from syndication. UCLA: 27 episodes; 1951–1953; some with commercials. MOB: 1 episode; 1951 (premiere).

Andy Griffith Show, The. CBS; 1960–1968. An immensely popular sit-com featuring Andy Griffith as the sheriff of the small town of Mayberry, North Carolina. The show revolves around the personal relationships of the crime-free community. *Gomer Pyle, U.S.M.C.* and *Mayberry R.F.D.* were spin-offs. UCLA: 3 episodes; 1961–1966; some with commercials. MOB: 1 episode; 1960 (premiere).

As the World Turns. CBS; 1956–present. Long-running daytime soap opera created by Irna Phillips. Along with *The Edge of Night*, television's first thirty-minute soap opera. UCLA: 8 episodes; 1958–1986; some with commercials. MOB: 1 episode; 1961; with commercials.

Bachelor Father. CBS/NBC/ABC; 1957–1962. In this domestic comedy an unmarried Hollywood attorney (John Forsythe) discovers fatherhood when his orphaned niece (Noreen Corcoran) comes to live with him. MOB: 2 episodes; 1960.

Betty Hutton Show, The. CBS; 1959–1960. This unsuccessful sit-com stars popular film star Betty Hutton as a former showgirl turned manicurist who inherits a millionaire's estate and becomes the guardian of his three children. UCLA: 1 episode; 1959.

Beverly Hillbillies, The. CBS; 1962–1971. This hugely successful sit-com concerns a family of poor mountain people who suddenly become very wealthy. The series was the top-rated show on TV during its first two seasons and remained popular until CBS cancelled it in the early 1970s to make room for more urban-oriented programs. It stars Buddy Ebsen, Irene Ryan, Donna Douglas, Max Baer, Jr. and Nancy Kulp. UCLA: 1 episode (pilot entitled *The Hillbillies of Beverly Hills*); with commercials. MOB: 2 episodes; 1962 (premiere), 1971.

Bewitched. ABC; 1964–1972. This sit-com stars Elizabeth Montgomery as a pretty young witch who marries a mortal and tries earnestly to leave her supernatural powers behind. In 1966 the couple's first child, Tabitha, was born; she also had supernatural powers. A short-lived series based on the character of Tabitha, starring Lisa Hartman, aired on CBS in the late 1970s. UCLA: 5 episodes; 1966; some with commercials. MOB: 3 episodes; 1964 (premiere)–1972.

Big Valley, The. ABC; 1965–1969. Barbara Stanwyck stars as the matriarch of a rich, ranching family in the 1870s. This program was essentially ABC's version of *Bonanza.* Stanwyck's character, Virginia Barkley, tightly controlled the family empire and the comings and goings of her four adult children played by Richard Long, Lee Majors, Linda Evans and Peter Breck. UCLA: 77 episodes; 1965–1969; some with commercials.

Bing Crosby Show, The. ABC; 1964–1965. In this domestic sit-com Crosby plays Bing Collins, a former singer who has become an architect but often performs a song or two. His wife, Ellie, is played by Beverly Garland; Diane Sherry is their daughter Janice; and Carol Faylen is daughter Joyce. MOB: 2 episodes; 1964 (premiere), 1965; one with commercials.

Blondie. NBC; 1957. The first of two, short-lived adaptations of Chic Young's popular comic strip about hapless Dagwood Bumstead and his wife Blondie. Starring Arthur Lake (who played Dagwood in a series of 1940s films) and Pamela Britton, this series was a Hal Roach Studios production. UCLA: 7 episodes (including pilot); 1957; some with commercials.

Bob Cummings Show, The. CBS; 1955–1959. Film star Bob Cummings plays swinging bachelor photographer Bob Collins in this very successful sit-com. Bob lives with his widowed sister (Rosemary De Camp) and her girl-crazy teenage son (Dwayne Hickman). Episodes frequently concern Bob's relationships with scores of beautiful models. UCLA: 168 episodes; 1955–1959; some with commercials.

Bonanza. NBC; 1959–1973. One of the longest running and most successful series in TV history, *Bonanza* concerns the lives of the Cartwrights, a wealthy family of Nevada landowners that consists of a father and his three adult sons. Episodes range from standard western situations to highly dramatic character studies to out-and-out comedies. The series stars Lorne Greene, Dan Blocker, Michael Landon, and for the first six years, Pernell Roberts. UCLA: 2 episodes; 1961, 1970.

Brady Bunch, The. ABC; 1969–1974. This sit-com concerns a widow with three daughters who marries a widower with three sons. Episodes center on the trials and tribulations of a large, loving, middle-class family. In an attempt to revive the format of the show, NBC aired *The Brady Bunch Hour* in 1977, but this show lasted only five months. An animated spin-off aired on ABC from 1972–1974. UCLA: 11 episodes (including pilot); 1969–1974.

Bringing Up Buddy. CBS; 1961–1962. This sit-com stars Frank Aletter as a bachelor investment broker making his home with his two maiden aunts. Stories often concern Buddy's efforts to overcome his aunts' attempts to find him a wife. WC: 1 episode; 1961.

Courtship of Eddie's Father, The. ABC; 1969–1972. This sit-com concerns a widowed publisher (Bill Bixby) and his young son who continually tries to get his father to remarry. The series is based on a novel by Mark Tobey. UCLA: 1 episode; 1969.

Danny Thomas Show, The. ABC; 1953–1957; CBS, 1957–1964. This long-running sit-com stars comedian, Danny Thomas, as nightclub singer/comedian, Danny Williams, who is married with two children. Originally titled *Make Room For Daddy,* this show was retitled in 1957. In the new version, Thomas plays the same character, now a widower, who in 1957 marries Marjorie Lord, a widowed nurse. A third child is also added to the cast. Episodes often deal with how the loud, but soft-hearted father is upstaged by his precocious children. UCLA: 20 episodes; 1957–1960; some with commercials. MOB: 1 episode; 1954; with commercials.

Date With The Angels. ABC; 1957–1958. Betty White stars in this domestic sitcom about a new bride and her insurance salesman husband (Bill Williams). Also featured are an assortment of friends and neighbors. UCLA: 37 episodes; 1957–1958.

Days of Our Lives, The. NBC; 1956–present. A long-running daytime soap opera created by Ted Corday, Irna Phillips and Allan Chase. UCLA: 1 episode; 1969.

December Bride. CBS; 1954–1959. A sit-com about a lively widow (Spring Byington) who moves in with her daughter and son-in-law. Harry Morgan plays Pete, the next-door neighbor, and Verna Felton is Lily's best friend Hilda. MOB: 8 episodes; 1954 (premiere)–1959; some with commercials.

Dennis Day Show, The. NBC; 1952–1954. Singer Dennis Day plays a young bachelor living in a luxurious Hollywood apartment in this series (also known as *The RCA Victor Show*) that was seen bi-weekly, alternating with *The Ezio Pinza Show*. Also featured is Cliff Arquette (in his "Charley Weaver" character) and Hal March as Dennis's girl-crazy neighbor. The first season was shot live, but subsequent shows were filmed. UCLA: 3 episodes; 1953–1954; some with commercials. WC: 2 episodes; 1954; with commercials.

Dennis O'Keefe Show, The. CBS; 1959–1960. Film star O'Keefe plays syndicated columnist Hal Towne, a widower with a precocious ten-year-old son and a housekeeper named Sarge. Set in Los Angeles, episodes often deal with Towne's work and romantic life. UCLA: 1 episode; 1959; with commercials.

Dennis the Menace. CBS; 1959–1963. Based on Hank Ketcham's famous cartoon character, and starring Jay North as Dennis, this sit-com centers on how Dennis, while always trying to be helpful, manages to make a mess of things. Many episodes concern Dennis's neighbor, Mr. Wilson, who was played from 1959 to 1962 by Joseph Kearns. After Kearns's death, Gale Gordon joins the cast as Mr. Wilson's brother John. UCLA: 1 episode; 1962; with commercials.

Dick Van Dyke Show, The. CBS; 1961–1966. Dick Van Dyke stars as TV writer Rob Petrie. Mary Tyler Moore rose to stardom as Rob's wife Laura and Rose Marie, Morie Amsterdam and Carl Reiner rounded out the cast. A multi-Emmy winning show, the series often deals with Rob's work environment and his home life. Many episodes feature flashbacks to Rob and Laura's courtship, the early years of marriage, and the development of Rob's career. UCLA: 15 episodes; 1962–1966; some with commercials. MOB: 5 episodes; 1961–1966. WC: 1 episode; 1961.

Donna Reed Show, The. ABC; 1958–1966. Film star Donna Reed plays housewife Donna Stone in this long-running sit-com which features Carl Betz as her doctor husband and Paul Peterson, Shelley Fabares and later on, Patty Peterson as the couple's children. One of TV's most solid nuclear families, the Stones deal with all of the standard TV family problems. The show won many awards from parent, medical and educational groups. UCLA: 4 episodes; 1959–1961; some with commercials. MOB: 2 episodes; 1958 (premiere), 1959; one with commercials.

Edge of Night, The. CBS/ABC; 1956–present. Created by Irving Vendig, this daytime program is a rather unusual soap opera which focuses on crime stories. After its first few seasons, it converted to a more traditional soap opera format. UCLA: 1 episode; 1971; with commercials.

Empire. NBC; 1962–1963; ABC; 1964. This one-hour dramatic series stars Richard Egan, Terry Moore, Ryan O'Neil and Charles Bronson and is set on a large ranch in modern-day New Mexico. The show ceased production at the end of the 1962–1963 season, but NBC retained Egan's character for a half-hour show titled *Redigo,* which aired for thirteen weeks in the fall of 1963. In 1964, ABC aired reruns of the original hour-long episodes. UCLA: 2 episodes; 1963.

Ethel and Albert. NBC; 1953–1954; CBS; 1955; ABC; 1955–1956. This live sit-com originally aired on radio in the 1930s. It first appeared on TV as a featured sketch on *The Kate Smith Hour.* Peggy Lynch, who created the characters for radio, stars as Ethel. Alan Bunce, who also worked on the radio series, stars as Albert. Stories center on Ethel and Albert Arbuckle, a middle-aged married couple who are forced to deal with the little crises of everyday life in the town of Sandy Harbor. CBS carried the show in the summer of 1955 as a replacement for *December Bride.* ABC aired filmed episodes in the fall of that year. UCLA: 2 episodes; 1953.

Family Affair. CBS; 1966–1971. This sit-com concerns a carefree bachelor (Brian Keith) who, after the death of his brother and sister-in-law, becomes the guardian of his three nephews and nieces. Assisting him is his English butler, Mr. French, played by Sebastian Cabot. The show was produced by Don Fedderson Productions. UCLA: 111 episodes; 1966–1971; some with commercials.

Farmer's Daughter, The. ABC; 1963–1966. Based on the 1947 movie starring Loretta Young, this sit-com concerns a naive Swedish farm girl (Ingrid Stevens) who comes to Washington, D.C. to work for a congressman (William Windom) as the governess for his two sons. After two years, the two married, but the show was cancelled soon after. UCLA: 3 episodes; 1963–1964. MOB: 3 episodes; 1963 (premiere)–1966 (final).

Father Knows Best. CBS; 1954–1955; NBC; 1955–1958; CBS; 1958–1962. This quintessential 1950s wholesome, family sit-com stars Robert Young and Jane Wyatt as the parents of a typical trio of children played by Elinor Donahue, Billy Gray and Lauren Chapin. Episodes center on the problems of growing up in an idealized world. UCLA: 36 episodes; 1954–1962; some with commercials; two clips are dubbed into Japanese and German. MOB: 2 episodes; 1955, 1957.

Father of the Bride. CBS; 1961–1962. This family sit-com is based on the book by Edward Streeter and the 1950 film of the same name. Leon Ames and Ruth Warrick star as the parents of bride, Myra Fahey. Episodes concern the adjustments parents are forced to make when their children grow up and marry. UCLA: 1 episode; 1962.

Fibber McGee and Molly. NBC; 1959–1960. One of the most popular radio series of all time was brought to TV with Bob Sweeney and Cathy Lewis as the title characters. However, what worked on radio (e.g., Fibber's overcrowded closet) did not make a successful transition to TV. The show lasted only six months. Many episodes concern Fibber's tendency to overstate (hence the name "Fibber") and Molly's efforts to resolve the problems Fibber's antics cause. UCLA: 1 episode; 1959. MOB: 2 episodes; 1959.

General Hospital. ABC; 1963. Created by Doris and Frank Hurley, this daytime soap opera underwent a tremendous transformation under the stewardship of producer Gloria Monty in the late 1970s. The sagas of Luke and Laura, plus guest appearances by stars such as Elizabeth Taylor, drew new (and younger) viewers to the soap opera genre. The success of the youth-oriented format spawned numerous teenage-centered stories on competing serials. UCLA: 1 episode; 1964.

George Burns and Gracie Allen Show, The. CBS; 1950–1958. A popular sit-com which integrates vaudeville and variety show performances with stories centered around domestic life. George Burns and Gracie Allen, a popular vaudeville act, first appeared in this series on radio and later transferred the series to television. Of special note is Burns's direct address to the audience. The first season was shot live in New York. Subsequent seasons were filmed in Los Angeles. UCLA: 16 episodes; 1950–1958; some with commercials. MOB: 4 episodes; circa 1950–1957.

Ghost and Mrs. Muir, The. NBC; 1968–1970. This sit-com is based on the 1947 film about a recently widowed writer who moves to a New England cottage with her two children and discovers that the house is haunted by the ghost of a nineteenth-century sea captain. Although he initially resents the family's intrusion, the ghost eventually learns to care for them fondly. Hope Lange and Edward Mulhare star in the series. UCLA: 6 episodes; 1968–1970; some with commercials.

Gidget. ABC; 1965–1966. Sally Fields plays Gidget Laurence, a teenage girl with teenage problems. Her father (Don Porter), a widower, offers advice. Gidget's older sister, Anne (Betty Connor), is married to a psychiatrist (Peter Deuel). MOB: 3 episodes; 1965 (premiere)–1966.

Goldbergs, The. CBS; 1949–1951; NBC; 1952; DuMont; 1954; syndicated; 1955. Created by Gertrude Berg (who starred as Molly Goldberg) on radio in 1929, this hit radio show became one of TV's first popular sit-coms. This program centers on the life of a Jewish family residing in the Bronx. In the final syndicated season, the Goldbergs move from their tenement apartment into a suburban neighborhood, thus mirroring the experiences of many second-generation Jews. From 1949 to 1954 the show was aired live. The 1955 season was filmed. UCLA: 42 episodes; 1954–1955; some with commercials. MOB: 4 episodes; 1949–1956; some with commercials.

The Great Guildersleeve. Syndicated; 1955. A spin-off of the popular radio show, *Fibber McGee and Molly,* this program revolves around the escapades of a bombastic politician and his family. UCLA: 2 episodes; nd.

Green Acres. CBS; 1965–1971. Oliver and Lisa Douglas (Eddie Albert and Eva Gabor) leave New York and try to make a life in the rural setting of Hooterville (also the home of *Petticoat Junction*). Oliver has always wanted to live in the country, but Lisa, a chic urbanite, is less enthusiastic. MOB: 2 episodes; 1965 (premiere), 1968.

Guiding Light, The. CBS; 1952–present. This daytime soap opera has the distinction of being the longest running program in history. Created by Irna Phillips for radio in 1937, the television version began in 1952 and ran concurrently with its radio predecessor for four years. Although the radio show was cancelled, the television series has continued to prosper for over thirty-five years. UCLA: 3 episodes plus an electronic press kit; 1952–1966. MOB: 1 episode; 1956; with commercials.

Guns of Will Sonnett, The. ABC; 1967–1969. This half-hour western stars Walter Brennan as a former Cavalry scout who raises his grandson after the boy's father becomes an outlaw. Episodes center on the efforts of the two to locate the boy's father. UCLA: 4 episodes; 1967–1969; some with commercials.

Hathaways, The. ABC; 1961–1962. This sit-com stars Jack Weston and Peggy Cass as a husband and wife who agree to take in a family of performing chimps, which they soon begin to treat as their own children. UCLA: 2 episodes (including pilot); 1961.

Hazel. NBC; 1961–1965; CBS; 1965–1966. This sit-com is based on the popular cartoons of Ted Key which appeared in the *Saturday Evening Post.* Shirley Booth plays the title role, a maid/housekeeper for a highly successful lawyer (Don DeFore). In the 1965–1966 season, Hazel changes employers, but the plots remain essentially the same. UCLA: 8 episodes; 1961–1963. MOB: 3 episodes; 1961 (premiere)– 1966.

He and She. CBS; 1967–1970. Richard Benjamin and Paula Prentiss star as a young married couple living in New York City who are forced to deal with a variety of eccentric neighbors and friends. The series was produced by David Susskind's Talent Associates Company. UCLA: 6 episodes; 1967–1968; some with commercials.

Here's Lucy. CBS; 1968–1974. A direct successor to *The Lucy Show* (with a slight format change), this sit-com stars Lucille Ball, Gale Gordon and Ball's two children, Lucy and Desi Arnaz, Jr. Ball plays her usual scatterbrained character and Gordon plays her blustering foil. UCLA: 3 episodes; 1970–1971; some with commercials.

Hey, Jeannie. CBS; 1956–1957. This sit-com is about a sweet, young Scottish girl who moves to New York City with no job and no place to live. Immediately after her arrival, however, she meets a kindly cab driver who offers to become her sponsor. Jeannie moves in with him and his sister and tries to learn about America. Jeannie Carson, Allen Jenkins and Jane Dulo star. UCLA: 28 episodes; 1956–1957; some with commercials.

Honeymooners, The. CBS; 1955–1956. This sit-com, starring Jackie Gleason as bus driver Ralph Kramden and Art Carney as sewer worker Ed Norton, is one of the best and best-remembered series of all time. Also featured in the cast are Audrey Meadows and Joyce Randolph. It was first seen in 1951 as a sketch on DuMont's *Cavalcade of Stars.* The thirty-nine episodes filmed for CBS have remained in syndication constantly since their initial run. UCLA: 2 episodes; 1956. MOB: 4 episodes; 1955–1956; some with commercials; and 50 of the "Lost Episodes;" 1952–1969; some with commercials. WC: 2 episodes; 1955.

I Dream of Jeannie. NBC; 1965–1970. Jeannie (Barbara Eden), a woman with supernatural powers who lives in a bottle, is discovered by an astronaut (Larry Hagman). She subsequently becomes his "slave" and refers to him as "master." Like Samantha in *Bewitched,* Jeannie is continually at pains to behave like a normal housewife in spite of her magical abilities. MOB: 1 episode; 1968.

I Love Lucy. CBS; 1951–1961. This program was TV's first smash hit sit-com and is perhaps the most popular series in TV history. It was shot on film by Lucy and Desi's Desilu company. UCLA: 17 episodes; 1951–1954; some with commercials. MOB: 9 episodes; 1951 (premiere)–1958; one with commercials. WC: 1 episode; 1955.

I Married Joan. NBC; 1952–1955. This domestic sit-com stars Joan Davis as Joan Stevens and Jim Backus as her husband, Judge Bradley Stevens. The series was owned by Davis's production company. UCLA: 98 episodes; 1952–1955. MOB: 2 episodes; nd.

I Married Joan

Jackson and Jill. Syndicated; 1949. One of television's very first sit-coms, this series of thirteen filmed half-hour shows involves the laughable misadventures of two scatterbrained newlyweds played by Helen Chapman and Todd Karns. The series was produced by Jerry Fairbanks, Inc. and NBC Films. UCLA: 6 episodes; 1949.

Jamie. ABC; 1953–1954. This family sit-com deals with the relationship between a boy and his grandfather. Child star Brandon De Wilde (the young boy from *Shane*) plays Jamie, an eleven-year-old orphan living with his grandfather, aunt and cousin. The series was broadcast live from New York. The pilot had been broadcast as part of *ABC Album*. MOB: 3 episodes; 1953–1954. WC: 5 episodes; 1953–1954; some with commercials.

Jean Arthur Show, The. CBS; 1966. This short-lived (four months) sit-com stars actress Jean Arthur as widowed defense attorney Patricia Marshall whose comic involvements with her family and clients provide the show's plots. UCLA: 1 episode; 1966.

Joey Bishop Show, The. ABC; 1961–1965. This popular sit-com stars deadpan comic Joey Bishop as a press agent. In the second season the show was revamped with the star playing a Johnny Carson-type TV talkshow host. This format produced a veritable parade of guest stars, all playing themselves. UCLA: 132 episodes; 1961–1965.

Julia. NBC; 1968–1971. In this sit-com singer Diahann Carroll portrays a nurse and single mother whose husband was killed in Vietnam. UCLA: 2 episodes; 1968, 1969. MOB: 4 episodes; 1968 (premiere)–1970; some with commercials.

King's Row. ABC; 1955–1956. Based on a Hollywood film, this prime-time soap opera centers on the adventures of young psychiatrist Parris Mitchell (Jack Kelly). The small minds of the small town create numerous obstacles to the young doctor's methods. UCLA: 1 episode; 1955.

Leave It to Beaver. ABC; 1957–1963. This domestic comedy revolves around the escapades of eight-year-old Beaver (Jerry Mathis) and his twelve-year-old brother Wally (Tony Dow). As the show progressed and the boys aged, the stories concentrated more on Wally and various "teenage troubles." The "perfect" homemaker-mother June (Barbara Billingsly), the stern but understanding father Ward (Hugh Beaumont), and their children lived in an idealized suburban neighborhood. UCLA: 1 episode; nd; with commercials. MOB: 2 episodes; 1958–1963 (final); with commercials.

Life of Riley, The. NBC; 1949–1950, 1953–1958. William Bendix originated the role of Chester A. Riley for a radio comedy, but Riley's first television portrayal was played by Jackie Gleason. The show's second television run again features Bendix as the outspoken, working-class father. Rosemary DeCamp plays Riley's wife, Peg. MOB: 1 episode; 1954.

Life with Father. CBS; 1953–1955. Better known as a technical triumph (the first live color series for network television originating in Hollywood) than for its lasting appeal, this nostalgic, autobiographical series was based on Clarence Day, Jr.'s *New Yorker* articles and the popular film. The show centers around the stern patriarch of a turn-of-the-century family. UCLA: 1 episode; 1955. MOB: 2 episodes; 1953, 1955.

Long Hot Summer, The. ABC; 1965–1966. This prime-time serial drama was based on the film of the same name. Ben Quick (Roy Thinnes) returns to his hometown in the South and attempts to clear the name of his father, who was accused of murder. The program also stars Edmond O'Brien, Dan O'Herlihy, Nancy Malone, Lana Wood, and Paul Geary. MOB: 1 episode; 1965 (premiere).

Love of Life. CBS; 1951–1980. Created by John Hess, this daytime soap opera has the distinction of being produced in its later years by Darryl and Dwayne Hickman, the stars of *The Many Loves of Dobie Gillis.* UCLA: 4 episodes; 1963–1967; some with commercials.

Love that Jill. ABC; 1958. Real-life married couple Robert Sterling and Anne Jeffreys star as rival heads of New York model agencies. Stories revolve around their fights over various beautiful models. UCLA: 3 episodes; 1958; some with commercials.

Lucy-Desi Comedy Hour, The. CBS; 1962–1967. This summer series consisted of re-broadcasts of one hour specials made by the *I Love Lucy* cast from 1957 to around 1960. The programs usually revolve around travel to an "exciting" location and the presence of various guest stars. UCLA: 2 episodes; 1958 (reruns).

Lucy Show, The. CBS; 1962–1974. Lucille Ball's post-Desi sit-com cast her as a widow with teenage children and stars Gale Gordon as her ever-suffering foil. The show undergoes several changes during its twelve year run, including location (from Connecticut to San Francisco to Los Angeles), Lucy's job (from bank clerk to employment agent), and casting (her real children join the cast in 1968 at which time the program name is changed to *Here's Lucy.*) UCLA: 8 episodes; 1962–1971; some with commercials.

Magnificent Montague, The. Broadcast origin unknown; 1958. This sit-com features a pompous stage actor forced to become a radio star because of financial difficulties. The show stars Sir Cedric Hardwicke. WC: 3 episodes; 1958.

Make Room For Daddy. See *Danny Thomas Show, The.*

Mama (aka *I Remember Mama*). CBS; 1949–1956. A much loved sentimental domestic comedy/drama which revolves around a Norwegian-American family living in San Francisco at the turn of the century. The program is narrated by the eldest daughter Katrin, in a nostalgic flashback style. With the exception of a short Sunday afternoon run in 1956, the majority of the programs were shot live. UCLA: 10 episodes plus some out-takes; 1952–1956; some with commercials. MOB: 32 episodes; 1950–1957.

Many Loves of Dobie Gillis, The. CBS; 1959–1963. Featuring the mishaps of a money/car/girl-crazy teenager and his beatnik buddy Maynard, this sit-com is notable for early TV appearances by Warren Beatty (as the rich and snobby Milton) and Tuesday Weld (as the want-to-be rich and snobby Thalia Menninger). Dobie (Dwayne Hickman) spends most of his time bemoaning his middle-class status and searching for get-rich-quick schemes. UCLA: 6 episodes; 1959–1960.

Marge and Gower Ghampion Show, The. CBS; 1957. A "real-life" oriented sit-com in which Gower plays a choreographer and Marge plays his dancing partner. The program is based on actual experiences, with the couple dancing at least once per program. The series alternated with *The Jack Benny Show* on Sunday nights. UCLA: 6 episodes; 1957; some with commercials.

Marge and Jeff. DuMont; 1953–1954. Marge Green wrote this nightly fifteen minute domestic comedy about a young Manhattan couple. She also stars as Marge Greene. Jeff Greene is played by Jess Cain. MOB: 4 episodes; circa 1954.

Marriage, The. NBC; 1954. This was the first network series to be regularly telecast in color. The comedy situations revolve around a New York lawyer and his wife, a former department store buyer who has difficulty with her newly acquired house-wife status. Telecast live, this six-week series stars Hume Cronyn and Jessica Tandy in the roles they originated on radio. UCLA: 4 episodes; 1954.

Mr. and Mrs. North. CBS/NBC; 1952–1954. This is a comedy-mystery about the adventures of a crime novelist and his seemingly naive, but successfully sleuthing wife. The program sprang from radio, but its origins go back to a Broadway play, a theatrical film and a series of stories for *The New Yorker*. UCLA: 1 episode; 1954.

Mr. Ed. CBS; 1961–1965. Alan Young plays Wilber Post, a former architect who, along with his wife, purchases a ranch home complete with a talking horse. The situations revolve around the complications engendered by the fact that Mr. Ed spoke only to Wilber. UCLA: 4 episodes; 1961–1965; some with commercials.

My Favorite Martian. CBS; 1963–1966. Bill Bixby plays Tim O'Hara who discovers Ray Walston, a Martian, and adopts him as his "Uncle." Uncle Martin's alien powers result in mishaps. UCLA: 2 episodes; 1963, 1966.

My Friend Irma. CBS; 1952–1954. Born on radio in 1947, this popular sit-com follows the antics of "dumb-blonde" Marie Wilson as an unorthodox secretary and her sensible roommate. UCLA: 1 episode; 1952; with commercials.

My Little Margie. CBS/NBC; 1952–1955. Gale Storm plays Margie Albright, a twenty-one-year-old woman who is determined to prevent her eligible widower father (Charles Farrell) from remarrying. This story is set in Manhattan and situations deal with the tenacious daughter's schemes both to gain her own freedom and maintain her father's. UCLA: 4 episodes; 1954; some with commercials. MOB: 1 episode; nd.

My Living Doll. CBS; 1964–1965. Julie Newmar plays the beautiful robot who wanders into psychiatrist Robert McDonald's office. McDonald (Bob Cummings) adopts her as his "niece," and proceeds to train her to be the "perfect" woman. UCLA: 5 episodes; 1964–1965; some with commercials.

My Sister Eileen. CBS; 1960–1961. Based on a book and two movies, this comedy deals with two sisters who move from Ohio to New York to pursue writing and acting careers. UCLA: 1 episode; 1960 (pilot).

My Three Sons. ABC/CBS; 1960–1972. This popular domestic comedy stars Fred MacMurray as the head of a male-only family. Steve Douglas, a consulting aviation engineer, is a widower living in a midwestern city with his three sons and his father-in-law (William Frawley). During the program's twelve year run, the eldest son, Mike, married and moved away and was replaced by the adopted youngster, Ernie. With the death of Frawley, William Demerest became the surrogate mother, "Uncle Charley." UCLA: 20 episodes; 1960–1965 (including pilot); some with commercials. MOB: 2 episodes; 1960 (premiere), 1965; one with commercials.

Never Too Young. ABC; 1965–1966. This daytime serial is aimed at a young audience, set in Malibu and focuses on the escapades of teenagers. The cast includes some TV notables such as Tony Dow from *Leave It to Beaver* and Tommy Reddig from *Lassie*. UCLA: 1 episode; 1966; with commercials.

One Man's Family. NBC; 1949–1952. This soap opera began on radio in 1932 and made the transition to television with an all new cast. The program deals with the trials and tribulations of San Franciscan banker, Henry Barbour, and his family. It ran both in prime time and daytime. UCLA: 10 episodes; 1952; some with commercials.

Our Miss Brooks. CBS; 1952–1956. Starring Eve Arden, this sit-com originated on CBS radio and was heard on both radio and television throughout the mid-

1950s. Arden plays a high school English teacher. Her interaction with the supporting cast of teachers and students comprises the stories. UCLA: 17 episodes; 1952–1955; some with commercials. WC: 1 episode; 1954.

Patty Duke Show, The. ABC; 1963–1966. Patty Duke plays both Patty and Cathy Lane, a pair of look-alike cousins. Cathy, a sophisticated English girl, lives with Patty's family. Patty, a spunky Brooklyn teenager finds numerous ways to take advantage of having an identical cousin. MOB: 4 episodes; 1965–1966.

Peyton Place. ABC; 1964–1969. This serial is the first long-running, prime-time soap opera. Based on a best-selling novel and a 1957 movie, it details the romance and scandal of Peyton Place, a New England town. The large cast includes Mia Farrow, Ryan O'Neal, Dorothy Malone, Gena Rowlands, Lee Grant and Mariette Hartley. MOB: 1 episode; circa 1969.

Real McCoys, The. ABC/CBS; 1957–1963. A rural family comedy set in northern California. *The Real McCoys* features Walter Brennan as Grandpa Amos McCoy, who looks after his orphaned grandchildren. Richard Crenna plays the oldest grandson Luke; Kathy Nolan is Luke's wife "Sugar Babe;" Michael Winkelman is Little Luke; and Lydia Reed is granddaughter, Hassie. MOB: 2 episodes; 1957 (premiere), 1962; one with commercials.

Rifleman, The. ABC; 1958–1963. Single father Lucas McCain (Chuck Connors) and his son Mark (former mouseketeer Johnny Crawford) struggle for survival and humanity in the old West. UCLA: 23 episodes; 1958–1963.

Ruggles, The. ABC; 1949–1952. Produced live from ABC's Hollywood station, KECA–TV, this domestic comedy stars Charlie Ruggles as "himself," a harassed husband and father struggling with the typical needs of a suburban family. UCLA: 13 episodes; 1950–1952; some with commercials.

Sally. NBC; 1957–1958. Joan Caulfield plays the paid companion of a wealthy widow (Marion Lorne). The women run a department store and travel to foreign lands. UCLA: 15 episodes; nd.

Sky King. ABC; 1952–1954. Crimefighter/pilot Kirby Grant uses an airplane to capture wrongdoers with the help of his niece Penny and nephew Clipper. UCLA: 72 episodes plus opening trailers, Welches and Nabisco commercials featuring the cast members; 1952–1954; some with commercials.

That Girl. ABC; 1966–1971. Marlo Thomas stars as Ann Marie, single girl and struggling actress. Stories revolve around Ann's conflicts with her overprotective father, her various audition mishaps and her romance with junior executive Don Hollinger. UCLA: 2 episodes; 1967; with commercials.

This Is Alice. Syndicated; 1958. This family comedy is set in Atlanta and centers on the adventures of nine-year-old Alice. UCLA: preprint only.

To Rome with Love. CBS; 1969–1971. Widower college professor Michael Endicott (John Forsythe), his father-in-law (Walter Brennan) and Michael's three daughters leave Iowa and settle in Rome. UCLA: 32 episodes; 1969–1970; some with commercials.

Topper. CBS/ABC/NBC; 1953–1956. Based on the popular film series, this program focuses on banker Cosmo Topper's benign harassment by ghosts George and Marion Kirby. UCLA: 1 episode plus some segments; 1953 (pilot).

Wren's Nest. ABC; 1949. Real-life marrieds star in this very early domestic comedy focusing on suburban life with twelve-year-old twins. UCLA: 1 episode; 1949.

Young Doctor Malone. NBC; 1958–1963. This daytime serial drama originated on radio and continued on radio until 1960. Its televised version incorporates many characters from a previous serial, *Today Is Ours*. The show takes place in Valley Hospital, located in the town of Three Oaks and concerns two generations of the Malone family. MOB: 1 episode; 1962; with commercials.

Young Marrieds. This late afternoon soap opera is aimed at younger audiences. It deals with the dilemmas of young couples in suburbia. UCLA: 7 episodes; 1964–1966; some with commercials.

The Beverly Hillbillies

The Museum of Broadcast Communications at River City
800 South Wells Street
Chicago, IL 60607
(312) 987–1500

The Museum of Broadcast Communications at River City was founded in 1987 by the National Academy of Television Arts and Sciences as a way to commemorate its 25th anniversary. All titles are instantly accessible by computer and archive patrons may do computer searches according to several different categories. The A.C. Nielsen, Jr., Research Center provides patrons with a study suite furnished with video and audio decks. The museum is open

Wednesday through Friday from noon to 5:00 PM, Saturdays from 10:00 AM
to 5:00 PM, and Sundays from noon to 5:00 PM. The suggested donation is
$3.00 for adults. The museum is closed to the public on Monday and Tuesday.

Holdings:

Addams Family, The. 1 episode; 1964.

Adventures of Ozzie and Harriet, The. 10 episodes; 1953–1961 and some
undated.

Amos 'n' Andy Show, The. 2 episodes; 1953 and undated.

Andy Griffith Show, The. 4 episodes; 1960–1964.

Angel. CBS; 1960–1961. Angel, a young French immigrant, moves to the U.S.
and becomes the bride of architect John Smith. Humor revolves around Angel's
befuddled attempts to adapt to an American lifestyle as neighbors Susie and
George look on with amusement. 1 episode; 1960; with commercials.

Bachelor Father. 4 episodes; 1961–1962; all with commercials.

Beulah Show, The. ABC; 1950–1953. Famous singer-actress Ethel Waters
(and after 1952, Louise Beavers) plays a black maid working for a white family. Beulah was previously a popular radio character in her supporting role in
Fibber McGee and Molly. 2 episodes; 1952, 1953.

Beverly Hillbillies, The. 1 episode; 1952.

Dark Shadows. ABC; 1966–1971. A campy, gothic soap opera that featured
the enigmatic ladykiller Barnabas Collins. Aging actress Joan Bennett plays a
supporting role. 3 episodes; 1967–1968.

Date with the Angels. 4 episodes; 1957 and undated; all with commercials.

Days of Our Lives, The. Audition tape that shows four actresses trying out for
the role of Dr. Laura Horton; 1968.

Dennis Day Show, The. 1 episode; 1953.

Dick Van Dyke Show, The. 21 episodes, including the premiere and a Christmas special; 1961–1966.

Donna Reed Show, The. 1 episode; 1962.

Ed Wynn Show, The. NBC; 1958–1959. Ed Wynn plays John Beamer, an
elderly widower raising his two orphaned granddaughters, Laurie, age 18, and
Midge, age 9. 1 episode; undated; with commercials.

Ethel and Albert. 6 episodes; 1953–1956; all with commercials.

Family Affair. 1 episode; 1968; with commercials.

Father Knows Best. 2 episodes; 1954, 1958; one with commercials.

George Burns and Gracie Allen Show, The. 6 episodes; 1950 (premiere) and
undated; all with commercials.

Goldbergs, The. 1 episode; 1951; with commercials.

Guiding Light, The. 4 episodes; 1953; all with commercials.

Hawkins Falls, Population 6,200. CBS; 1950–1955. A prime-time combination sit-com/light drama/variety show. Later, *Hawkins Falls* became a soap opera. It was set in a "typical" small town patterned after real-life Woodstock, Illinois. 2 episodes; 1950, 1955; with commercials.

Heaven for Betsy. CBS; 1952. Real-life newlyweds Jack Lemmon and Cynthia Stone play recently married Pete and Betsy Bell, who face comical difficulty adapting to married life. Betsy, a secretary-turned-housewife, regularly rescues Pete, an assistant buyer for the toy department of a suburban New York department store, from his poorly thought-out schemes. 1 episode; 1952.

Honeymooners, The. 43 episodes (including several of the lost episodes); 1952–1957.

I Love Lucy. 4 episodes; 1952–1956; one with commercials.

I Married Joan. 1 episode; 1952; with commercials.

Joey Bishop Show, The. 1 episode; 1963; with commercials.

Leave It to Beaver. 10 episodes; 1957 (premiere)–1963.

Life with Father. 1 episode; 1955; with commercials.

Life with Luigi. CBS; 1952. Irish-American actor J. Caroll Naish played an Italian immigrant who tried, with comic difficulties, to assimilate into American society. Although this show had been popular on radio since 1948, some found the television version's ethnic stereotyping offensive, advertisers wavered, and production was stopped. 2 episodes; 1952; one with commercials.

Love of Life. 2 episodes; 1955,1957; with commercials.

Love on a Rooftop. ABC; 1966–1971. Humor revolves around the mismatched love of newlyweds Julie (an art student from a wealthy family) and David (a working-class boy trying to become an architect). 1 episode; 1967.

Lucy Show, The. 1 episode; 1967.

Mama. 1 episode; 1950; with commercials.

Meet Corliss Archer. CBS; 1951–1955. Simulcast on television with the radio show of the same name, the series featured a typical high school girl and her relationships with her parents and boyfriend. 1 episode; 1955.

Mr. Adams and Eve. CBS; 1957–1958. Real-life husband and wife Howard Duff and Ida Lupino play film stars who deal with all the hassles anyone would ever expect to find at a studio as well as in their own domestic affairs. Scenarios were often based upon real-life occurrences experienced by Duff and Lupino. 1 episode; 1957; with commercials.

My Favorite Husband. CBS; 1953–1957. Based on the radio show of the same name, this series featured George Cooper, a banker, and his wife Liz, a scatterbrained housewife. The radio version starred Lucille Ball and was a prototype for *I Love Lucy.* 1 episode; 1954; with commercials.

My Little Margie. 2 episodes; 1954; with commercials.

My Living Doll. 1 episode; 1964; with commercials.

Norby. NBC; 1955. The first television series to be filmed in color featured Pearson Norby, a banker in a small upstate New York town, and his family. Episodes revolve around Norby's domestic and work-related problems. Sponsored by Eastman Kodak. 1 episode; 1955 (premiere); with commercials.

One Man's Family. 1 episode; with commercials.

Our Miss Brooks. 1 episode; 1953.

Topper. 1 episode; 1953; with commercials.

Valentine's Day. ABC; 1964–1965. Valentine Farrow is a suave young publishing executive in New York City who is continually chased by beautiful women. 1 episode; 1964; with commercials.

Family-Oriented Anthology Dramas and Related Programming on American Television, 1950–1960

William Lafferty

The following list gives the titles and approximate dates of original telecasts for network and syndicated anthology film dramas which either occasionally or often dealt with what can be considered "family-oriented" subject matter. Although the vast majority of these anthologies embraced a number of different genres, episodes dealing directly with domestic drama were often plentiful. For example, although Screen Gems' syndicated *Celebrity Playhouse* is best known for transferring the elements of Hollywood's contemporary "adult western" to video, the series also featured highly melodramatic stories such as "A Very Big Man" (with Pat O'Brien) and "Home Is the Soldier," both concerning marital discord. In the same manner, *Four Star Playhouse* is perhaps best known for Dick Powell's Will Dante episodes, but the presence of Ida Lupino as a partner in *Four Star*, as well as an occasional director and frequent star, resulted in some very unusual, almost quirky episodes dealing primarily with social and domestic issues seen from a woman's perspective. Meanwhile, a series like *Fireside Theater*, although also encompassing many different genres, invariably embodied themes related directly to traditional family values.

Listed first are those series known to have been heavily oriented toward "family drama," followed by anthologies in which such drama was not the primary focus, but which nevertheless include examples. The third section indicates titles which are not strictly speaking filmed anthologies, but which could prove valuable as sources of 1950s-era "family drama."

Anthologies Most "Family-Oriented"

1. *Fireside Theatre.* NBC; April 1949–August 1955. This is an excellent source of programming concerning familial relations, as reflected (or refracted) through a 1950s sensibility. Syndicated titles include *Royal Playhouse, TV Theater, Theatre Time,* and others. Owned by Procter & Gamble, 1951–1958, this program evolved into *Jane Wyman Theater.* UCLA: 1 episode; 1953.

2. *Ford Television Theater*. NBC; ABC; October 1952–June 1957. This is another excellent source. This program was syndicated as *All-Star Theater, Award Theater, Key Club Playhouse,* etc. UCLA: 4 episodes; 1952–1954.

3. *Four Star Playhouse*. CBS; September 1952–September 1956. The program includes some very interesting episodes, particularly those directed by and/or starring Ida Lupino. UCLA: 12 episodes; 1952–1955. MOB: 1 episode; 1950.

4. *General Electric Theater*. CBS; February 1953–September 1962. As with the previous three entries, this is an excellent source of domestic melodramas, although comedy was a favored genre. The primary syndication title was *Your Star Showcase*. UCLA: 18 episodes; 1953–1958. MOB: 1 episode; 1961.

5. *Ida Lupino Theater*. Syndicated; 1956. Little is known about this syndicated series, but with Lupino's imprimatur as hostess, it is inevitable that the subject matter of her contemporary *Four Star Playhouse* work would be mirrored in this series.

6. *Jane Wyman Presents the Fireside Theatre/Jane Wyman Theater*. This is a continuation of *Fireside Theatre*, with Wyman (who gained her industry reputation and clout as a star in Sirk melodramas) as hostess and occasional star. The series was produced through her production company.

7. *June Allyson Show*. CBS; June 1959–June 1961. Produced by Dick Powell, Allyson's husband, this anthology (as with virtually all hosted by women), included many episodes with a heavy "human interest" emphasis.

8. *Loretta Young Theater*. NBC; August 1954–September 1961. The quintessential family anthology, with Young (in earlier episodes) reading a viewer's letter as an introduction to the story, and concluding with Biblical quotations. Unfortunately, these introductions (including her swirling entrance) and endings do not appear in syndicated prints. UCLA: complete run; 1954–1961. MOB: 1 episode; 1959.

9. *Schlitz Playhouse of Stars*. CBS: May 1952–June 1959 (filmed version). This is another valuable anthology, often dealing with domestic matters handled in an overtly melodramatic manner. The primary syndication title was *Spotlight Playhouse*, although it existed under many other titles in syndication. UCLA: 8 episodes; 1952–1958.

10. *Silver Theater*. CBS; October 1949–June 1950. Sponsored by the International Sterling Company, this program was one of the first anthologies on film (despire some reference works which claim it was live). It had been on radio for many years, broadcasting essentially human interest dramas. UCLA: 2 episodes; 1950.

Other Anthologies Useful as Sources of Family-Oriented Programming

1. *Adorn Playhouse*. CBS; May–July 1957. A summer replacement sponsored by Adorn shampoo, this series featured "human interest" episodes culled from previously broadcast *Schlitz Playhouse of Stars* seasons.

2. *Alcoa/Goodyear Theater*. NBC; September 1958–May 1960. *Alcoa Theater* and *Goodyear Theater* appeared on alternate weeks and were syndicated under the shared title of *Award Theater*. These programs are now telecast on Arts & Entertainment cable under the (misleading) title *The Golden Age of Television*. UCLA: has a complete run of *Alcoa Theater*, 1957–1960; and 3 episodes of *Goodyear Theater*, 1958–1960.

3. *Celebrity Playhouse*. Syndicated; 1955–1956. UCLA: 17 episodes; 1955–1956.

4. *Curtain Call Theater*. NBC; summer replacement; June–September 1952. This anthology was comprised of previously broadcast anthology episodes, particularly from *Fireside Theater*. UCLA: 10 episodes; 1952.

5. *David Niven Theater*. NBC; April 1959–September 1959.

6. *Douglas Fairbanks, Jr., Presents the Rheingold Theater*. Syndicated; 1953–1957. UCLA: 35 episodes; nd.

7. *The Errol Flynn Theater*. DuMont; March 1957–July 1957, and syndicated.

8. *Gruen Guild Playhouse*. ABC; DuMont; September 1951–September 1952. UCLA: 2 episodes; 1952.

9. *Lilli Palmer Theater*. Syndicated; 1956.

10. *My Favorite Story*. Syndicated; 1953–1954. WC: 78 episodes; 1953–1954.

11. *Pepsi-Cola Playhouse*. ABC; October 1953–July 1955.

12. *Rebound*. ABC; DuMont; February 1952–January 1953.

13. *Short Story Theater*, aka *Little Theater*. Syndicated; 1952; 15 minutes.

14. *Target*. Syndicated; 1951.

15. *TV Reader's Digest*. ABC; January 1955–July 1956. The program is comprised of adaptations of stories which appeared in *The Reader's Digest*. UCLA: 1 episode; nd.

16. *The 20th Century–Fox Hour*. CBS; October 1955–September 1957. This anthology featured adaptations of Fox feature films. UCLA: 4 episodes; 1956–1957.

Programs of Related Interest

1. *Boss Lady*. NBC; DuMont; July 1952–September 1952. This is a sit-com produced by Procter & Gamble, focusing upon Lynn Bari, operator of a construction company, and the difficulties she faces both with her family and in a male-dominated profession.

2. *Cosmopolitan Theatre.* DuMont; October–December 1951. Although broadcast live, many DuMont kinescopes still survive, including, perhaps, episodes of this hour-long anthology drama which were adapted from stories in *Cosmopolitan Magazine.*

3. *Faith Baldwin's Theater of Romance.* ABC; January 1951–October 1951. The series was broadcast live but might still exist in kinescope. The title indicates its orientation.

4. *Matinee Theater.* NBC; October 1955–June 1958. These were live, daily dramas, telecast during the afternoon from the West Coast. Many must still exist (somewhere) on kinescope, probably in NBC's recent kinescope donation to the Library of Congress. UCLA: 10 episodes; 1955–1958.

5. *Mr. Adams and Eve.* This series was a sit-com, produced by and starring Howard Duff, directed and starring his wife, Ida Lupino, with executive producer Collier Young, Ida Lupino's ex-husband. Set in the Hollywood industry, with Duff and Lupino as a husband-and-wife acting team.

6. *Window.* CBS; July–August 1955. This program was a brief summer replacement consisting of dramatic episodes dealing with personal problems, often family-oriented, such as female alcoholism in "A Domestic Dilemma," with Jason Robards, Jr., and Geraldine Page. It was apparently produced live, but kinescopes might still exist.

A Note on Alternative Sources of Television Programming for Research
William Lafferty

Past television programming can serve historians not only as invaluable research material for reconstructing the evolution of the television medium itself, but also for helping to determine the shifting social, cultural, and political fabric of the United States over the past forty years.[1] As this source guide indicates, archives, particularly within the past decade, have devoted considerable funds and effort to acquiring and preserving television programming and making that programming accessible to researchers. Generally speaking, however, archives maintain only that programming donated to them and which their overseers deem to be the most worthy in terms of historical, aesthetic, or social value. As a result, out of the millions of American television programming hours produced locally, on the networks, or for syndication, and recorded on film or videotape during the medium's history, only a minuscule percentage resides today in archives, and that preserved programming represents the acquisition and selection criteria of those archives. Particularly with entertainment programming, there is always the risk that only those programs which have been validated by audience popularity and commercial success will be deemed worthy of preservation. This observation is certainly not meant to condemn archives and their policies. Any archive's major role is specifically the selection of material for its collection which conforms to the archive's particular mission and which will be of the greatest use and value to the greatest number of researchers. Obviously, not all the millions of feet of film and tape produced by television can be, or shoud be, preserved, a situation which makes selection both inevitable and desirable. However, there is always the possibility that the collections of the nation's television archives will offer little material of value to an individual researcher's particular project. When this is the case, the researcher must explore alternative sources of programming. The two primary alternative sources of past television programming available to researchers include the burgeoning commercial videocassette market and the largely underground collectors' market.

With the overwhelming proliferation of videotape cassette recorders over the past few years, a small but growing segment of the pre-recorded cassette industry is carving out a niche in that market by offering tapes of vintage television programming. Primarily culled from kinescopes and film prints in private collections, these tapes represent a wide, eclectic variety of programs, ranging from early soap operas, largely forgotten syndicated anthologies, live "golden age" drama, variety and musical programs, situation comedies, and even commercials. Three dealers are perhaps the most visible today within the commercial trade and offer the largest variety of titles:

1. *Mike LeBell Video*, 1101 West Crenshaw Blvd., Suite 104, Los Angeles, California 90038, (213) 938-3333. Mike LeBell also offers vintage films, but his selection of rare television programs is outstanding, especially his filmed dramatic series, both network and syndicated. His situation comedies range from the pilot for radio's *Duffy's Tavern* to the early and popular *The Goldbergs*, while drama runs the gamut from relatively forgotten syndicated filmed anthologies like *The Errol Flynn Theater* to *The United States Steel Hour*'s staging of "Bang the Drum Slowly" with Paul Newman. LeBell advertises that most of his network programming contains the original commercials. A large catalogue is available.

2. *Shokus Video*, Post Office Box 8434, Van Nuys, California 91409, (818) 704-0400. Unlike Video Yesteryear (below) or Mike LeBell, Shokus concentrates on television. Its catalogue and updated flyers also indicate a wide variety of genres, with situation comedies, variety, and game shows well represented.

3. *Video Yesteryear*, Box C, Sandy Hook, Connecticut 06482, (800) 243-0987. In addition to a huge list of old film titles, Video Yesteryear also offers a large selection of television programming, with a particular emphasis on live, "golden age" drama, especially *Studio One*. The variety genre is also well represented, ranging from *Ted Mack's Original Amateur Hour* to *The Colgate Comedy Hour* to *Hulabaloo*. Video Yesteryear offers a large catalogue with frequent updates.

As the pre-recorded videocassette industry expands, it is almost inevitable that more firms will begin to specialize in early television, resulting in the commercial preservation of previously "lost" programming.

The second source for television programming is the collectors market. For decades film collectors have traded or sold prints among themselves. Although the questions of copyright have always clouded the legality of this activity, it appears today that collectors, if it is manifest that they trade, buy, or sell for personal use only, are free to pursue their avocation openly. As a result, enthusiast publications like *Classic Images* and regional and national collectors conventions thrive. Lately, television programming has become more visible in the collectors market. Two publications in particular offer copious advertisements offering often rare and obscure television programs, mostly on film but occasionally on tape, to the collector:

1. *The Big Reel*, Empire Publishing, Inc., Route #3, Box 83, Madison, North Carolina, (919) 427–5850. Although primarily directed at collectors of movie memorabilia and prints, *The Big Reel* is a monthly publication which includes many advertisements from collectors who offer kinescopes and prints of vintage television (primarily entertainment programming) and videocassettes. Commercial outfits like Mike LeBell also advertise in its pages. *The Big Reel* is an excellent means by which a researcher can tap into the huge collector trade, where most of today's extant television programming can be found. Indeed, with increasing frequency researchers themselves advertise in its pages, announcing what titles they need in the hope that some collector might have that rare print or kinescope, and be willing to part with it (for a price) or, more advantageous to all, supply a videotape of it.

2. *The TV Collector*, Post Office Box 188, Needham, Massachusetts 02192, (617) 238–1179. As its title indicates, *The TV Collector* specializes in television. A small publication appearing about six times a year, it includes features on past television programs (with credits and synopses for all episodes) and actors, as well as a large classified section where advertisers can list available titles both for sale and purchase. The magazine also offers for sale videocassettes of older programs, especially soap operas and commercials.

To illustrate how these alternative sources can be used by a researcher, consider a hypothetical project: By tracing the career of Betty White, a comedienne whose professional life has coincided with the evolution of television, perhaps a thesis concerning the shifting nature of female stars on television might arise. Although published sources concerning White and the place of women within the performing end of the industry can be assembled, how can one obtain actual examples of her television performances throughout her career of over thirty years? Obviously, her current program, *The Golden Girls*, is still telecast, and given its popularity, will be for many years once it is stripped for syndication. Her performances as Sue Ann Nivens on *The Mary Tyler Moore Show* exist in syndication, but also in the MTM archive at the Wisconsin Center for Film and Theater Research, as does her short-lived MTM situation comedy *The Betty White Show*. White also appears in syndication in her role on *Mama's Family*. This covers, though, only her more recent appearances; if no archive contains any of her earlier programs, how can such a research project continue?

It happens that *The TV Collector* sells a videocassette of the original *Betty White Show*, a variety-interview program telecast on NBC in 1954. Recently in *The Big Reel* a collector advertised prints of her 1957 situation comedy,

Date with the Angels. Mike LeBell Video offers a videocassette of her 1953 situation comedy *Life with Elizabeth*, paired with an episode of *I Married Joan*. Perhaps an advertisement in *The TV Collector* might tap into that immense, uncatalogued national television archive that the VCR has spawned, uncovering a White fan who taped her 1983 game show *Just Men*. Although only a few examples of her performances are represented, by exploiting alternative sources of television programming a much wider historical span of her career can be studied.

Two other sources should be mentioned, sources which, through their obviousness, might be overlooked by researchers: distributors and cable. A frequently fruitful avenue for researchers in locating and using previously syndicated programming is to contact the distributors which presently hold rights to the programming. Some large distributors, like MCA and Republic (formerly NTA), will rent prints from their television libraries to researchers, while others will offer to screen them on the distributor's premises.

Given the insatiable demand for programming spawned by cable television, it appears that virtually any program, despite its age or previous success, can find a video home, explaining perhaps why some distributors keep their old television product available. Over the past three years, cable networks have raided television history to provide needed and relatively inexpensive programming. Some specialize in recent fare (such as Arts & Entertainment's acquisition of *Buffalo Bill*), some in the obscure (USA's resurrection of the mid-1960s situation comedy *Good Morning, World*), some in previously popular but unavailable programs (Nickelodeon's reintroduction of shows like *Car 54, Where Are You?*) to a new generation of television viewers. Meanwhile, cable networks like Nickelodeon and CBN recycle important programs from television's past, like *Route 66* and *Gunsmoke*.

NOTE

1. Evidence of this current emphasis upon film and television as tools for historical inquiry is the National Endowment for the Humanities project "The Historian and the Moving-Image Media"; for a description of the project, see *IAMHIST Newsletter* 21 (August 1987), pp. 22–23.

Contributors

Contributors

Sarah Berry is a doctoral candidate in Cinema Studies at New York University. She is writing a dissertation on the representation of communications technology in early film and has been working in television production in Berlin.

Aniko Bodroghkozy is a doctoral student in the Department of Communication Arts, University of Wisconsin-Madison. Her dissertation will deal with 1960s youth rebellions and popular culture in the United States.

Julie D'Acci is Assistant Professor at the University of Wisconsin-Madison. Her book, *Women, Television and the Case of Cagney and Lacey,* is forthcoming from the University of North Carolina Press.

Robert H. Deming teaches film and television studies at SUNY-College at Fredonia and is working on a book on culture studies approaches to television studies and another on representations of masculinity, 1890–1990.

Daniel Einstein has been the television archivist at the UCLA Film and Television Archive since 1979 and has completed the master's program in the Department of Theater, Film and Television at UCLA. He has written articles on television and film for *Emmy Magazine*, *Magill's Survey of Cinema*, and other publications; has taught film studies courses at a Los Angeles community college; and is the author of *Special Edition: A Guide to Network Television Documentary Series and Special News Reports, 1955–1979* (Scarecrow Press).

Sandy Flitterman-Lewis is the author of *To Desire Differently: Feminism and the French Cinema* (University of Illinois Press, 1990) and coauthor of the forthcoming *New Vocabularies in (Film) Semiotics* (Routledge, Chapman and Hall, 1992). She has essays on television in

279

Regarding Television (University Publications of America, 1983) and *Channels of Discourse* (University of North Carolina Press, 1987). She is Associate Professor of English and Cinema Studies at Rutgers University in New Brunswick, New Jersey.

Mary Beth Haralovich teaches film and television studies at the University of Arizona in Tucson. Recent publications include an analysis of television series design and popular appeal in *Magnum, p.i.* in the *Journal of Film and Video* and a study of entertainment and censorship in the 1930s Hollywood "proletarian woman's film" in *Screen.*

Lynne Joyrich is Assistant Professor at the University of Wisconsin-Milwaukee where she teaches in the Modern Studies and Film Studies programs. Her work on feminism and television has been published in *Camera Obscura* and in the collection *Logics of Television* and *Modernity and Mass Culture* (both from Indiana University Press).

William Lafferty is Chair and Associate Professor in the Department of Theatre Arts at Wright State University. His writing on American broadcasting and film history has appeared in a wide variety of journals and anthologies, most recently a chapter, "Feature Films on Prime-Time Television," in *Hollywood in the Age of Television* (Unwin Hyman, 1990).

Nina C. Leibman is Visiting Assistant Professor at Loyola Marymount University, teaching courses in film and television history and theory. Her articles have appeared in *Cinema Journal*, the *Journal of Film and Video*, *Quarterly Review of Film Studies*, *Literature in Performance*, the *Journal of Popular Film and Television*, and *Wide Angle*. She is currently working on a book analyzing the representation of the American family in film and television from 1954–1963.

George Lipsitz is Professor of Ethnic Studies at the University of California, San Diego, and is the author of *Time Passages: Collective Memory and American Popular Culture* (University of Minnesota Press, 1990) and *A Life in the Struggle: Ivory Perry and the Culture of Opposition* (Temple University Press, 1988).

Denise Mann has published work on television, women, and consumerism in *Camera Obscura*, the *Quarterly Review of Film and Video*, and in the recent collection, *Star Texts: Image and Performance in Films and Television* (Wayne State University Press, 1991). She was an associate editor of *Camera Obscura* for six years and is currently writing screenplays in Los Angeles.

Lynn Spigel is Assistant Professor of Cinema and Television at the University of Southern California. She is coeditor of *Camera Obscura, A Journal of Feminism and Film Theory.* Spigel is author of *Make Room for TV: Television and the Family Ideal in Postwar America* (University of Chicago Press, 1992) and coeditor of *Close Encounters: Film, Feminism, and Science Fiction* (University of Minnesota Press, 1991).

Jillian Steinberger is a graduate student in the Department of Communication Arts at the University of Wisconsin-Madison. She is working on feminist theory and the politics of popular culture.

Randall Vogt is a doctoral candidate in the Department of Communication Arts at the University of Wisconsin-Madison. He is writing his dissertation on the television industry in the 1950s.

Index

Index

Compiled by Robin Jackson